Mark's Memory of the Future

# Mark's Memory of the Future

## A Study in the Art of Theology

by

Bascom Wallis

**BIBAL Press**
Publishing agency of BIBAL Corporation
*Berkeley Institute of Biblical Archaeology & Literature*

Mark's Memory of the Future: A Study in the Art of Theology

Copyright © 1995
by BIBAL Press

No part of this book may be reproduced in any manner whatsoever without written permission of the publisher or author except brief quotations embodied in critical articles or reviews.

Most biblical quotations are from the *New Revised Standard Version Bible*, copyright 1989, by the Division of Christian Education of the National Council of the Churches of Christ in the United States of America.

### Library of Congress Cataloging-in-Publication Data

Wallis, Bascom, 1934-
    Mark's memory of the future : a study in the art of theology / by Bascom Wallis.
       p.  cm.
    Includes bibliographical references.
    ISBN 0-941037-34-7
    1. Bible. N.T. Mark--Criticism, interpretation, etc. I. Title.
BS2585.2.W33 1995

95-16050
CIP

Published by BIBAL Press
P.O. Box 821653
N. Richland Hills, TX 76182

Printed by Griffin Printing, Sacramento, CA
Cover by KC Scott, Ashfield, MA

... for Barbara

# CONTENTS

Preface .................................................... ix

Introduction: Mark's Religious Text ............................. 1

Chapter 1  **The Shape of Mark's Gospel** ................ 11

Chapter 2  **Concentric Constructions** ................... 33

Chapter 3  **Healing Many As a Recursion** ............... 51

Chapter 4  **The Twelve** ................................... 77

Chapter 5  **The Feedings** ............................... 105

Chapter 6  **Healing the Blind** .......................... 131

Chapter 7  **Jerusalem** .................................. 169

Epilogue ................................................... 201

Appendix: Mark's Concentric Constructions and the
          Synoptic Problem ................................. 211

Notes ...................................................... 219

Works Cited ................................................ 233

# Preface

This little book grows from my lifelong concern with the New Testament, especially Mark's gospel. In my undergraduate days in the nineteen-fifties, I first encountered and struggled with form critics like Bultmann and Dibelius. From the very beginning, my research was a quest. I struggled not only with intellectual problems but also with problems of faith. Later, as an English teacher, I learned to use the methods of literary criticism to analyze the text of the New Testament and discovered that the struggle had become a meditation that enabled me to articulate my faith. It is in the spirit, then, of quest, meditation, and adventure that I offer this little book for both the layperson and the scholar. The literary methods of inquiry are here employed not to seek out artifice or ornament, but as tools for discovering treasures. I sincerely hope that the readers of this book, whatever their religion may be, will share the sense of adventure.

The writing of the book has introduced me to some good people, and I would like to thank them now. I wish to express my gratitude to William Scott of BIBAL Press for his patient support and encouragement. To Cheryl Brown, of Fuller Theological Seminary, I owe many thanks for editing the manuscript of this book and for her many helpful suggestions.

I also want to thank Arthur Patzia, director of the Fuller extension at Menlo Park for his teachings about the New Testament and for his reading a draft of the manuscript. For him I wrote the research paper which proved to be the seed of this book. Two other members of the Menlo Park faculty deserve thanks as well: I give heartfelt thanks to Duane Christensen for reading various drafts of the manuscript and for his guiding it toward publication. John Koeker encouraged me to continue my research into the New Testament. He is the best listener I have ever known, and it was primarily his enthusiastic encouragement which led me to write the book. I also wish to thank Cecil White, the director of McKeon Memorial Library at St. Patrick's Seminary in Menlo Park. Because of Cecil, it was always good to go to "St. Pat's." He and Sister Patricia Wittman, SHF, provided cheerful help to me during the long seasons of research.

My wife Barbara's faith made the writing possible, and I dedicate this book to her.

# Introduction
## Mark's Religious Text

Mark's story of the Christ is the gospel most written about by modern critics. Mark's gospel attracts so much attention because most critics consider his to be the first-written and also because of the intriguing problems it presents. Stripped of most of the parables and sayings of Jesus which are present in the other synoptic gospels, Matthew and Luke, this gospel at first glance would seem to be a condensed biography of Jesus of Nazareth. The emphasis is upon narrative action, as if the author did not wish to be troubled by too much talk but wished instead to write a suspenseful drama of Jesus' life. But even though Mark's emphasis is upon story, as opposed to sayings, the gospel drama is actually formed from a group of smaller stories. One of the early schools of biblical criticism, the form critics, demonstrated that Mark, as well as the other gospels, are not primarily biographical but are works composed from these inherited stories, passed down in various forms to the evangelists.[1]

The evangelists, however, did not hand down this inherited material in an unmodified state. Later critics, now called redaction critics, emphasized that the gospel writers were indeed theologians who shaped their inherited materials to meet the needs of their churches.[2] Even in Mark's gospel, which omits the Sermon on the Mount and the parables, the critic will discover a complex network of inherited traditions modified to meet the needs of Mark's church. Probably written in Rome around the year 70 CE,[3] this gospel may indeed be read as a guide for initiates into the new faith — a guide into the form and content of the new religion. Whatever the nature of his inherited traditions, Mark has given a unique form to this work, creating the new genre of gospel. Recent literary criticism, however, has discovered a unity in the complexity of Mark's text, and once aware of this unity, the reader can both appreciate the profundity of Mark's art and better understand his theology.

A close study of this gospel, using the methods of literary criticism, can reveal many remarkable features. A portrait of Jesus, for example, can be observed emerging from Mark's text, and it is a special kind of portrait. Even though not strictly biographical in any modern conception of that genre, Mark's gospel does reflect the basic image of Jesus which the disciples and the early church wished to be remembered. This memory is preserved in carefully selected actions and sayings probably intended for catechism or liturgy.

Most importantly for Christianity, however, Mark also constructs a portrait of the risen Christ. The believer is introduced, in addition to the picture of a person, to the glories of the new faith, with its hope of resurrection and eternal life. Mark seems to have been most strongly concerned, in editing and composing his story, with introducing the initiate, or new believer, into the problems of this new faith. The basic problem which must have confronted most believers was establishing a personal relationship with the risen Christ. The believer, or the one who wants to believe, was then and is now still presented with the paradox of a glorious Lord who died a shameful death upon the cross. How can one, in public ritual or in private prayer, experience a vital communion with this Lord?

Mark's task, in creating a written gospel, was to construct a religious text which was far more than an apology. He wrote in such a way as to make the original experience of Jesus and the disciples available to the believer. Mark set himself the task, therefore, of identifying the essential nature of Jesus of Nazareth. Working with memories and traditions embedded in liturgies and catechism, as well as with other oral traditions, he wanted to recreate the experience of Jesus and the disciples so that the new believer could share fully in the experience of faith. Much of the uniqueness of this gospel would derive from the faith that the risen Christ was still present to the church. Not only Jesus of Nazareth must be remembered, but also the nature of the risen Christ who is continuous with that historical personality. Because of the transcendent nature of this new faith, it was, therefore, necessary to define the nature of the Christ who still lives. The portrait of Jesus, as Mark and the other evangelists present it, is also the portrait of the risen Christ.

In reading Mark, one experiences the shock of opening a packet of photographs and observing that most of them are double exposures. Behind the subject of Jesus of Nazareth stands another image, a mysterious figure in the background. Mark's gospel is such a doubly exposed photograph. His story is constructed to tell not only about Jesus of Nazareth's experiences in the regions of the Jordan, in Galilee and Jerusalem; his story is also written to illuminate that figure standing within and behind the portrait of Jesus. The character and actions of Jesus become the character and actions of a Christ still living and present to the believer.

This double exposure achieved in the person of Jesus is an example of how Mark, and the oral tradition before him, construct religious symbols related to personal experience. The title of this book, *Mark's Memory of the Future*, is intended to convey Mark's art of presenting the present-and-future Christ in the person of Jesus of Nazareth. To have faith is to experience a brief taste of the future: "Faith is the assurance of things hoped for" (Heb 11:1). At Pentecost, the future again appeared in the present, in the Holy Spirit, to give a foretaste of the approaching kingdom. This future is not an abstraction, however. Mark sees Jesus of Nazareth as a messenger from that same future which faith and spirit give a taste of in present time.

In the person of Jesus, the Christian remembers the future. That future which moves always toward us is also God who moves steadily toward us. When Jesus stood upon the mount of transfiguration (9:2-8), for example, "he was transfigured before them, and his clothes became dazzling white, such as no one on earth could bleach them" (9:2-3). This scene, several critics suggest, may be a resurrection scene brought forward by Mark to stand at the center of his gospel.[4] Whether it is or not, it is certainly a disclosure of Mark's method of double exposure. During the transfiguration, Jesus of Nazareth becomes, in the present, the future risen Christ. In this scene, the three disciples view the future in the present. This evangelist, who writes often of faith and who implies much about spirit, fuses all time into a double exposure, not only in the transfiguration but in nearly every presentation of Jesus. When Jesus of Nazareth steps onto the world's stage, he prefigures the future resurrection experienced by the disciples and Mark's early church. He also prefigures the risen Christ of the present time. Jesus of Nazareth, then, is the memory of the future.

Here, then, is a relationship between the shape and meaning of a necessarily new genre of writing. In fact, Mark's gospel is a wedding of form and content designed to confront the enigma of Jesus and to answer the question: "What was and is the character of this man who rose from the dead?" This complicated process of composition had begun, of course, in the oral traditions many years before Mark shaped his written gospel. All the elements of this gospel, its "inward parts," were arranged to answer the religious questions raised by the life, death and resurrection of the Christ. Mark's gospel is, therefore, a religious text written for religious purposes.

Even though the text is a religious one, most modern critics will still insist that the gospel can be read and criticized the same as any other work of literature, whether religious or secular. Such a statement, however, must be radically qualified. Any analysis of any literary work must be guided, to some extent, by the genre of that work. The problem that arises from treating Mark's gospel as if it were secular literature is that when the critic does attempt to impose genre, that imposition is usually a secular one. The religious quality which defines Mark's unique genre is lost. It is not that modern critics neglect to impose genre; it is that they often impose an incorrect genre as the dominant influence. For example, Mark simply will not respond to being interpreted as a documentary biography, as a memoir, or as an allegory. Neither can it be read, even though literary criticism be applied, as a short story or novel.

This study will reveal that Mark did probably use other genres, especially the narratives of the Hebrew Scriptures and even Greek tragic drama, as we shall see in the epilogue of this book. These borrowed genres must certainly be taken into consideration in the analysis of the religious text. We must not, however, interpret the entire gospel through the lens of borrowed genres, but determine the nature of the religious text which the evangelist created—whatever forms he may have used. In specific regard to Mark's gospel, his new genre uses tragic drama and Hebrew Scripture in startling new ways determined by his religious purposes. His new genre snatches a grace beyond the reach of art by synthesizing the old with the new.

In order to offer intelligent interpretation, in other words, the critic must know something about the form or class of literature to which a text belongs or aspires. Mark is a religious text; and to be understood adequately, it must finally be read—whatever other operations may be performed upon it—as a religious text. It is as surely a religious work, in the broadest sense, as is Buddha's *Fire Sermon* or *The Diamond Sutra* from later Buddhist traditions. Many religious texts address the experience of the reader or listener in order to change attitudes—more than that—to change the person!

The critic, as well as the general reader, must, therefore, be aware of crucial differences in the ways that plot, character, setting, and symbolism in the gospel text are used to communicate religious belief and experience. Too much biblical criticism has proceeded as though examining food recipes, modern novels, or stamp collections without allowing the text to speak for itself and from its own integrity.

Luke Johnson states the problem clearly when he says that an inadequacy of historical criticism "has been its inability to deal with the religious content of the writings" of the New Testament "except in a comparative, developmental, or theological fashion. And although form criticism tried to align religious settings and literary forms, it did so by abstracting the forms of the smaller literary units from the larger literary setting. The connections between the logic of the literary works and the logic of the religious experiences or convictions they express still require examination." Historians, Johnson says, "have shied away from asking the question of origination in the strictest sense—from asking what sort of religious experience gave rise to the Christian movement and motivated the writings that now interpret it. In short, the historical model is of little help for interpreting the canonical writings of the NT as religious literature."

Johnson asks for a model which "would recognize the value of studying the normative collection of a religious tradition on its own terms, as the classic expression of that tradition" and "would respect the anthropological, historical, literary, and religious dimensions of the writings. It would allow the study of their individual production, without forgetting their eventual anthological status. It would be able to ask the question of origination in specifically religious terms. It would be able to recognize the specific and distinct voice of each writing. It would recognize that those who canonized the NT writings found an implied harmony that distinguished these voices from others."[5] I certainly agree with Johnson's assessment of the problem. The often unanalyzed dictum that religious work may be analyzed just as any secular text has led to some unfortunate and potentially destructive mistakes. This study takes into account the symbolic nature of the text and interprets it in light of its religious purpose.

The methods of literary criticism are well suited, I believe, for the analysis of this gospel story, because such criticism offers a method willing to listen to symbolic language and action. Because the unique nature of the New Testament is too often ignored, modern criticism of these texts is frequently reductionist and skeptical. A few critics seem to feel that debunking the gospel should be their primary aim, and their hostility is often misidentified as integrity.

The purpose of interpretation of any religious text must not be merely to debunk or discredit the text in the light of an anti-religious bias, nor to demonstrate one's sophisticated ability to demythologize. Approaching the gospel as religious text, good critics will accept the discipline imposed by their method, whether anthropological, sociological, historical, etc. They will, in all cases, follow the scientific method while attempting to elucidate the text's meaning for both the believer and the nonbeliever. An empathetic attitude (not necessarily sympathetic) is a basic requirement for the understanding of religious beliefs, whether one accepts those beliefs or not. Such interpretation would not be weakened by empathy, but strengthened so as to gain insights otherwise unavailable. Criticism of religious texts must employ the highest standards of biblical criticism and must not become sentimental or impressionistic. It must, rather, always be an inductive attempt to answer basic questions about the text.[6]

The modern reader of Mark's gospel must read critically and perceptively if the Christian story is to be so interpreted as to apply to the living of a Christian life. An important question to be asked of Mark by a modern reader is the relationship of the shape of his text to the theology of the author and to the experiences he seeks to communicate. What does Mark say, in first century forms, to a reader at the beginning of the twenty-first century? In such an analysis, the reader must be open to any structural clues which could reveal the author's intentions as well as to clues revealing his expectations concerning the readers' response. All the nuances available to a first-century reader can never be fully discerned by the critic, but it will prove possible to identify and interpret some of the structural signals which Mark sent to his first readers.

Charles H. Talbert has, as an example, uncovered and analyzed the "architecture" of Luke's gospel and of Acts.[7] After defining the structures he has discovered, he proceeds to show the relationship of those structures to the theology of the writer. Talbert provides a fine example for critics wishing to employ the methods of literary criticism, because he is never impressionistic, but always listens attentively to the text. He invites the reader not to read into the text, but to attempt to interpret it only after careful and close analysis. The challenge for the critic of Mark's gospel, then, is to attempt to see it through new eyes, to look closely at it, as if seeing it for the first time.

# INTRODUCTION

This book will attempt to meet that challenge, always asking the question: "Does Mark provide any structural signals which help our understanding of his meaning?"

Mark carefully folds and bends his story so that scenes begin to reflect one another. When the angel at the tomb sends the disciples back to Galilee, there is the intriguing possibility that Mark is sending the reader back once again to read the story of Jesus. After all, was that not the original experience of the disciples? After the resurrection they relived the story of Jesus and were forced to see, by way of the double exposure provided by an active interpretative memory, the real significance of Jesus' life. Having misunderstood the call during the first mission with Jesus of Nazareth, they now must, after his death, go out with the risen Christ on a second mission,[8] which will be founded upon their interpretation of the first adventure. Conversion to the new faith, in effect, will consist in the mimesis, or imitation, of the disciple's struggle to understand Jesus. The disciples converted people by inviting them to relive their own experiences! That is precisely why the four gospels take the form they do: they invite the reader to imitate the struggles of Jesus of Nazareth so that they may be able, as a consequence, to understand the risen Christ.

Mark gives insight into his intentions as craftsman and his ideas as theologian, for instance, by creating, in the first half of his gospel, four large sections which I shall call "envelopes." He creates these envelopes by enclosing portions of his text with doublets. A doublet may be defined, for the purposes of this inquiry, as a verse or passage repeated later in the text. This repetition need not be verbatim or word-for-word, but should be close enough in form and/or content that the verses could be called twins. Furthermore, literary criticism can help to show how Mark constructs the first half of his gospel from the four envelopes:

"Healing Many" (1:32 - 3:12)
"The Twelve" (3:13 - 6:13)
"The Feedings" (6:30 - 8:10)
"Healing the Blind" (8:22 - 10:52)

Each of these sections, in other words, is enclosed by virtually the same passage, one of which is placed at the beginning of the section, the other at the end.

Identifying these envelopes, as well as the other sections, establishes the basic research question which organizes this book: "In addition to the presence of the doublets which define its limits, does each envelope have a definable structure?" We will analyze the structure of individual envelopes and make comparisons between the envelopes. The structural integrity of each envelope must be demonstrated. Uncovering this integrity can provide valuable insights into the author's craft.

Mark's gospel, as is often said, consists of a passion narrative preceded by a long introduction. His prologue (1:1-31) and the envelopes themselves (1:32 - 10:52) will comprise an introduction to the Jerusalem section with its presentation of Jesus' passion (11:1 - 15:20). The epilogue (15:21 - 16:8) — the narrative of Jesus' death, burial and resurrection — will conclude the gospel by paralleling the prologue. In the Jerusalem section and prologue, too, will be a gathering together of the major themes of the first four envelopes. An analysis of this relationship should help to clarify the shape of the entire gospel.

The rather unusual form of this book about Mark grows from an effort to understand the relationship between religious art and theology and to explain that relationship to a lay audience as well as to meet the standards required by New Testament scholars. In this introduction, a brief comment is in order concerning the book's organization. Some helpful suggestions can perhaps be made for lay persons, for this book is written essentially for them. The book's form is determined primarily by an inductive method of carefully drawing conclusions from as much evidence as possible. This procedure has led to the inclusion of copious examples and careful analysis of small details. Such a method is obviously necessary if the conclusions of the work are to be validated by good logic, but it does sometimes create problems with style.

The first chapter, however, should be relatively easy to read. After a brief survey of basic critical tools, this chapter considers the relationship between Mark's beginning and his ending verses. An analysis of the full prologue and epilogue will reveal them to be the "bookends" of the gospel, much in the same way that the doublets are frames for the smaller envelopes. Although some readers might find the intense focus on textual detail in chapter 2 to be irritating, it will show how Mark was influenced by the form of chiasmus or concentric construction. Its purpose is to give an overview of the entire gospel

INTRODUCTION 9

by highlighting the basic patterns and themes. Since these patterns do literally provide a diagram of Mark's methods, they should clarify much of the book's content.

Throughout the whole book my goal has been to integrate the many examples and details into a readable style which would reach out beyond an audience of scholars. I have been encouraged by the fact that Schillebeeckx's book on Jesus,[9] though quite scholarly in nature, obviously was widely read. His readability was due to the clarity conferred by his style and also to the sense of adventure and excitement he conveyed concerning his life-long research into the life and teachings of Jesus. I have taken care, therefore, to achieve clarity by defining carefully the terminology used, and whenever possible, by avoiding, or at least defining, the jargon which so frequently attaches itself to the different kinds of literary and biblical criticism. Specific examples should help with the analysis and understanding of the material, which though technical at times, is not really difficult. The reader should find the concluding summaries of most chapters helpful in following the development of ideas.

After the second chapter, the book is able to follow the three envelopes in the order Mark presents them. Chapter 3, for example, will focus upon the "Healing Many" envelope, drawing together conclusions from the previous sections in order to illustrate clearly how Mark intends to organize this and the other envelopes. The book's epilogue will discuss Jesus as both a tragic and triumphant figure. Finally, for those interested, the appendix comments briefly on the relevance of this analysis to the synoptic problem, and offers suggestions for further research.

If the reader is not distracted by a new and sometimes strange terminology, my inductive approach to the gradually unfolding patterns of Mark's gospel will perhaps provide some measure of interest or even some excitement. As much as possible, my goal has been to present the paths of analysis so that the reader may share my own sense of discovery.

# 1
# The Shape of Mark's Gospel

The beginning and ending of Mark's gospel stand in significant relationship to one another. In the first scenes, for instance, John baptizes Jesus, who descends into the water and then ascends to be confirmed by the voice from heaven to be God's Son. In the last scenes of the gospel Jesus descends into the grave, but then ascends as resurrected Lord, confirmed by the angel at the empty tomb. This baptism at the beginning and the crucifixion, burial, and resurrection at the end stand as bookends on either side of the gospel story.[10]

As noted in the introduction, Mark forms the envelopes by placing portions of his text between doublets. Mark signals, in the large framework of the gospel, a principle he will apply to those smaller parts of the gospel called envelopes in this analysis. The basic research question guiding this analysis is whether there is a structural integrity within the portions of gospel text framed by doublets, which are themselves bookends which he utilizes on a large or small scale or both. If it can be demonstrated, for instance, that the baptism, death, burial, and resurrection contain significant parallels which state the basic themes of the gospel, then it becomes much more probable that Mark would use similar small constructions to border his smaller envelopes. Not only can this broad focus provide an initial overview of Mark's structure, it can also supply the reader with an introductory glimpse of the shape from front to back.

This analysis starts with these beginning and concluding parallel scenes for the following reasons: 1) they give an excellent opportunity to discover, at the outset, some of the basic themes which unify the entire gospel story, and these themes will prove to be some of the same ones which organize the envelopes; 2) a comparison of beginning and ending will also facilitate, in a clear way, the introduction of the basic critical vocabulary to be used in this book.

This chapter, therefore, is divided into three parts: the first subsection defines and briefly discusses the basic tools of literary criticism; the second part takes a close look at the basic framework of the gospel, as provided by baptism and resurrection; the third part identifies Mark's prologue as including much more than the beginning scenes. This analysis should set the reader on guard against reading this gospel only in a linear way, looking only for one thing after another or for a smooth chronological continuity. The gospel may indeed be read (and usually is) in such a way, but so much can be lost. To read this gospel as chronological documentary is to drive upon a very bumpy road, an unnecessary detour taken by tourists. The bumps in that road are usually created by the "awkward transitions" which form critics find so significant. The bumpy road is there; but if it is only a detour or frontage road, and not the main highway, why drive on it? Mark's story is not, therefore, designed simply for reading from beginning to end. The linear story is transformed into religious text through its many inner parallels.

## The Gospel as Literature

For the interpretation of a written text, the basic tools of literary criticism are plot, character, symbol, and theme. Very briefly, these must be defined before taking a close look at Mark's gospel. Aristotle gave us a useful definition of plot in his *Poetics*. He defines plot as an organically connected series of episodes proceeding from one to another in a probable manner.[11] Mark's plot consists of a chronological progression of episodes moving from the river Jordan to the empty tomb. The manner in which Mark has connected his episodes, the ways he has juxtaposed them, the probable relationships which he intended between each and among many of them, these are the elements of plot which must be examined in our analysis.

Kingsbury defines a plot sequence "as governed by time and causality so as to reach ... (a) climax and to elicit from the reader one desired response." Mark's plot, Kingsbury believes, has as its beginning the baptism scenes and the temptation (1:2-12), its middle from the beginnings of the Galilean ministry through the healing of the man at Bethsaida (1:13 - 8:26), and its end from Peter's confession through the empty tomb (8:27 - 16:8.).[12] We shall examine other ideas concerning the general structure of the gospel; the point now is that we should realize that the evangelist probably had some ideas about structure which guided him in the composition of the text. Kingsbury shows how conflict moves the plot forward. Jesus' struggles, in other words, move the plot toward Jerusalem and beyond.[13] Another critic, James Williams, has written that Mark emphasized plot from the beginning of the gospel to its end, deliberately developing it so as to intimately connect all the gospel's scenes.[14] Mark's special attitude toward his material transforms his own idea of plot. The story he tells, after all, is to be a model for living. In the first encounter with Jesus, the reader/listener[15] is an observer of the action. Gradually, however, Mark invites the reader to identify with the disciples' struggles so that both disciples and readers are drawn into the action. After the resurrection as noted in the introduction, both are required to go again to Galilee and to reenact the gospel plot. The second time they are empowered by the risen Christ. Mark has thus taken a special view of plot as a model for mimesis, or imitation.

Mark's plot is also special because of the strange way it was put together from the oral tradition. Mark's plot appears to have been at least partly composed by his stringing together of smaller inherited units, called pericopes. This critical term derives from two Greek words meaning "cut around"; in other words, a pericope is a story "scissored," as it were, from one tradition and then pasted into another. The scenes depicting Jesus' baptism or his transfiguration, for instance, are each a pericope. So named by form critics, they seem to represent independent units of tradition inherited by the evangelists. They probably represent the form taken by these stories during the period of oral transmission preceding the writing of the Gospels. Travis writes that the stories circulated as independent units because "the acts and sayings of Jesus would be recounted by preachers and teachers as occasion demanded." He goes on to say that we "cannot imagine the apostles giving a series of lectures in the temple precincts on the life of Jesus. Rather they would use some particular story or word of Jesus to bring home some point in the course of their preaching. This is why when we look, for example, at Mark 2:1 - 3:6 we find a collection of short paragraphs (pericopes), each complete in itself and with no essential connection with what precedes or follows."[16]

Mark's unique style, therefore, derives to a large extent from the way he presents the plot, or action, through a series of these pericopes, often with only the briefest of transitions between them.

Mark may have composed some of these units himself; he may have reshaped others for their special use in his gospel. The result of his combination of them is a series of scenes often abruptly juxtaposed. This abruptness is not really confusing, however, because Mark's transitions keep the story moving quickly from one scene to the next. Consisting often of short phrases like "they went on from there," or "they came to," the transitions do, after all, make obvious Mark's basic chronological pattern. The effect of these brief scenes upon the reader is like seeing a group of statues arranged in a symbolic line or like seeing pictures framed in a line along a wall. Mark's plot, like medieval statuary, is presented almost as a tactile event to the illiterate. The story of Jesus is an orally shaped story meant to emblazon a series of scenes on the mind of the reader.

"A poem," wrote Archibald Macleish, "should not mean, but be."[17] Therefore while we are dealing with an epic plot, we are presented with a work intended for the common person. We are discovering, however, that this is an intricately crafted work involving the highest achievements of narrative art. Scholars may say that Mark is clumsy when they compare him to Homer,[18] but one must not overlook the profundity of Mark's religious art. The major idea for the reader to keep in mind is the multifaceted quality of the pericopes, how they reflect the light from one to another, so that all are bound not only in a rigid linear formation, but also carefully arranged as interconnected scenes, each in some way reflecting the light of the whole gospel.

Although accused of clumsiness, Mark has nonetheless given a significant chronological and symbolic order to various units of tradition. Most importantly, these strange and abrupt episodes are saved from disorder by their presentation as a dramatic plot. Stripped of discursive transitions which would probably only get in the way, Mark's story is a hard-hitting drama. One after another, in powerful succession, these small scenes confront and challenge the reader, who now must be audience as well. With their dialogue consisting mostly of direct quotations, these scenes move through complicating actions toward a climax, or high point. Mark the narrator has, in effect, placed Jesus' story on stage for us.

There is a strong likelihood that Mark presents the gospel plot as a tragic series of episodes. This is not to say that he changed the story but that both he and the oral tradition may have absorbed the influence of Greek drama.[19] Augustine Stock has observed that there was probably a Greek theater in Sepphoris—not far from Nazareth—during the lifetime of Jesus.[20] He also analyzes the Gospels to show how there is evidence, in the three synoptic gospels, of allusions to the stage, so that one may wonder whether not only Mark but also Jesus himself may have been aware of Greek tragedy. Stock convincingly argues that the synoptic traditions were aware of and perhaps influenced by Greek ideas about tragedy.[21] Mark's stage, at the beginning of his story, is set in the wilderness near the Jordan river. This stage will widen to include Capernaum and much of Galilee. As Jesus moves toward Jerusalem, the stage will expand further, until finally, with the resurrection, all heaven and earth are included in the scope of the gospel!

Mark's plot, then, is not only a dramatic one but is also, in many respects, an epic plot, which usually shows the great conflicts of great heroes and the nations they represent. The Hebrew Scriptures, which are closely interwoven into the New Testament by direct quotes and typological allusion, also were epic in scope, moving outward from garden to exile to promised land, involving the fate of a nation and of a people. Like the Greek epics, the Hebrew epic needs a large stage. The Christian epic, inheriting that Judaic stage and extending salvation to all humankind, needs an even larger one. John Milton found the right genre when he dramatized the Christian story as *Paradise Lost* and *Paradise Regained*. Mark is certainly aware that he borrows from the epic genre, especially in its ancient Hebrew mode, when he begins with his own genesis: the creative voice of God, and the divine messengers of John the Baptist and the dove. His conclusion, too, is epic, involving the fate of all humankind and creation itself. The resurrection of Jesus is a new genesis which extends the first creation by fulfilling its destiny as the new creation of the kingdom of God. The stately majesty of the story of Jesus comes not only from the dignity of his character, but also from the epic context in which he moves. Mark, composer and editor, is guided primarily by this model, especially its Hebrew Scriptures form.

Another important element which informs and organizes Mark's story, both within and among the envelopes, is his method of characterization. Or perhaps we should say the purpose of his characterization is what is important. Each of the characters is heavily influenced by symbolism; John the Baptist, as an example, was seen to incorporate many of the qualities of Elijah. He looms large as a character of mythic stature, representing the prophetic tradition of

Hebrew Scripture. The character of Jesus is christological, determined by Mark's purpose of conveying the experience of the risen Christ within the person of Jesus of Nazareth. We shall begin to analyze this phenomenon in some detail within this chapter, and continue to watch its development right up to and including the resurrection.

In addition to this theologization of character in regard to Jesus, the characters of Simon Peter and the other disciples are often presented as foils to the character of Jesus. Their traits, especially their ignorance and slowness to learn, are shaped by Mark's teaching purposes. Simon Peter, James, John, and the other disciples do indeed receive some bad press, but I believe that the first-century Christian would surely have understood that what was communicated was not the slow wit of the first disciples, but the necessity for correct understanding of Christian teaching.

The fate of the initiate/audience is involved with the fate of Jesus of Nazareth; and he or she is invited to share, through the struggles of the disciples, the experiences of Jesus' earthly life in order to know the character and living presence of the risen Christ. This most severe of gospels, one so utterly limited to action and so economical in its presentation of Jesus' teaching, makes essentially the same demands upon the reader as does the gospel of John. That demand is to understand and experience the deepest mystery of the Christian faith, the mystery of the person of the risen Christ.

This drama, moreover, is a form which invites the reader to share the experiences on stage with the actors. The disciples, after they were convinced of Jesus' resurrection, reinterpreted their own lives through the lens of the resurrection. They had to be aware, as they told and retold the gospel story, how their own lives formed a pattern which would also characterize the lives of each new believer. The new believer, after the crucifixion, would now experience, with the risen Christ, many of the same struggles and insights which the disciples had experienced both with Jesus of Nazareth and later in the pentecostal experiences. There would be no effective way, surely, of proclaiming the new faith in some dry theological tract.

The gospel, the good news, is inseparable from story as it turns out. The life of Jesus of Nazareth is here within the story, but we cannot be sure—from a modern point of view—how much documentary reality it contains: the color of Jesus' sandals when he arrived in Jerusalem, the exact sizes of crowds, the weather, etc. But we do have, in the plot and character, as remembered and preserved by the early church and Mark, what they wanted the initiate to know about this man and his fate. We must read the gospel in the light of this assumed purpose. Thus, to investigate the evangelist's characterization of Jesus is also to follow the development of his christology. The uncovering of Jesus' character, his identity, is primarily a vital part of the process of salvation (soteriology). The study of character, then, as well as the study of plot provides a light which helps the critic understand Mark's theology. Kingsbury says it well.

> In telling of Jesus ... Mark interrelates identity with destiny. Not until Jesus' destiny of death on the cross has been narrated does any human other than Jesus himself perceive the mystery of his identity as the Son of God, the kingly figure in whom God is decisively at work ... By tracing the contours not only of Jesus' ministry but also of the gradual unveiling of his identity, one can highlight this interrelatedness of identity and destiny.[22]

Plot itself, in Mark, therefore, becomes a vital contributor to characterization.

These literary categories we are employing are indispensable as tools, but they rarely exist independently, that is without some interrelationship. Narrative, for example, is rarely simply narrative of a sort that does not contribute to characterization. Greek drama frequently demonstrates that humankind's character is its fate; thus a person's actions—his or her plot, karma, fate—are related to one's character. In the same way, a theme could hardly exist without a narrative, characterization, etc. This interdependence is especially prominent in the discussion of symbolism.

Mark's text, as religious writing, reveals symbolism, for instance, on several levels: character, action, and dialogue. Most characters are symbolic; and much of the action, setting, and dialogue is symbolic as well. When we discuss symbolism we usually discuss it in relation to one of the other categories. John the Baptist is symbolic of Elijah, that is to say, he represents Elijah at least in that figure's relationship to end time. This symbolic connection is intensified in Mark by the clothing John wore and by the fact that he lived in the wilderness. The greatest danger in finding and analyzing symbols, of course, is that they can be oversimplified and can become reductive; that is to say that if one merely states that John the Baptist only represents Elijah, that oversimplification would distort one's interpretation. But mere symbol-hunting will not do; in all good writing the relationships of symbol to narrative, character, and theme must be explored thoroughly. We must be especially careful not to read into the text but, as modern critical theory insists, to allow the text to speak for itself.

My own method is to some extent structural in the sense that I am searching for structural signals and attempting to relate the different parts of Mark's gospel to the whole. Most symbolism in good literature must be interpreted carefully in the light of the whole text. This is true not only in modern novels such as *The Scarlet Letter* or *Moby Dick*, where the large symbols dominate the text, but especially in regard to the religious symbolism of the Christian Gospels. Mark's symbolism is intimately related with other elements of his story.

Jesus' actions are sometimes reminiscent of Elijah's actions, as when Jesus feeds the five thousand and later the four thousand. On the mount of transfiguration, Jesus' garments shine brightly; and we remember Moses on another mountain, Sinai, where after he received the commandments from God, his face glowed. This symbolism is double-edged. The beholders view the past in the transfigured Jesus, to be sure. They also experience a memory of the future: the coming resurrection of Christ and his future presence among his people. Most of Jesus' teaching is pregnant with allusive symbols, as when he speaks of the fig tree and the seasons, or when he teaches about sowing a seed.

Much of this symbolism is rooted in a process similar to midrash, a kind of interpretation found in rabbinic literature and which "related the teachings of rabbinic Judaism to the biblical text." Midrash "assumes that the biblical text has an inexhaustible fund of meaning that is relevant to and adequate for every question and situation."[23] Much of Mark's symbolism is of the nature of Haggadah, which is a midrash interpreting

> the historical and religious passages of Jewish Scripture that are not legal in character ... Many stories and legends came to be told about such central figures in Israel's history as Adam, Enoch, Abraham, Joseph, and Moses ... Unlike

the strict logic of legal interpretation, Haggadah could give free play to the imagination. [Haggadic expositions are not bound to the previous tradition], but the story had to remain within the bounds of what was acceptable to the religious community.[24]

Bailey defines midrash as a literary genre, "a type of literature, oral or written, which stands in direct relationship to a fixed canonical text, considered to be authoritative and the revealed word of God by the midrashist and his audience, in which this canonical text is explicitly cited or alluded to." Four subforms are observed by Bailey. He notices these in the letters of Paul, but obviously intends to demonstrate their prevalence in intertestamental times. These forms are 1) running commentary, 2) *pēšer* interpretation, 3) typological interpretation, and 4) allegorical interpretation.[25] Bailey emphasizes, then, that

> postbiblical Judaism developed a number of literary forms that can be legitimately classified as midrash ... Like the Qumran community, the Christians quoted and interpreted passages in the sacred Scriptures retrospectively in light of what they were convinced was God's revelatory activity and in the firm conviction that they were living in the end-times... [The Christians, however, believing Jesus to be the promised Messiah] looked to the Scriptures for confirmation that Jesus' activities, crucifixion, and resurrection made sense christologically.[26]

The early church obviously made use of this genre, as it naturally would, since the first members were all Jews. Thus, in the Elijah cycle of stories, there are obvious parallels with Jesus' words and actions, just as there are many important parallels between Jesus and Moses. These and other typologies find expression in the story of Jesus as it has been preserved for us. The New Testament looks to the future, but it is intentionally and inextricably interwoven with the past, and this fact gives the symbolism much of its flavor.

The final critical term, "theme," represents a very important critical tool, especially in this analysis. Like symbolism, theme can only be understood when analyzed in the light of narrative and character. It enters into other elements in the story and could not really exist without them. Often misdefined as a central idea of a work, theme is actually an organizing principle of a text. Only in the most amateurish writing could theme be conceived of as a sugar-coated pill or a simple moralistic message. No intelligent person would interpret the theme of *Moby Dick*, for example, as being "Don't mess with white whales!" Theme, rather, usually reflects the author's guiding organizational idea. The finished writing reflects this theme in the way architecture, for instance, often reflects some principle which guided the architect. For example, in Mark, the theme of identity is one of the dominant themes; plot, character, and symbol all involve, in some way, the theme concerning the riddle of Christ's true identity.

In the great works of literature—the Greek tragedies, Shakespeare's works, the Hebrew Scriptures—themes are often symphonic in nature. Introduced perhaps in an inconspicuous way, these ideas temporarily are muted and subdued, then reemerge—again and again—to culminate in climactic passages. It is very instructive, with this in mind, to examine *Hamlet* or *Oedipus* or many of the stories of the Hebrew Bible, such as those in the book of Genesis or the story of Job. When studying such patterns, it is important to exercise care to demonstrate, inductively and with a careful eye on the text, the relationship of these themes to other elements in the work—setting, plot, and character, for instance. The guiding principle must always be the avoidance of extreme subjectivity. The best literary analysis is not motivated by a search for ornament or esthetic surprises, but for insights leading to a sound interpretation.

## Bookends

The discussion of Mark's unique genre and unusual style should help us understand his opening verses introducing John the Baptist. Mark's introduction both looks back to the Hebrew Scriptures and points forward to the life of Jesus. In addition, Mark's concluding verses about the empty tomb will reflect the ideas of his introduction, thus looking back upon the life of Jesus and forward to the life of the church. At the inception of the gospel, John the Baptist also stands as a Janus[27] figure, looking back to the prophets and forward to the ministry of Jesus:

## THE SHAPE OF MARK'S GOSPEL

> The beginning of the good news of Jesus Christ, the Son of God. As it is written in the prophet Isaiah, "See, I am sending my messenger ahead of you, who will prepare your way; the voice of one crying out in the wilderness: 'Prepare the way of the Lord, Make his paths straight'".[28] John the baptizer appeared in the wilderness, proclaiming a baptism of repentance for the forgiveness of sins. And people from the whole Judean countryside and all the people of Jerusalem were going out to him, and were baptized by him in the river Jordan, confessing their sins. Now John was clothed with camel's hair, with a leather belt around his waist, and he ate locusts and wild honey. He proclaimed, "The one who is more powerful than I is coming after me; I am not worthy to stoop down and untie the thong of his sandals. I have baptized you with water; but he will baptize you with the Holy Spirit" (Mark 1:1-8).

So begins the prologue of the gospel. And at the end, in the last verses of the epilogue (16:1-8), Mark writes,

> When the Sabbath was over, Mary Magdalene, and Mary the mother of James, and Salome bought spices, so that they might go and anoint him. And very early on the first day of the week, when the sun had risen, they went to the tomb. They had been saying to one another, "Who will roll away the stone for us from the entrance to the tomb?" When they looked up, they saw that the stone, which was very large, had already been rolled back. As they entered the tomb, they saw a young man, dressed in a white robe, sitting on the right side; and they were alarmed. But he said to them, "Do not be alarmed; you are looking for Jesus of Nazareth, who was crucified. He has been raised; he is not here. Look, there is the place they laid him. But go, tell his disciples and Peter that he is going ahead of you to Galilee; there you will see him, just as he told you. So they went out and fled from the tomb, for terror and amazement had seized them; and they said nothing to anyone, for they were afraid.

Augustine Stock and other recent critics[29] have noticed strong parallels between these passages at the beginning and end of Mark's gospel. Both John the Baptist in the introduction, for example, and the angel (or young man) in the empty tomb are prophets foretelling the advent of Jesus: the first tells that one greater than John will arrive; and the young man, in the second instance, informs the women that Jesus may be seen in Galilee. Both herald, then, a beginning of Jesus' ministry. John in the first scene announces the beginning of Jesus' ministry in Galilee and Jerusalem; the resurrection announces the second ministry—the new mission which begins after the death of Jesus of Nazareth. As sometimes in classical drama, the reader encounters, in both prologue and epilogue, a messenger from God whose monologue introduces the spectators to the action. Both sections involve a divine pronouncement, and both involve a descent and an ascent. During the baptism there is a descent into the water and a rising up: "And just as he was coming up out of the water, he saw the heavens torn apart and the Spirit descending like a dove on him. And a voice came from heaven, 'You are my Son, the Beloved; with you I am well pleased'" (1:10-11).

The tomb will be another place into which Jesus descends at burial and from which he later will ascend. Furthermore, after the resurrection, the church has reached the point prophesied by John when he said that Jesus would baptize with the Holy Spirit. Stock notices as well the connections of the first and last scenes with the transfiguration scene which appears near the mathematical center of the gospel. In each of those three scenes, he calls attention to the descriptions of special garments (for instance, John's camel's hair apparel and the white linen garment worn by the young man at the tomb). Both of the garments are eschatological symbols. John's camel's hair recalls Elijah, and at the tomb, the angel's white apparel echoes the epiphanies in Hebrew Scriptures and in intertestamental literature. In the transfiguration scene, Jesus' garments become "dazzling white, such as no one on earth could bleach them" (9:3).

Mark uses his first scenes not only to parallel his last scenes, but also to look backward to the Hebrew Scriptures and thus to establish immediately the relationship of the new religion with Judaism. This theological, chronological, and dramatic link between the Hebrew Scriptures and the New Testament occurs in the person of John the Baptist. These relationships are established not only by explicit quotations and by the connotations provided by symbolism. The messengers of King Ahaziah describe the appearance of Elijah the Tishbite: "A hairy man, with a leather belt around his waist" (2 Kgs 1:8). John's physical appearance helps establish the Elijah typology, introducing as well a major theme which will surface and submerge several times throughout the story. A link is thus established through the Elijah symbol, not only with the past but also with the present and the future; for during the intertestamental period, many expected the return of Elijah. They believed that his return would herald the end of the age.

Mark, interestingly enough, begins by quoting a prophecy of Malachi, but mistakenly attributes it to Isaiah, who is the author of the remainder of the quotation. Malachi wrote: "See, I am sending my messenger to prepare the way before me, and the Lord whom you seek will suddenly come to his temple" (3:1). As Stock points out, "This passage has an important bearing on Jesus' cleansing of the temple" (Mark 12:15).[30] At the end of his prophecy, Malachi reveals that the messenger will be Elijah: "Lo, I will send you Elijah the prophet before the great and terrible day of the Lord comes" (4:5). As an Elijah figure, John the Baptist stands as a major symbol at the doorway connecting the two testaments, both explicitly in his prophecy and implicitly in his physical appearance.[31]

John's name is mentioned again in the gospel. Jesus' mission begins with the arrest of John (1:14), and concurrently with the death of John (6:14-29) Jesus sends out the twelve disciples and feeds the five thousand. Jesus clearly refers to John (9:9-12) as he and the disciples are descending the mount of transfiguration, identifying him there with Elijah.

John the Baptist is important to Mark because on the levels of narrative, symbol, and theme, he functions as a unifier of Mark's text as well as a counterpoint, or foil, to Jesus of Nazareth, who will do some of the same things that John did, and then more. John invited Jews to join a new Israel. Jesus, on the other hand, would bring the Holy Spirit, "the gift of the final time which will—quite differently from the waters of the Jordan—purify, sanctify, and bind believers to God in a lasting community. Baptism with the Spirit will be poured out on all flesh. The prophet Ezekiel had also foretold: 'I will sprinkle clean water upon you, and you shall be clean ... A new heart I will give you, and a new spirit I will put within you, and make you follow in my statutes ... You shall be my people and I will be your God'" (Ezek 36:25-28).[32]

Even though John's prophecies do apply to Jesus as the expected Messiah, John would be greatly surprised at what Jesus will become. According to the Q tradition, John was surprised: "Are you the one who is to come, or are we to wait for another?" (Matt 11:2; see also Luke 7:9). John the Baptist does not prophesy, for instance, concerning the Suffering Servant which Jesus would become — that the promise of the Spirit which Jesus would bring would be fulfilled by his shameful death upon the cross. What John's prophecies give is a blank outline to be filled in by Mark. Or, to change the metaphor, John provides the blank canvas upon which the portrait of Jesus is to be painted, filled with the details of his ministry. John's prophecy must be, in a sense, dramatically completed by the evangelist, if Jesus is to be presented to the new believer as the Son of God. If Mark is successfully to write a book for initiates into the new faith, he must somehow dramatize the theological differences which occur when God's Son is identified by a messianic formula[33] and later when Jesus is portrayed as the suffering Son of Man. It is largely for this reason that Mark is necessarily full of surprises which become an essential part of the good news. Because they expect a messianic king of great power, a king who will establish his glory upon this earth, the disciples themselves will constantly be surprised at the unfolding identity of Jesus. Mark apparently felt that christology could best be expressed by this gradual and dramatic revelation of Jesus' true identity.

The plot of the greatest story ever told is from its first lines a series of attempts to identify Jesus. This process is effective as narrative because of the constant tension it generates; the process is effective as a teaching device, because the evangelist is able to use the inherited story of Jesus of Nazareth in such a way as to instruct the initiate gradually concerning the identity of the risen Christ. Mark deftly arranges the scenes and sayings of the gospel to reveal the identity of Jesus through a series of affirmations and negations. Remarkably, the evangelist will accomplish his purpose without being in the least destructive of tradition. The picture of Jesus he is painting will constantly change, but nothing of Hebrew tradition will be destroyed, wasted, or lost. The negations concerning Jesus' identity are without exception creative because they are always incomplete affirmations of Jesus. Each of these incomplete affirmations, such as John the Baptist's prophecies, will be made complete by some later surprising episode in the life of Christ. Thus, we can reach at any point into this gospel and find a true statement about Jesus' identity (even, ironically, from the demons and other hostile detractors).

To find Mark's christology, however, we must read this gospel as a whole, from beginning to end, and be aware of the metamorphoses involved. Jesus changes (only apparently) from scene to scene, as different aspects of his person are dramatically defined. Mark's *tour de force* is his ability to integrate his picture of Christ into one unified portrait which includes and yet transcends its individual features. The four envelopes will represent four thematic units used by Mark to paint this christological portrait of the Christ as Jesus approaches the cross and resurrection. In spite of the dramatic confusion concerning Jesus' identity, however, Mark will ultimately demonstrate his agreement with the author of Hebrews: "Jesus Christ is the same yesterday and today and forever" (13:8).

## The Prologue

Mark's full prologue consists of scenes intended to introduce the basic themes of the gospel. Many of these introductory themes are to be reflected in the conclusion, or epilogue, of the gospel. The descent and ascent associated with baptism are later reflected in the descent into and the ascent from the grave. In addition, the temptation in the wilderness is later reflected by the crucifixion in a desolate place. As Augustine Stock observes, new life begins both in wilderness and in tomb: just as Israel found sustenance and new beginning in the wilderness, so the new covenant will find its beginning in a place associated with desolation.[34]

In his temptation scene of only two verses, Mark does not use, for whatever reason, the longer, more dramatically realized scenes of Matthew or Luke. Mark does, nonetheless, introduce here a darker theme which becomes more pronounced as Jesus begins his ministry and his journey toward the cross. For similarly to the John-Elijah symbolism, the symbols of evil first appear in the prologue and persist as the gospel unfolds. Evil thus is a unifying theme. Even though never again in the gospel will Satan appear, his influence will be felt through his legion of demons.

In the context of this large theme, as Jesus confronts the evil of the world, the demons (as well as the persons or elements they inhabit) convulse in the presence of the messenger. These convulsions occur not only in the exorcisms of people but also in Jesus' confrontations with the powers which temporarily govern nature. The divine messenger, Jesus, must walk across a stormy sea.

It is as if the approach of the kingdom and its messenger force a metaphysical breach, as if God's approach to humankind forces an area of storm and turbulence. As Stock puts it, "Jesus'... mission is rooted in his power over the elements, over demons, and over death."[35] The confrontation with Satan here in the temptation scene is thematically related to the exorcisms, and the healings.

The debates, which often bring vitriolic, threatening actions from the Pharisees and the authorities, are also related to this theme of evil. There is a convulsive reaction not only among the powers which rule nature, but also from the powers which govern the world. Jesus' appearance amongst humankind, then, is intrinsically related to the conflict between two ages — the present age and the coming kingdom. These so-called ages are actually states of being. As Kelber says, "Jesus' exorcising ministry amounts to a clash between two kingdoms. As he brings his newly gained authority into play, by actualizing his new word of teaching, he makes a reality of God's rule on earth. To do battle on behalf of the kingdom of God is the intrinsic purpose of the exorcism."[36] The sea and the wind react to the harbinger of the new age because Jesus has been given power over them. Demons control nature, therefore, as surely as they control human beings. Jesus of Nazareth threatens them; they recognize him, and react violently. The foreshadowing of evil in the temptation scene provides an early example of how Mark uses symphonic imagery. There is only a hint of the theme now, but it will reappear at intervals, finally reaching its high point at Golgotha.[37]

In this temptation scene, another theme is briefly introduced: the wilderness. A harsh, lonely place, it is associated with the "wild beasts" (v. 13). Stock sees this wilderness as "a place of testing and grace."[38] It will include all those places in Mark described by the Greek word *eremos*, which is used to refer to the lonely places such as the mountains to which Jesus withdraws and the lonely places encountered in the feedings of the multitudes. The wilderness is Jesus' place apart, then — not just a specific region in Palestine. Appropriately, this theme will reach its high points at Gethsemane and at the tomb. It is as if, in these first scenes, the reader is presented with miniatures, small scenes unfolding in rapid succession, scenes which sound the initial notes of themes which will later dominate the gospel as Jesus' portrait continues to unfold.

If that portrait is present to us only in outline at the beginning of Mark, so are Jesus' teachings largely held back for the time being. In the first three chapters, Mark will quote Jesus, but not at length, and it is only in Mark's fourth chapter, with its parables, that he will take a first close look at Jesus' teachings. The reason for this initial reluctance becomes clear as the gospel continues; Mark sees Jesus' message as being incorporated essentially within Jesus' person and his actions. His gospel is consequently stripped down to action; the only lengthy teachings occur in chapters four and thirteen. Much of his teaching is embodied, not in long orations, but in the dramatic clashes with Pharisees and other opponents. At the very beginning of his gospel, however, Mark wants only to give the teachings in broad outline: "Now after John was arrested, Jesus came into Galilee, proclaiming the good news of God, and saying, 'The time is fulfilled, and the kingdom of God has come near; repent, and believe in the good news'" (1:14-15). Two of these themes have already appeared. John the Baptist (as Elijah) has signaled the end time and has offered baptism as a mode of repentance (though John doesn't forgive sins).

The "believe in the good news" injunction, is usually viewed as an author-to-reader comment.[39] It also seems to me to be directed particularly to the initiate, the new Christian. Mark says, in essence, "Believe in the gospel story which I shall now relate for you." This tripartite statement of Jesus' message then proceeds to give only the broadest of outlines, because Mark wants to move quickly into the action of the gospel story—the call of the first disciples.

> As Jesus passed along the Sea of Galilee, he saw Simon and his brother Andrew casting a net into the sea—for they were fishermen. And Jesus said to them, "Follow me and I will make you fish for people." And immediately they left their nets and followed him. As he went a little farther, he saw James son of Zebedee and his brother John, who were in their boat mending the nets. Immediately he called them; and they left their father Zebedee in the boat with the hired men, and followed him (1:16-20).

In the prologue so far, we have encountered prophecies, the voice of God, the opening of the heavens, and the appearance of Satan. Jesus now moves, however, from "supernatural" regions toward the world of humans so that Simon, Andrew, James and John can be introduced. Even with this summoning of the four disciples, Mark's world nonetheless retains some of its mythic dimensions. This is a beautiful passage, shaped lovingly into simple rhythms. The characters, presented with only a few brush strokes, are larger than life. Even on the basis of an incomplete identification of him, the disciples are still able to make an unconditional response to his call. The passage thus introduces a basic theme in which the righteous response to the messenger is expressed as an unhesitating willingness to follow him. As one of Mark's symphonic themes, it will reach its high point in Mark's ninth chapter. The righteous, or right, response to Jesus is critical because the kind of response made will determine who can be healed or who can answer the call (negatively demonstrated in the rich man's refusal to follow Jesus, 10:17-22).

Thus we see that Mark's prologue is a special kind of introduction in which the central themes which dominate the body of the gospel are anticipated by the evangelist. This method is apparent as well in the confrontation, in the Capernaum synagogue, with the demoniac:

> They went to Capernaum; and when the Sabbath came, he entered the synagogue and taught. They were astounded at his teaching, for he taught them as one having authority, and not as the scribes. Just then there was in their synagogue a man with an unclean spirit, and he cried out, "What have you to do with us, Jesus of Nazareth? Have you come to destroy us? I know who you are, the Holy One of God." But Jesus rebuked him, saying, " Be silent, and come out of him!" (1:21-26).

The demon knows that Jesus is the "Holy One of God" (v. 24) and he recognizes the threat from Jesus to the realm of evil. It is his "I know who you are," statement which continues the identity theme introduced by John and by God's voice from heaven. There is a continuity, too, with John's triumphant prophecy and with God's announcement, which is, in a strange way, repeated by the demon. By introducing Jesus as an exorcist, recognized by the demon, Mark is telling us, in effect, what we have already suspected: John's predictions and the voice from heaven have given us Jesus only in the broadest outline. His defining qualities are not yet understood by a first-time reader, nor are they understood by the disciples. The demon does not know all either. "What have you to do with us, Jesus of Nazareth?" (1:24). This is a question which is also asked by the reader, and it is a question which can only be answered by the full narration of the gospel story. The riddle of Christ's identity becomes the shaper of the story, then, as each scene relates a bit more about Jesus. The gradual revelation of Jesus' character also proves to be the gradual shaping of Mark's theology.

Mark's identity theme nourishes the theme of teaching, and his method of development has for its purpose the instruction of both the disciples and the reader. In Mark's presentation they will both learn about Jesus in the same scope of dramatic, recreated time. The new believer, as well as the disciples, will often have difficulty understanding Mark's instructions concerning the identity of Jesus. That is because Mark's presentation of Jesus involves a constant process of metamorphosis, with Jesus appearing to be somewhat different in each scene, as each action or teaching has added to his developing portrait. After a while, the reader understands that any picture of Jesus is an incomplete portrait which must wait for the coming scenes for its completion.

The disciples, however, do not get that idea; and their ignorance of Jesus' identity becomes the basis for their blunders. Mark uses the disciples' mistakes, furthermore, as catechesis to instruct the initiate! We are, of course, identifying with a first-time reader or listener; and we know from a second reading that Jesus only apparently changes from scene to scene. His power is complete from the first scenes, as are his compassion and love. What Mark is doing, then, is not changing the picture of Jesus so much as he is filling it out by constant dramatic additions. He demonstrates the fullness of the gospel as present in each of its separate parts.

The identity theme involves the intertwining of two other themes, as well: the theme of power and the theme of the Suffering Servant. In this Capernaum synagogue, Jesus acts immediately to establish himself as servant of all. His powers are placed at the service of humankind as he displays compassion for the suffering and as he identifies with the social outcast. From now on, in scene after scene, Jesus adds to his own portrait not just by his healings and exorcisms as demonstrations of his power, but also by this attitude toward human suffering. When God encounters humankind through his messenger, he moves immediately toward the broken, hurt outcasts of this world. Jesus, who heals the possessed man in this early scene, has already taken up his cross.

Because the Suffering Servant theme is only hinted at early in the gospel, Jesus is only later seen to have possessed this nature from the beginning. The man baptized in the Jordan river was already giving of himself in the first scenes, but it takes the movement toward the cross to develop the picture fully. Because of Mark's dramatic method, the Jesus of this gospel is always Jesus Incognito. That point must be grasped if the reader is to understand Mark's method of relating the gospel story. He is, as we observed earlier, interested not only in portraying Jesus of Nazareth, but also in teaching christology. The qualities of character displayed by the historical Jesus remain the eternal characteristics of the risen Christ. This eternal nature was present in the man Jesus.

It is in this same Capernaum synagogue scene that Mark's chorus makes its first entrance. Used by the Greeks to comment upon the action and thus to universalize it, the chorus was an important part of their plays. Sometimes, as in Sophocles' *Oedipus the King*, it functions as a character within the play, displaying an intense interest in each new development and assuming an apprehensive posture toward unfolding events in which it may also participate. In Mark's gospel drama, as in Sophocles' play, the chorus is closely related to the identity theme. Typically, in Mark, they ask a question, usually in awe, about Jesus' identity and then add some additional comments about him which often serve to summarize the scene:

> They were all amazed, and they kept on asking one another, "What is this? A new teaching—with authority! He commands even the unclean spirits, and they obey him." At once his fame began to spread throughout the surrounding region of Galilee (1:27-28).

If John's prophecy is really only an outline, the chorus here takes an early step toward filling in that outline. At Capernaum, the chorus highlights the central idea of *exousia*, or authority; they confirm that Jesus has been given a special authorization by God. A corollary is thus established in relationship to the divine pronouncement, "You are my beloved Son" (v. 11). Mark uses the chorus, then, as a christological tool which highlights themes, two of which appear in these early pronouncements by the chorus: the theme of identity and the closely allied theme of spreading fame.

## THE SHAPE OF MARK'S GOSPEL

The chorus, in addition to being a commentator, assumes the role of a character in Mark's drama in the sense that they contribute to the development of plot. They often represent the forces brought to bear on Jesus which bring severe stresses into his life. By proclaiming his fame (and the misunderstanding of his mission), they feed the nemesis which grows ever stronger as the story moves toward Jerusalem. These choric responses are also a unifying element in that their constant reappearance provide a thematic strand weaving in and out of the action. At this initial point, the chorus-character is filled with awe; later, at Nazareth or at the trial before Pilate, we shall see their hostility and fickleness.

After this first appearance of the chorus, the healing of Peter's mother-in-law provides a transition between the prologue and the first envelope.[40] The supernatural regions of the introduction are beginning to give way to the hustle and hubbub of the human world, the dirt and dust, and the cries of the suffering. The refocusing began, at least a bit, when the four disciples were named. Now we see Peter's mother-in-law:

> As soon as they left the synagogue, they entered the house of Simon and Andrew, with James and John. Now Simon's mother-in-law was in bed with a fever, and they told him about her at once. He came and took her by the hand and lifted her up. Then the fever left her, and she began to serve them (1:29-31).

The reader remembers that earlier, in verses 16-20, the disciples made an immediate and unconditional response to Jesus' call. In this scene, even though her service to Jesus may not involve formal discipleship, Peter's mother-in-law does provide a positive example of how to receive Jesus into one's life. In the examples provided by both the calling of the four and the healing of this woman, Mark is not only recounting the history of Jesus of Nazareth, he is also demonstrating the response to be made to the risen Christ. This is the technique of double exposure which defines the character of this religious text. What Jesus does, Christ has done, is doing, and will do again. Stock comments on this doubly exposed quality of Mark's pictures of Jesus: "The ability of Jesus to heal physical ailments points to a more important reality: the risen Christ will heal the spiritual blindness of those who follow him in the post resurrection period."[41]

In the same way, the mother-in-law (healed of her fever) rose from her sick bed and served Jesus and the disciples. The prologue, which the evangelist uses to introduce basic themes, ends here, just before the first half of the healing-many doublet.

# 2
# Concentric Constructions

With Jesus' healing of the paralytic (2:1-12), Mark begins to organize his story according to a strange pattern, called a chiasmus or concentric construction. The following diagram is suggested by Joanna Dewey in her book, *Marcan Public Debate*.[42] It provides an apt introduction to a rather complicated subject by illustrating a final critical tool to be employed in this analysis. Occurring not long after the baptism scenes, this structure describes much of the second chapter of Mark, along with the first verses of the third chapter. A detailed discussion of each term in the diagram will soon follow, but here it is important to understand the whole pattern:

  A    Healing of the paralytic (2:1-12).
      B    Calling of Levi (2:13-17).
          C    Question about fasting: (2:18-22) including central logia: the bridegroom and the new teachings.
      B´   Plucking grain on the Sabbath (2:23-28).
  A´  Healing of the man with the withered hand (3:1 - 3:6).

Notice how this construction doubles back upon itself. The A and B terms are paralleled by the A´ and B´ terms. The pattern, therefore, is like the letter V, tipped over on its side. The central term, C, forms the tip of the "V" at the center, which happens to be composed mostly of Jesus sayings.

These constructions in their simplest form are easy to recognize; and they are, at least in regard to their structure, fairly easy to define. Bailey[43] says that a concentric construction or chiasmus, is "a stylistic literary figure which consists of a series of two or more elements followed by a presentation of corresponding elements in reverse order." He describes them as a kind of inverted parallelism. Welch says that such a construction is a "two-part structure or system in which the second half is a mirror image of the first, i.e., where the first term recurs last and the last first." He notes that the term(s) in the center are usually the most important. "The basic figure of chiasm simply involves the reversal of order of words in balancing clauses or phrases."[44] One can identify the construction usually by the repetition of key words and phrases or often by the repetition of key ideas. Formal parallels can be established by repetitions of grammatical and syntactical patterns. A familiar jingle employs, for example, the form of a concentric construction:

A   Old King Cole
   B   Was a merry old soul
   B´  And a merry old soul
A´  Was he

Dewey uses the phrase, "concentric construction," to define the structure, in preference to the old term, "chiasmus." I will follow this practice as much as possible, since the (latinized) Greek term seems stilted and less descriptive to the modern reader.[45] Originally, however, chiasmus was a good description, with the force of its Greek meaning, which is "a cross, or something shaped like a cross: two pieces of wood, for instance, or a bandage placed crosswise around the chest."[46] When used in its literary sense, it refers to this strange construction which doubles back upon itself. However, it is usually diagramed more as a "V" resting on its side, really, than as a cross. The jingle provides a good example because in it one can see the A−B, then B´−A´ of the chiasmus.

An excellent study of concentric constructions in the Bible is offered by Nils Lund in his *Chiasmus in the New Testament*, a standard study to which Dewey expresses her indebtedness. John Welch (mentioned above) and Lund have made, it seems to me, the best studies of these forms. Welch presents a helpful historical survey of this construction. Then, as editor, he gathers articles which provide examples from many primitive cultures, but especially from the Judaic and Hellenic traditions.

Welch writes that a large amount of chiasmus can be found in ancient literature, especially in Greek and Latin. Both he and C. H. Talbert[47] find many concentric constructions in Homer's epics. Welch notes that these constructions often are small, occurring within the structure of one line, although larger ones, extending over several lines, may be found.[48] Almost every page of Virgil, according to Welch, includes concentric constructions.[49]

The use of concentric constructions in ancient Judaism is confirmed by their abundant occurrence in Hebrew Scripture. These constructions occur in both short and long forms, and Lund gives examples of both types. From the Psalms, he gives an example of an eight-line construction:

```
A    The idols of the heathens are silver and gold:
  B    The work of men's hands;
    C    They have mouths, but they speak not;
      D    They have eyes, but they see not;
      D'   They have ears, but they hear not
    C'   Neither is there any breath in their mouth;
  B'   They who make them are like unto them:
A'   So are all they who put their trust in them (Ps 135:15-18).
```

Even a simple list can be cast into a concentric construction:

```
A    And he had sheep and oxen,
  B    And he asses,
    C    And men servants,
    C'   And maid servants,
  B'   And she asses,
A'   And camels (Gen 12:16).
```

From Num 15: 35-36:

```
A    And Yahweh said unto Moses:
  B    He shall surely be put to death, the man,
    C    They shall stone him with stones,
      D    All the congregation without the camp.
        E    And they brought him,
      D'   All the congregation without the camp
    C'   And stoned him with stones
  B'   To death
A'   As Yahweh commanded Moses.[50]
```

Lund also analyzes the longer concentric constructions found in the Bible and establishes the fact that entire sections of the Hebrew Bible were composed (and obviously memorized) using this tool. He finds examples in the third and fourth chapters of Genesis and gives many examples from Leviticus, for it seems that many of the laws expressed in the Pentateuch were cast as concentric constructions.[51]

It should hardly be surprising to find many examples of concentric constructions, both long and short, in the New Testament as well. Here is a group of writings composed within the framework of the oral traditions which were probably both Aramaic and Greek. Bailey, writing about the history of such constructions, shares the following insights: "Chiasms offer us a glimpse into the patterns of thought of ancients. Relatively unconcerned about a linear or logical flow of ideas, biblical communities relished sayings and stories that were memorable, and they thus appreciated repetition that we might consider redundant." Because of their usefulness to oral instruction and to memory, an "extended chiastic design could provide the structure for recalling a longer sequence of verses or stories. In a worship setting, separate groups in the choir or congregation could recite the contrasting parts. So, for ancients the chiasm was not only aesthetically valued but also practically functional." And he adds, interestingly enough, that in our present "post-literary" world, "it might be critically important for us in the church to become more sensitive to the rhetorical dynamics of the chiastic form and its implications for our actual practice in worship and scriptural transmission"[52]

The teachings of Jesus offer many examples of concentric constructions:

```
A    The Sabbath
     B    was made for humankind,
     B´   and not humankind
A´   for the Sabbath (Mark 2:27).

A    And no one puts new wine into old wineskins;
     B    otherwise, the wine will burst the skins,
     B´   and the wine is lost, and so are the skins;
A´   but one puts new wine into fresh wineskins (Mark 2:22-23).
```

Lund convincingly argues that the entire Sermon on the Mount in Matthew's gospel (4:25 - 8:1) is carefully built from a series of these concentric constructions (Lund, 241.) The larger these constructions become, the less exact the parallels become. But that did not stop the ancients from using them! Later in this analysis, these longer constructions will be defined as recursions.

Lund finds one of these long concentric constructions in Matthew's missionary discourse (10:5 - 11:1).[53]

```
A    Jesus and the twelve: the scope of the mission: "the house of
     Israel" (10:6).
  B    Instructions to the disciples: "receive," "food" (10:8, 10).
    C    Testimony under persecution: from strangers: "not
         worthy" (10:13).
      D    Comfort under persecution: "be not anxious"
           (10:19).
        E    The master's own example is recalled: "fear
             them not" (10:26).
      D´   Comfort under persecution: "be not afraid"
           (10:28, 31).
    C´   Testimony under persecution: "from their own
         household" (10:37ff).
  B´   Instructions to the churches: "receive," "to drink" (10:42ff).
A´   Jesus and the twelve: the scope of the mission: "their cities"
     (11:1).[54]
```

Given the prevalence of concentric constructions in Judaic writing, it would not be surprising if Jesus cast his teachings in this form. But it does not really matter if some of his teachings were altered in form by the early church for its own mnemonic or liturgical purposes. Many large sections of the New Testament are organized by means of such constructions. Welch, observing the large amount of material so organized, reaches an interesting conclusion:

> serious readers of the NT cannot afford to proceed with these texts without an awareness of chiasmus as a basic element in the literary composition of the New Testament. Chiasmus has been found to be particularly influential in the books of James, Galatians, 1 Corinthians, Hebrews, Ephesians, Colossians, Philemon,

1 Timothy, 1 Timothy, Jude, Revelation and in certain respects in the four gospels as well ... students of the New Testament should not be reluctant to observe chiastic patterns in most parts of the book ... [for] chiasmus may often supply the needed element of order, or coherent structure, which draws to one's attention the central meaning and fundamental artistry of the writing being studied. Such are benefits which, when found, cannot and will not be ignored.[55]

It is particularly interesting to find so many concentric constructions operating within the letters of Paul. He seems to have composed the seventh chapter of Corinthians as a chiasmus,[56] and it can be argued as well that the entire book of Philemon is also a chiasmus! If Paul indeed organizes his material in such a way, he is composing the longer concentric recursions, just as Mark did. In these longer constructions, or recursions, one would find the organization to be basically topical, with fewer line-by-line parallels. What these examples may reflect, therefore, is a method of outlining used by Paul. He writes most of his letters to be read aloud to an audience, and his concentric constructions may also be a memory aid to his listeners, to aid them in remembering the thoughts he shares.

Paul also employs the smaller constructions. As an example, consider Gal 4:1-7.[57]

```
A    The heir remains a child and servant (4:1).
  B    Until the time appointed of the father (4:2).
    C    When that time came, God sent forth his Son (4:4).
      D    Made under the law (4:4).
      D´   To redeem those under the law (4:5).
    C´   Because you are sons, God sent forth the Spirit of his
         Son (4:6).
  B´   That you cry Abba, Father (4:6).
A´   That you are no more a servant but a son and heir (4:7).
```

As further examples from the writings of Paul, one could also consider Ephesians 11-22 to be a concentric construction (see also Eph 5:5). In Col 3:3-4:

```
A    For you have died,
  B    And your life
    C    Is hidden
      D    With Christ
        E    In God
      D´   When Christ
    C´   Is manifested
  B´   [who is your life],
A´   Then you also will be revealed with him in glory.⁵⁸
```

On and on these examples could continue. Lund's examples are especially instructive because they demonstrate that not only are the sayings of Jesus organized concentrically in the synoptic gospels, but also the doings of Jesus. This idea is extremely important for our analysis in helping us to understand how Mark organizes his material within larger recursive structures. The evangelist will, for instance, often establish thematic comparisons among the doings of Jesus and then relate those doings to a sayings section of the envelope; then he will relate more doings which will parallel both the previous actions and the sayings. Lund first identified a concentric construction in the second and third chapters of Mark, where Dewey finds a pattern. Lund's pattern is closer to the envelope, because he does include the two healing-many passages as the outer frames. His interesting inclusion from Matthew suggests, too, that a basic concentric form may underlie both traditions:

By the seaside: "all the multitude."
  Scribes and Pharisees: Why eat with sinners?
    Justifying example: A proverb about the physician.
      Jesus' disciples and the Pharisees: Why not fast?
        Justifying example: A proverb about the sons of the bridechamber.
          The guiding principle: The new patch on the old garment.
          The guiding principle: The new wine in the old skins.
        Jesus' disciples and the Pharisees: Why do it on the Sabbath?
      Justifying example: David and the priests.
    Pharisees and Herodians: Is it lawful on the Sabbath day?
    Justifying example: the sheep in the pit (Matt 12:11).
  By the seaside: "A great multitude," with other details.
                           (Mark 2:13 - 3:8)⁵⁹

Many of the examples given so far intrigue the reader to look into the parallels established and to interpret meaning in the light of the ensuing comparisons and contrast. Concentric constructions involve more than artifice contrived for esthetic effect. Their mnemonic function has already been discussed, but most interesting for this analysis is the effect of the construction's form upon its contents. The examples already given in this chapter indicate that, within the construction itself, the most important term is placed, as Bailey noted, at the center. Welch says it very well:

> An emphatic focus on the center can be employed by a skillful composer to elevate the importance of a central concept or to dramatize a radical shift of events at the turning point ... the remainder of the system can be used with equal effectiveness as a framework through which the author may compare, contrast, juxtapose, complement, or complete each of the flanking elements in the chiastic system.[60]

Rereading the Bible with these constructions in mind can certainly enrich the reading experience and enhance interpretation. The chiastic form can be exegetically significant, Welch continues, "because its presence can require reinterpretation of text."[61]

These concentric constructions may offer a key to the ancient mind which can aid in the interpretation of Mark's gospel. It can help the modern scholar understand the ancient mind and not "unwittingly impute too much modern mentality to the ancient author. Their "thoughts are not necessarily our thoughts," Welch says, "and our designs rarely theirs, for ancient rhetoric and modern prose do not strive to achieve the same ideals ... Modern style is linear, syllogistic and involves a continuous flow of ideas" and "Circuitousness and repetitiveness are shunned in most circumstances. But in ancient writings, repetition, redundancy, and parallelism thrive." Repetition often had an express pedagogical purpose for the ancients, and "double structures carried moral implications for the ancient mind as well." Repetition and parallelism facilitate memory by providing an organization in a time when writing "did not make use of paragraphs, punctuation, capitalization and other such synthetic devices to communicate the conclusion of one idea and the commencement of the next." Concentric constructions could also be liturgical, suitable for "ritual settings and may well have been affected on certain occasions to facilitate alternate recitation, e.g., by the opposite divisions of the choir in Jewish worship."[62]

The form and content of Mark's gospel, therefore, may be analyzed by using the concentric construction as a literary tool. Joanna Dewey, with whose diagram this section began, uses this tool with great skill in her analysis of Mark.

## Joanna Dewey

There is virtually a consensus among scholars who have closely examined Mark's early chapters that they contain at least one concentric construction, especially in the activities and sayings of Jesus after his arrival in Capernaum (1:21 - 3:12).[63] Joanna Dewey's insightful analysis provides at this point an excellent entrance into an application of concentric constructions to Mark. By taking advantage of her insights, we will be able to reach some firm conclusions about how Mark constructs the envelopes studied in this book. As previously noted, her conception differs from mine (and from Lund's) in that she neither includes the doublets nor the healing of the leper.

For convenience, Dewey's diagram is repeated:

A   2:1-12. The healing of the paralytic.
    B   2:13-17. The call of Levi/eating with sinners.
        C   2:18-22. The sayings on fasting and on the old and the new.
    B´  2:23-27. Plucking grain on the Sabbath.
A´  3:1-6. The healing on the Sabbath.[64]

Remembering what we said earlier about the relationship of form and meaning, it is important to pay close attention to Dewey's comments here:

> The two healings (A and A´) are parallel to each other. The call of Levi and the plucking of grain (B and B´) have many parallel elements. The question of fasting (C) is a middle unit without a parallel pericope. It is related to B and B´ in one way and to A and A´ in a different way.[65]

In the A section, Jesus is seen at home in Capernaum, where he is depicted by Mark as speaking to the people. "Then some people came, bringing to him a paralyzed man, carried by four of them" (2:3). In the following verses (2:4-12), Mark narrates the story. Because they cannot force their way through the crowd, in order to approach Jesus, the men actually remove a portion of the roof above Jesus, and then lower the paralytic down, still on his mat, so that Jesus may heal him. Dewey parallels this episode across the construction to A´, the healings of the paralytic (A) and of the man with the withered hand (A´).

At the close of the construction (A´), Jesus is seen entering a synagogue in an unidentified locale. He is there confronted by a man with a withered hand, and the Pharisees and Herodians watched Jesus to see whether he "would cure him on the Sabbath, so that they might accuse him" (3:2). Mark has Jesus himself pose the central question to his hostile audience: "Is it lawful to do good or to do harm on the Sabbath, to save life or to kill?" (3:3). When they make no response, he "looked around at them with anger; he was grieved at their hardness of heart" (3:4-5). He then healed the man's hand, and "the Pharisees went out and immediately conspired with the Herodians ... how to destroy him" (3:6).

In both these scenes, she observes that the miracle narrative is interrupted so that Jesus may speak to his opponents. Then the narrative begins again. Jesus then speaks to the one being healed. This structure is characteristic of these two scenes in Mark and in their synoptic parallels. She also notes structural similarities achieved by the repetition of Greek words and phrases. The introductions of both scenes are nearly identical. Both scenes, furthermore, are set indoors, and in neither scene do the opponents of Jesus openly express their opposition. In both, Jesus takes the initiative while the opponents react. She also cites further parallels: 1) in each, the word *heart* appears, the first uses of the word in the gospel; 2) Jesus responds with a counter-question; 3) the healings are not exorcisms or cleansings, but restorations of body; 4) resurrection symbolism is present in both; 5) the verb *egeiro* (to raise) is used; and 6) each story is completed by the response of the bystanders. Dewey notes emphatically that these parallels are detailed and explicit; they are not vague and merely formal.[66]

The section which she identifies as B tells of Jesus' call to Levi (2:13-17). Walking out "beside the sea," Jesus is surrounded by a large crowd and is teaching them. He sees Levi "sitting at the tax booth" and says to him, "Follow Me." And Levi gets up and follows him. Mark immediately shifts to Levi's house, where many tax collectors and sinners are also sitting with Jesus and his disciples. The Pharisees, observing that he was eating with such people, are offended. When Jesus hears of their reaction, however, he says, "Those who are well have no need of a physician, but those who are sick; I have come to call not the righteous but sinners."

Before focusing on the parallelism present in B and B´, the controversies over eating with sinners and plucking grain on the Sabbath, Dewey first makes a very interesting observation which illustrates the rich allusions which can be offered to the reader within such concentric structures. "B is set in relationship to A, and B´ to A´. A and B concern sin/sinners. In both, the crowd (and the larger group of tax collectors and sinners) plays an important role. B´ and A´ are concerned with violation of the Sabbath law." Both "arms" of the construction have strong connections with the central point C. We shall discuss such relationships in more detail later. In regard to B and B´, she writes that the parallelism is "strongly marked." In both stories (B and B´), Jesus is outdoors. In the first he is beside the sea; in the second, he is walking through the fields. Both stories, as well, close with a proverb which has christological significance. Eating, she observes, is also a central part of each of these controversies.[67]

The centerpiece of the construction is C, the sayings concerning fasting and the old and the new. In this central section, Jesus responds to objections that he and his disciples, unlike the disciples of John and of the Pharisees, do not fast. Both Dewey[68] and Lund affirm that the important points of a concentric construction are placed at the center. This center establishes a relationship with the extremes of A and A´. This is one of the chiastic "laws" which Lund discusses. He also finds other laws:

> These laws are the following: 1) *the centre is always the turning point*. The center, as we shall see, may consist of one, two, three, or even four lines. 2) At the centre there is often a change in the trend of thought, and an antithetic idea is introduced ... For want of a better name, we shall designate this feature *the law of the shift at the centre*. 3) Identical ideas are often distributed in a fashion that they *occur in the extremes and at the centre*. 4) There are also

many instances of ideas occurring at the center of one system and recurring in the extremes of a corresponding system, the second system evidently having been constructed to match the first. We shall call this feature *the law of shift from centre to the extremes*. 5) There is a definite tendency of certain terms to gravitate toward certain positions within a given system, such as the divine names in the psalms ... 6) Larger units are frequently introduced and concluded by *frame-passages*.[69]

In this section of Mark, this is certainly true; for at the center of his construction the evangelist has placed the teachings of Jesus that concern the newness of his message and activity. Also in the center appears the bridegroom symbol, with all its apocalyptic and christological overtones. Here Jesus says that new wine is for new skins and also affirms that he and his disciples are different from John the Baptist and his disciples. While the bridegroom is among them, these disciples will not fast; but they will later, when he is taken from him.

The center is, then, a turning point, a kind of hinge. What is on one side of that hinge either reinforces the other side or is contrapuntally related to it. In the section which we are analyzing, the episodes following the sayings of Jesus about newness are related in a special way to the episodes A and B which preceded the sayings. Many of Lund's "laws" are operating here. The second parts of the construction, the episodes occurring after the central part C, begin to mirror their twins (which occur before C) in a special way. These parallels Dewey describes as "closely interwoven." A and A´ can be seen as "ring compositions, with the miracle at the beginning and the end. B might be described as two situations with one dominical response (23:13-14, 15-16, 17), and B´ as one situation with two dominical responses (2:23-24, 25-26, 27-28)." B and B´ are concerned with eating, as we have already seen, but notice that C is concerned with fasting. In B, "Jesus eats with the wrong people. In C, the disciples do not fast. In B´, Jesus cites the example of David eating unlawful food." Most importantly, Dewey, who is thoroughly familiar with Lund, notices the climactic progression of episodes. Not only is there a startling advance in christological identity, there is also a dramatic increase in hostility toward Jesus, running through the controversies with the Pharisees and culminating in the enemies of Jesus plotting to destroy him.[70]

The central sayings at C, in Dewey's construction, unify the construction by applying the newness of Jesus' message to A and B and B´ and A´. In other words, the healing of the paralytic and the call to Levi are referred to in C, and their significance is heightened. Similarly, the plucking of grain at B´ illustrates the radical newness of Jesus' person and message, as does A´ when Jesus defies the establishment once again. Dewey comments on this unity: "Perhaps the most important function of the symmetrical pattern in 2:1 - 3:6 is to create," Dewey says, "a coherent literary unity out of episodic incidents, to bind the incidents into an organic whole." This group of episodes therefore shows that "the opponents objected to Jesus' activity as a whole, and to the messianic claim which was the basis of Jesus' actions." Also, this literary unity shows that "the individual parts of the section can only be fully understood in the context of the larger structure."[71] This second "arm" of the construction (B´ and A´) not only intensifies conflict with Pharisees, it also dramatically intensifies Jesus' sayings about old and new. In Jesus' life we do indeed see the bursting of the wineskins and the ripping of the patch from the garment.

Dewey obviously believes that when attempting to identify concentric constructions, the critic must, above all, avoid extreme subjectivity. Otherwise, once aware of these constructions, the incautious critic could begin to see them everywhere. Welch states the problem as follows: "Since the modern mind is not rehearsed in the use, appreciation or even the recognition of chiasmus, a most important question arises over what criteria must be met before it becomes reasonable to speak of chiasmus, let alone of a particular chiastic arrangement, within a given text." The primary concern, he goes on to say, must be objectivity.[72]

Dewey's discussion of criteria is the most thorough I have encountered. She certainly attempts to establish linguistic and formal criteria, as well as criteria applying to content. Parallelism of content, she observes, is of importance as a criterion. It may be general or specific, "synonymous or antithetic." The parallelism, of course, should be manifestly clear on some level. In the content of the passage or passages involved, a parallel may be established between settings of the stories involved, or there may be parallels in character. *In regard to parallels of content, one should be careful not to move beyond "manifest content" and not to indulge in abstract interpretations which are not supported by the text.*[73]

Welch is also anxious to establish specific criteria. His criteria may be summarized as follows: 1) inverted parallel sequences "must be evidenced in the text" and not imposed upon the text; 2) the "second half of the system should tend to repeat the first half ... in a recognizably inverted order; 3) if there are two central sections, their juxtaposition should be "marked and highly accentuated; and 4) in regard to longer passages, they are "more defensibly chiastic where the same text also contains a fair amount of short chiasmus and other forms of parallelism as well." In summary, Welch is requiring clarity or what he calls "apparentness" achieved by 1) repetition, 2) balance, 3) inversion, 4) both focus and shift at center, and 5) "density of parallel forms." Some subjectivity, he insists, is inevitable. He states that some of the examples in his book are "proposed" to be concentric constructions. In his words, "They are proposed as what appears to be the most natural and meaningful analysis of the text under study."[74]

D. L. Clark also generally approves of Dewey's criteria and, like Welch, he warns against dogmatism. Clark notes that concentric constructions are representatives of a "wider phenomenon embraced by the term 'recursion,' a tendency of ancient writers to use inverted orders of expression similar to but not necessarily identical to chiasms." What makes identification of chiasm difficult is that *"different types of recursion may interpenetrate one another"* (italics his). He continues to say that "if the method of recognizing literary units by means of noticing parallelisms of content, form, language and setting is valid only where its results confirm views already held for other reasons, is it really worth the trouble? ... And it must be emphasized again that multiple levels of patterning may coexist, superimposed and interpenetrating. The recognition of one of them does not necessarily involve the repudiation of others. This whole question, however, though raised from a linguistic perspective, must ultimately be settled by biblical scholars in the overall context of their discipline."[75]

Even in the light of these rigorous criteria, I am convinced that Dewey demonstrates beyond any reasonable doubt that this portion of Mark's text is at least one of those longer recursions which fulfills most of the criteria for the identification of smaller concentric constructions. Because she does not distinguish between criteria to be applied to shorter constructions and those to be applied to the longer, recursive patterns, however, Dewey cannot find larger concentric constructions elsewhere in Mark. Her construction, essentially detached from the form of the gospel, simply floats around like an iceberg which is not really moored in the context of the gospel. This is in no way to denigrate her excellent analysis; it is merely to say that, in her interpretation, this one section of Mark exhibits the only formal large concentric construction which her criteria will allow her to accept.

At this point, my own analysis reaches a critical point. Dewey's criteria, which are derived from analysis of smaller constructions, cannot be applied to longer recursions which are unlike them in many ways. If one does attempt to apply these criteria, something similar to the Heisenberg Indeterminacy Principle occurs: the application of her critical method disturbs or destroys the pattern analyzed. In fact, any attempt to apply these criteria to long constructions would eliminate most of them from the Hebrew Scriptures, from the New Testament, and from most classical literature. Criteria requiring rigid symmetry would certainly dissolve most of Mark's constructions.[76] For instance, Lund's diagram of Matthew's material, in the preceding section, would surely have to be discarded, as would most of the long patterns discovered in Paul's letters.

However correct Dewey is in insisting on rigid criteria for the identification of concentric constructions, she errs in deriving those criteria from the wrong model. In other words, the longer recursions themselves need closer study so that criteria may be found which would enhance the ability to identify and discuss them. The dogmatic introduction of the wrong criteria prevents the kind of inductive analysis necessary for the discovery of Mark's unique constructions! A recursion, as Mark uses it to form his envelopes, does indeed fulfill some of the criteria for the smaller chiasm which it imitates, but it discards others, in order to parallel larger themes, topics, and ideas occurring in larger blocks of material.

Thus, it is an unrealistic either/or which introduces the confusion. Biblical criticism still seems to insist that no large concentric construction can exist unless it exhibits the same structure of the small chiasmus. If the long construction deviates even in the smallest way, then it must be dogmatically rejected; it is not worthy of being a true chiasmus. In effect, then, the longer constructions are denied their integrity because they are not always like the smaller constructions. This is a fallacious procedure, much like refusing to accept a large elephant as an animal simply because it does not have all the attributes of a mouse.

The rigid criteria of Dewey, Lund, and Welch serve the admirable purpose of showing that they refused to be irresponsible persons who find such constructions everywhere and recklessly read into Scripture whatever parallels they wish to find. But when unrealistically applied to larger sections of text, these criteria, which insist on verbatim repetition or close stylistic and grammatical parallels, hold Mark's gospel in a cold, mathematical embrace. Criteria designed to accredit longer constructions should be derived from a close analysis of those constructions. Mark certainly did not throw up his hands and refuse to use recursions because they were too long and informal to be called a perfect chiasmus!

As we have observed, Welch and Lund themselves have emphatically pointed out how, especially in regard to longer constructions, ancient writers almost never attempt to construct perfect chiastic constructions! In the shorter formulations, yes. In Leviticus, especially, as well as in other biblical passages, we see perfect short concentric constructions. In the longer passages, even in the best examples given in his book, Welch is constrained to insist that such constructions, if and when they exist, are never tightly constructed, but are suggested by a loose, though often convincing, parallelism. By Welch's own admission he could not, applying the most rigid formal tests, even have compiled his anthology!

What these critics are discovering in the Bible as well as in other ancient writings is a literary method of organization simply taken for granted by ancient writers. It was probably taken for granted because it had been so obviously present in most of the ancient oral traditions. Perhaps it was customary for a writer to conceive an outline similar in form to that of a small chiasmus and then to write a longer work which relaxed the rigid requirements of small perfect constructions in order to allow for larger bodies of material which would be paralleled section by section rather than line by line.

Even though her own criteria prevent her from seeing Mark's method in this section and in much of his gospel, Joanna Dewey's excellent analysis nonetheless remains valuable in showing how even the longer constructions can be interlaced with formal parallels. In demonstrating the presence of an almost perfect longer construction, she may point toward a more formal oral tradition inherited by Mark.

The evangelist by his use of doublets and the inclusion of the leper story, in other words, may have diluted an inherited formal construction similar to the one identified by Dewey.

# 3
# Healing Many as a Recursion

A   Healing many people (1:29-34).
  B   Preaching tour (1:35-39).
    C   Healing leper (1:40-45).
      D   Healing paralytic (2:1-12).
        E   Calling Levi (2:13-17).
        E´   Fasting (2:18-22).
      D´   Plucking grain (2:23-28).
    C´   Healing withered hand (3:1-6).
  B´   Going out toward the sea (3:7-9).
A´   Healing many people (3:10-12).

In the preceding chapter, criteria were given for the establishment of the smaller construction called chiasmus or concentric construction. The judgment was reached that all these criteria can not be applied to the longer concentric constructions; therefore, a decision was also made, following D. L. Clark, to call these longer constructions recursions. Before proceeding, a formal definition of a recursion should be stated: a recursive structure frequently occurs when a large block of written material is patterned on the form of a chiasmus, or concentric construction. More informal in construction, then, than a small chiasmus composed of single lines, a recursion parallels groups of lines, whole paragraphs, or even longer sections of text. Many of the formal devices used by smaller chiasmus are also often used to parallel the terms of the recursion, but the larger structure usually depends upon similar topics or themes in each section of the text in order to establish symmetry. A recursion should, however, display at least the following characteristics: 1) it should, like the chiasmus, consist of two arms pointing toward the center of the construction; 2) noticeable parallels, topical and/or thematic, should exist between the two arms; and 3) both arms of the recursion should relate significantly to the ideas, themes, or topics of the center. The word "center" does not refer to a mathematically exact point but rather to those sayings or scenes which emphasize, near the center, the basic themes, ideas, and topics of the construction. These requirements are surely fundamental and should always be present if the construction is to be defined as a recursion. In this book, I have added another requirement in order better to avoid subjectivity: 4) only those portions of text enclosed by doublets and demonstrated to be recursive are identified as recursions. In order not to confuse this analysis, other speculations are identified as such or are relegated to footnotes. Easily identifiable small concentric constructions, of course, will be taken for granted if they fulfill the criteria.

The presence and position of the doublets, which frame the recursion, identify the structure we have called envelopes. The definition of envelope builds upon the preceding definition: *An envelope is a recursion enclosed within the borders of a doublet.* The doublets themselves therefore become functional within the envelope, since they establish parallels not only between their halves but also stand in a relationship to the terms of the recursion they both join and enclose. According to these defining characteristics most all the examples given in the preceding discussion qualify as small, symmetrical concentric constructions. Lund's conception of the longer construction in Matthew, however, must clearly be redefined as a recursion.

With these new definitions in mind, I shall attempt to demonstrate that it is doublets which identify all four envelopes and that the longer recursive pattern provides much of the structural integrity of the material between the doublets.

The diagram on the preceding page shows the recursive structure of Mark's "Healing Many" envelope. This recursion, as Mark employs it, retains some basic features of the small and formal concentric constructions. He signals, with his doublets, that he is self-consciously enclosing material. *The sayings center, furthermore, remains near the center of our envelope, and the rhythm is recursive,* at least in the tendency of the scenes placed after the sayings to change and refocus the parallel actions preceding the sayings center. This phenomenon is difficult to describe without using jargon, but if the reader has a firm conception of the sayings at the center and sees an arm of the construction extending into and away from the center, he or she can imagine a helpful visual image of this discursive rhythm. Mark apparently expresses his own preferences by retaining only parts of inherited constructions, which were in the rigid form of chiasmus. These, if they did exist, he must have recast for his own theological purposes between the doublet verses. It appears, then, that Mark himself was subjective in regard to these concentric constructions.

To serve as the bookends for his first envelope, Mark creates the first doublet[77] by the repetition of a scene in which Jesus is depicted as healing many people.

> That evening, at sundown, they brought to him all who were sick or possessed with demons. And the whole city was gathered around the door. And he cured many who were sick with various diseases, and cast out many demons; and he would not permit the demons to speak, because they knew him (1:32-34).

> Jesus departed with his disciples to the sea, and a great multitude from Galilee followed him; hearing all that he was doing, they came to him in great numbers from Judea, Jerusalem, Idumea, beyond the Jordan, and the region around Tyre and Sidon. He told his disciples to have a boat ready for him because of the crowd, so that they would not crush him; for he had cured many, so that all who had diseases pressed upon him to touch him. Whenever the unclean spirits saw him, they fell down before him and shouted, "You are the Son of God!" But he sternly ordered them not to make him known (3:7-12).

The formal parallels are established by the large crowd, which includes those brought to Jesus to be healed of disease or to be exorcised of demons and the messianic secret. Most critics have seen these passages, not as doublets or as frame passages, but as similar summary passages because they foreshorten the activity of Jesus by summarizing it.[78]

The two passages are interesting as well because they echo the activity of John the Baptist. "And people from the whole Judean countryside and all the people of Jerusalem were going out to him, and were baptized by him in the river Jordan, confessing their sins" (1:5). These correspondences give a unity to the gospel, in that Jesus' activity echoes (and supersedes) John's activity. Further support for Mark's use of them as frames will come with the analysis of the material they enclose; for we shall discover a structure not only in their repetition, but also in their relationship to this enclosed material.

It is interesting to notice in the second doublet (3:7-12) that Jesus outdoes John, attracting people from as far away as Tyre and Sidon, establishing a thematic connection in the borders of this envelope. Jesus is consciously and carefully compared to John the Baptist and shown to be superior to him, just as John had prophesied he would. Healing and exorcism have replaced baptism as the major activity; and whereas John is associated with the vicinity of the river Jordan, Jesus begins immediately to widen the circle of his influence.

The second pericope, labeled B, describes an incident occurring the next day which involves Jesus and his disciples:

> In the morning, while it was still very dark, he got up and went out to a deserted place, and there he prayed. And Simon and his companions hunted for him. When they found him, they said to him, "Everyone is searching for you." He answered, "Let us go on to the neighboring towns, so that I may proclaim the message there also; for that is what I came out to do." And he went throughout Galilee, proclaiming the message in their synagogues and casting out demons (1:35-39).

Now something happens here which will happen, as we shall see, in all the other envelopes. The second term, the B pericope, the one following the first half of the doublet, nearly always establishes a contrast with the preceding scene. There is thus an instance here of the affirmation/negation process referred to earlier (see page 24). The first half of the doublet will affirm some quality of Jesus, and the second pericope, the one immediately following, will negate the idea—not denying it, but simply demonstrating that it is an incomplete affirmation. For example, Jesus, in the first scene, is portrayed as a triumphant and charismatic healer and exorcist. The second scene, however, shows Jesus wishing to move away from this scene of early triumph. The obvious message is that Jesus is not to be limited or finite in his influence and power. There is certainly a christological contribution here; but from the point of view of technique, Mark is also revealing how the motor of his plot will run. Jesus will be affirmed as A, but B will show that A was an incomplete affirmation which must be complemented in some way.

These contradictions tend to continue throughout the course of each envelope. For instance, looking briefly ahead, the envelope called "The Twelve" will affirm Jesus' sharing of his mission with twelve disciples; but there is, in the last sentence, the statement that one of the twelve will betray him. The second pericope involves the harsh conflict with his opponents in which they accuse him of being in league with Beelzebul, and even shows that members of his own family are concerned with his sanity! In the next envelope, "The Feedings," the disciples, immediately following the feeding of the four thousand, demonstrate that they do not understand about the bread. In "Healing the Blind," the blind man's sight is restored; and Peter confesses that Jesus is the Christ. Immediately, however, Peter cautions Jesus not to go to Jerusalem, so that Jesus must address him with the harsh words, "Get behind me, Satan!" (8:33).

Here, the introduction shows Jesus among the crowds at Capernaum; and yet immediately thereafter, Jesus is deciding to leave! He is not only silencing the demons' identification of him and thus dampening the triumph the plot seems to be proclaiming, he is also refusing to conform to what his new disciples and the people of Capernaum think of him. This "metamorphosis" of Jesus will be continuous in this gospel. Each scene presents a new Jesus, even though he remains essentially the same "yesterday and today and forever" (Heb 13:8).

Peter's misunderstanding of Jesus in this Capernaum scene anticipates his later misunderstanding during and immediately after the transfiguration. His cautious reactions both to Jesus' leaving Capernaum and later to his entering Jerusalem provide excellent characterization for that newly chosen disciple or that initiate who wants to conceive of Jesus in some triumphalist way. Peter acts as a foil to Jesus. In fact, Peter seems greatly disturbed in this scene. He and those with him hunted for Jesus. The original Greek verb (*katedioko*) implies hunting, rather than seeking, or even can have the force of "hunting down."[79]

The disciples, time and again, want Jesus to display his glory on earth, not realizing that to remain in Capernaum would be to restrict the mission severely, or even to smother it. This is a major reason why Peter, here and at the transfiguration, tries to hinder the scope of Jesus' mission. Peter is "driving with his brakes on." This point is strongly emphasized by Mark in his gospel story, and it is obvious that he wants the initiate to learn from Peter's mistake and not to misinterpret the character of the Christ and the consequent character of his mission.

In using the term "negation" to describe Mark's method we mean only that the dramatic contrasts provided by Mark, in his arrangement of pericopes, give a constant commentary on the developing picture of Jesus. Mark organizes the Jesus story to represent to the initiate the experience of the disciples as they struggle from one incomplete identification of Christ to another more complete understanding of his nature. He perhaps presents a dramatic portrayal of the first disciples' struggle to understand the nature of Christ both before and after his death and resurrection. To what extent the material is intended as an argument against some competing triumphalist view is impossible to determine. But the complex method of affirmation/negation/repeated affirmation is undeniably present in the texture of Mark's work.

Mary S. Thompson has an interesting study of this phenomenon in *The Role of Disbelief in Mark*. Her study succeeds in demonstrating that Philip Shuler is incorrect to place Mark in the genre of laudatory encomium.[80] She defines many of the ways in which Mark's negations manifest themselves. She finds five categories of negative elements in Mark: 1) "lack of laudatory details of Jesus' life," 2) "treatment of miracles," 3) "constant lack of understanding," 4) "contrast with John the Baptizer," and 5) "minor details." She notes that in "some passages the negative elements are clear and precise; in others they tend to neutralize or mute a laudatory feature."[81]

Thompson remarks that the "procedure of subsuming the negative elements of the gospel under the affirmative had been so obvious down through the centuries that no one could seriously attempt to discredit it. However, the negative level has not been allowed to carry the weight it actually bears within the text. Scholars have been reluctant to allow the full weight of the negations to assume their proper significance within a negative level."[82] Her conclusions are disappointing in that she really never determines why Mark uses negative contrasts in such a way. She can only state generally that irony results from the contrasts. I would agree with this to some extent, in that Mark demands, as Kierkegaard would, a leap of faith in spite of "absurd" negations. But more analysis seems necessary to prove this point. Her concluding words tend to be tacked on, and do not really grow from her analysis:

> The negative elements, so emphatically presented, destroy any easy acceptance of the affirmative level. The proclamations must be seen, heard, perceived, understood, believed, precisely as proclamations. They are not proven by indisputably miraculous signs. They are not supported by a description of a loyal band of followers nor by a change in the operation of the religious establishment. Even when a spectacular event occurs, it never produces an affirmative response at all. The reader of Mark's gospel is going to have to base his belief, if such he has, on unproven proclamations that Jesus is Messiah and Son of God. In other words, faith in Jesus is just that — faith.[83]

It is better not to jump to any conclusions about Mark's theology simply on the basis of the presence of negations. What we shall attempt to do is to make some sense of the specific contrasts Mark employs in the envelopes. So far, for instance, we have observed how the second scene in each envelope negates the first scene, but only in the sense that it demonstrates that the christology implied by the first scene requires amplification.

Moving back now to the diagram of the first envelope, the A-B terms, in addition to exhibiting the linear relationship just discussed, reveal a concentric relationship as well within the structure of the recursion. For instance, Jesus' healing many (A) is followed by the preaching tour (B, 1:39), which dramatizes his decision to move beyond Capernaum; in the same way his second healing many (A´) is preceded, in recursive fashion, by his movement out toward the sea (B´).

> Jesus departed with his disciples to the sea, and a great multitude from Galilee followed him; hearing all that he was doing, they came to him in great numbers from Judea, Jerusalem, Idumea, beyond the Jordan, and the region around Tyre and Sidon (3:7-9).

This parallel, although brief, is an unmistakable echo of Jesus' going out in the first instance from Galilee to the surrounding area (1:39); this time he moves toward the sea. His popularity and the consequent seeking of him by many provide both a thematic parallel as well as a correspondence on the level of plot. In the first passage, everyone is searching for Jesus, in order to be taught and healed; here, in this second passage, a multitude follows him for the same reasons. The basic formal parallel is established by the repetition of the word "Galilee" (3:7).

The next pericope in this envelope, the healing of the leper, (1:40-45) is in some ways the most difficult in the entire gospel.

> And a leper came to him begging him, and kneeling said to him, "If you choose, you can make me clean." Moved with pity, Jesus stretched out his hand and touched him, and said to him, "I do choose. Be made clean!" After sternly warning him he sent him away at once, saying to him, "See that you say nothing to anyone; but go, show yourself to the priest, and offer for your cleansing what Moses commanded, as a testimony to them." But he went out and began to proclaim it freely, and to spread the word, so that Jesus could no longer go into a town openly, but stayed out in the country; and people came to him from every quarter (1:40-45).

There is some confusion both within the scene and between the scene and its context. There is a problem here within the scene because Jesus' attitude is somewhat uncharacteristic of him; he seems to be angry with the leper for some reason; and that sternness which he displays seems, unaccountably, to conflict with the statement that he was "moved with pity."[84] It has to be remembered that Mark is not writing a novel of manners and that almost everything he says is designed for theological purposes. But he is, as he should be, obviously trying to provide some sense of consistency of character, some connection between motive and action, in order to write a coherent narrative. Jesus' emotions tend to be unaccountably harsh, too, after the feeding of the four thousand when the disciples and Jesus are in the boat and he berates them severely for not understanding about the bread (Mark 8:14-21). Emotions there, at first perception at least, seem unsuited to the stimulus described within the context. Matthew and Luke soften both passages, as well as some of the rest of Mark's harshness (see Matt 8:1-4 and Luke 5:12-16).

D. E. Nineham suggests that the leper story, as Mark presents it, is actually a conflation of two stories. In one story, Jesus was pictured as being moved with pity, but in the other story he was shown to be angry with "the leprous spirit."[85] Perhaps this is the answer, but we must be wary of theories that explain Mark's awkwardness as due to inept editing on his part or his apparent artless unskillful response to his inherited material. There is further difficulty because Jesus behaves more conservatively here than he does in the rest of the gospel; he sends the man, after cleansing him, to a priest, "to offer for your cleansing what Moses commanded, for a proof to the people" (1:44). Neither does this scene fit smoothly into its context; it follows too abruptly upon Jesus' departure and there is no brief account of setting as there will be in the other healing passages. Suddenly there is the leper; he is healed; he is sent to a priest; Jesus moves on. There is not even the drawing of a moral, which we find at the end of the other healing passages.

There are, however, several clues which indicate Mark's intentions. In the place of the proverbial saying which one would expect as a part of the healing structure, Mark has placed a new sort of idea for emphasis: Jesus' growing popularity and the spread of his fame. Jesus does truly pity the leper, just as he obviously was compassionate toward those suffering in Capernaum, but he is facing the growing problem of fame. It had already begun with the crowds about his door; Mark does not explicitly say so, but Jesus seems harassed by the large numbers of people there. Although he leaves Capernaum to extend his ministry, not to escape crowds, it seems that fame and popularity do present a problem. And that problem is related to the messianic secret alluded to in 1:34b: "He would not permit the demons to speak, because they knew him."

Here, Jesus does not want the leper to tell about his healing; this directive is what stands in the emphatic position usually occupied by the proverb.

> After sternly warning him, he sent him away at once, saying to him, "See that you say nothing to anyone . . ." But he went out and began to proclaim it freely, and to spread the word, so that Jesus could no longer go into a town openly, but stayed out in the country; and people came to him from every quarter (1:43-45).

Jesus charges the leper sternly because he is not seeking fame. In fact, fame and what it implies about his role interferes with Jesus' purpose; he has only just left Capernaum in order to go on "to the next towns," but now he cannot enter a town.

In Mark's gospel, Jesus is threatened, not primarily by popularity and fame and crowds, but by the misunderstanding of his identity which is implied by fame and popularity. In this case, he is threatened by the premature (and thus incorrect) revelation of his role. It is very important for Mark's Jesus to be understood in the right way and, as a consequence, to be responded to in the right way. Consider how much of this gospel is devoted to the response of people to Jesus of Nazareth! Here we encounter, perhaps, Mark the teacher. Nothing is more important for the new member of the church than the correct understanding of Jesus as the Son of God. Jesus is not primarily a wonder worker. As Weeden has noted, it is as if Mark, throughout this gospel, is attempting to counteract triumphalism. Mark does not want to present Jesus simply as *theos aneir*, the divine holy man. According to Mark's presentation, Jesus' power is not revealed to work the crowds, and his works did not have the end of producing fame and reward. Mark evidently feels that he must make this absolutely clear. That may explain the harshness of Jesus' tone in this encounter with the leper.

Crowds can be dangerous. Jesus will later stand before crowds which call for his death, and many will mock him as he is led to the cross. Jesus does not seek the approval of the crowd. He searches for disciples, but that is a very different thing from seeking fame or encouraging others to seek it (as he will later try to explain to James and John). Mark, therefore, demonstrates that the growth of Jesus' popularity was against Jesus' will. Coming after the Capernaum episode, then, the healing of the leper develops the popularity theme as well as the related theme of identity which is stressed in the first half of the introductory doublet: Jesus does not yet want to be made known.[86]

At this point the recursion invites the reader to look ahead to discover the several concentric parallels between the leper scene (C, 1:40-45) and the healing of the man with the withered hand (C´, 3:1-3:6). Mark, in the withered-hand scene, does not refer to the Son of Man as he does in the leper scene, but the two scenes are allied in two basic ways. In both scenes, Jesus is confronted by a person with an infirmity. He also gives commands in C and in C´ in regard to the person to be healed: "Be made clean!" to the leper (1:41) and "Come forward" (3:3) and "Stretch out your hand" (3:5) to the man with the withered hand. In both scenes, Mark calls specific attention to an emotional reaction of Jesus. In the leper scene, Jesus is moved by pity; and in the second scene, "he was grieved at their hardness of heart." Also, there is a negative conclusion to both scenes. In the first, fame is becoming a problem "so that Jesus could no longer go into a town openly, but stayed out in the country" (1:45). The conclusion of the second scene, coming near the end of the second arm of the recursion, is sinister, as the Pharisees and Herodians conspire to destroy Jesus (3:6). The parallels here are not nearly so strong as they are in Dewey's analysis, but parallels do remain.

If the envelopes determine the basic structure of a recursion here, then an inherited chiasmus could have been inserted by Mark within the doublet he chose for framing this section. If he did make these changes, he kept his eye on the recursive form he has chosen for his envelopes, modifying that construction by placing scenes within the doublet halves.

The comparisons between C and C′ show how Mark invites the reader to move back and forth between the recursive order and the linear order of his gospel, and such a reading opens the way for the full impact of Mark's composition. By folding the linear order into recursive shape, he thus creates several levels of comparison while still retaining the flow of the basic gospel structure. Much of the explosive power of the gospel text comes from this careful construction of both linear and recursive order.

A linear analysis of this envelope indicates that the two scenes that follow the sayings—plucking grain and healing man with withered hand—sharpen the focus upon the Sabbath conflict while at the same time continuing the theme of Jesus' uniqueness. Furthermore, the hardness of heart of those Pharisees who object to the healing on the Sabbath of the man with the withered hand echoes the earlier attitude of the Pharisees who objected to Jesus eating with tax collectors and sinners (2:16).

After the leper scene, Mark portrays Jesus returning to Capernaum "after some days" (2:1). There is some awkwardness here, since Jesus has only shortly before declared his determination to move elsewhere. The exact geographical points are obviously of little concern to Mark, however. What he seems interested in portraying is the general extension of the ministry of Jesus. If Mark's characterization of Jesus is related to christology, so is Mark's plot. For theological reasons, movement away from provincialism is important. The peripatetic quality of Christ and his disciples is highlighted by Mark to demonstrate the ever-expanding circle and the always widening influence of Jesus and his message. This movement will be not only topographical, but becomes a sociological widening which denies class structure and universalizes Jesus' teachings, moving outward even toward Gentiles.

The plot progression continues with scene D, the healing of the paralytic. At this point, Jesus' fame has reached such proportions now that tiles must be removed from a roof in order to place a paralytic before the healer:

> When he returned to Capernaum after some days, it was reported that he was at home. So many gathered around that there was no longer room for them, not even in front of the door; and he was speaking the word to them. Then some people came, bringing to him a paralyzed man, carried by four of them. And when they could not bring him to Jesus because of the crowd, they removed the roof above him; and after having dug through it, they let down the mat on which the paralytic lay. When Jesus saw their faith, he said to the paralytic, "Son, your sins are forgiven." Now some of the scribes were sitting there, questioning in their hearts, "Why does this fellow speak in this way? It is blasphemy! Who can forgive sins but God alone?" At once Jesus perceived in his spirit that they were discussing these questions among themselves; and he said to them, "Why do you raise such questions in your hearts? Which is easier, to say to the paralytic, 'Your sins are forgiven,' or to say, 'Stand up and take your mat and walk'? But so that you may know that the Son of Man has authority on earth to forgive sins"—he said to the paralytic—"I say to you, stand up, take your mat and go to your home." And he stood up, and immediately took the mat and went out before all of them; so that they were all amazed and glorified God, saying, "We have never seen anything like this!" (2:1-12).

With this pericope, the envelope begins to assume a clear shape. First of all, Jesus' ministry is extended on a christological level. Now his divine power prevails not only over madness and disease but also over sin. Moving beyond Capernaum, then, means much more for Mark than geographical extension of ministry. Jesus speaks with authority and he also shares God's authority. The envelope begins a climactic ascent from the first day of healings in Capernaum into the radical assertion that Jesus is the Son of Man. Just what Jesus means by this title becomes clearer with the progression of the narrative as the listener understands the contexts in which this title occurs. The title, "Son of Man," Stock says "does not serve in Mark to tell us who Jesus is, nor is it just a substitute for 'a man' or the pronouns 'I' or 'men.'"[87] Some critics feel that Son of Man is merely an overly literal translation of the Hebrew phrase *ben 'ādām* (Aramaic *bar 'ēnāš*) which could mean, simply, "human." Stock, however, comments favorably upon Kingsbury's ideas. Son of Man, both critics say, was intended to be a title, and a majestic one. Mark has applied the title to the peculiar conditions of Jesus' ministry. Jesus, for instance, apparently associates the designation, Son of Man, with his earthly ministry as well as with his passion and resurrection. The term thus becomes unique; it can apply to Jesus in such a way that it can not be associated with any other person.[88]

As forgiver of sins, for instance, Jesus begins to assume an increasingly "first-person" stature. The Jesus who emerged from the wilderness seemed to be a third-person, "objective," Jesus who pointed beyond himself to a coming kingdom. Even though Jesus always speaks of the Son of Man in the third person, and even though he does not yet use the first person pronoun, he obviously refers to himself in this passage. We now move closer to a first-person Savior who is himself more involved personally in the power of the kingdom. He makes himself part of its arrival, for he is one who forgives sins from his person, not with a cleansing ritual like John. He shares divine power with God! Mark is making certain that the power of Jesus, already dissociated from desire for fame, is presented as the activity of God in the world. When Jesus forgives sins, the transcendent Christ begins to emerge.

In the paralytic scene, the theme of faith is introduced. Faith, in Mark, proves to be the response required when one is confronted with the Christ; for faith precedes healing. Faith is referred to only in passing here, in a dependent clause, "and when Jesus saw their faith." But Mark obviously wants to emphasize its importance in the plot of the story. The lowering of the man through the roof is not merely a sensational episode in a good story; it is an act of faith, an example of how humankind must respond to the approach of the messenger. Although this theme will be emphasized much more in some of the other envelopes, it is nonetheless important here in that it defines the proper response to Jesus, and later contrasts it with the hardness of heart of Jesus' opponents (3:5).

These opponents of Jesus are again like a chorus. As we have seen (p. 30), the crowd often functions in Mark as a chorus—a chorus which functions as a character. The comments and questions of hostile authorities also have a choric function, a hostile commentary upon Jesus' behavior. If Mark's gospel were a Greek drama performed on an ancient stage, one would expect to see a *choragos*, or chorus leader, step forward to confront Jesus with either awe or hostility. At the end of the drama, the hostile chorus dominates as the *choragos* becomes Pontius Pilate.

The chorus which appeared in the Capernaum synagogue was awed by Jesus, favorably impressed. In this paralytic scene, however, we hear the first discordant noises from humankind. And their discord is certainly intentionally paralleled with the reactions of the demons who possessed the man in the synagogue, as well as who will possess the Gerasene demoniac later. The hostile chorus is not complete without this undertone of the demoniac. If Mark were to be so performed on stage, perhaps it would be effective to costume a few members of the chorus as demons, for they achieve a demonic intensity again later at the trials before the Sanhedrin and before Pilate. In those instances the chorus will be virtually unified into one loud, noisy group. And certainly by the end of the gospel, the hostile chorus becomes the dominant voice, with only a few dissenters remaining; the centurion standing by the cross will understand something more about Jesus and identify him as the Son of God, and Joseph or Arimathea will also come forward to bury Jesus. So here again, we find the gradual growth of a theme which had its inception in Satan's temptation in the wilderness.

The recursive order reveals the alignment of this paralytic scene (D) and the plucking grain scene (D´).[89] As Welch has already pointed out, the existence of such alignments along the two arms of such constructions does not always imply that the author is making a profound comparison. The only comparisons often possible are topical in nature or (especially in a recursion) might often depend upon a comparison or contrast of themes. Even though the form of the recursion may be demonstrably more informal than the form of other concentric constructions, that fact in no way allows subjectivity of interpretation.

The next scene shows Jesus and his disciples in the fields, plucking grain on the Sabbath:

> One Sabbath he was going through the grainfields; and as they made their way his disciples began to pluck heads of grain. The Pharisees said to him, "Look, why are they doing what is not lawful on the Sabbath?" And he said to them, "Have you never read what David did, when he and his companions were hungry and in need of food? He entered the house of God, when Abiathar was high priest, and ate the bread of the presence, which it is not lawful for any but the priests to eat, and he gave some to his companions." Then he said to them, "The Sabbath was made for humankind, and not humankind for the Sabbath; so the Son of Man is lord even of the Sabbath" (2:23-27).

After Mark has placed the key statements of Jesus as the center piece of the envelope, he now turns back, as it were, to continue to illustrate how Jesus' message is new and different. In this pericope, the theme is related to Sabbath law, but it is the same theme of newness which continues to dominate this envelope and to provide much of its structural integrity. Jesus' newness is seen to be a transcendence of tradition, as he boldly compares the actions of his disciples with the actions of David and those with him when they ate the bread of the presence.

The Son of Man reference, which Mark has already used before the sayings in the scene with the paralytic, likely fell like a bombshell upon his listeners; and it is once again that reference which deepens the christology of this passage. Nineham's comments are instructive. Before the introduction of the Son of Man, he writes, "the argument is a general one about the right way of understanding the Law, and does not turn upon the special, eschatological status of Jesus." He continues:

> The dispute up to this point might have occurred between any two rabbis, and no doubt many of the more liberal rabbis of the time would very largely have agreed with Jesus. But in the last verse Jesus claims — or Mark claims for him, it is not clear which — that it is in virtue of his

eschatological status as Son of Man that he is "Lord of the Sabbath" and so can dispense his disciples. This statement brings the section formally into line with the previous conflict stories, and no doubt it was on the basis of it that the early (gentile) Christians felt justified in ceasing to observe the Sabbath and observing Sunday ('the Lord's day', e.g., Rev 1:10) instead.[90]

Once again, we see that even though Mark does not organize material in the way suggested by Dewey, he nevertheless establishes key parallels between two recursive twins. In Dewey's scheme, the plucking of grain is compared with the calling of Levi. In addition to the obvious parallels of Sabbath controversy, she establishes parallels regarding 1) both taking place outdoors, 2) both presenting a christological saying, and 3) both referring to eating.[91] In "Healing Many," the recursive parallels are perhaps stronger than the ones Dewey discovers in her arrangement. When the relationship of the paralytic scene at D is compared to its recursive twin, plucking grain on the Sabbath at D´, a strong similarity becomes obvious. In both scenes, Jesus refers to himself as the Son of Man. In the paralytic episode, Jesus affirms that "the Son of Man has authority on earth to forgive sins" (2:10). In the grain episode, Jesus affirms that "the Son of Man is lord even of the Sabbath" (2:28). Thus, even though this new parallel lacks the Sabbath healing correspondence as well as the topical parallel regarding eating, the Son of Man reference provides a strong binding similarity. In both the paralytic and grain scenes, Jesus is making a strong attack upon tradition. In the paralytic scene, Jesus forgives sin, a power heretofore relegated only to God. In the grain scene, Jesus once again defies traditions regarding Sabbath observance, and once again greatly offends the establishment. Both scenes, in the recursive arrangement, also involve Jesus asking a challenging question of hostile observers, and both include a christological pronouncement made by Jesus.

Because the Son of Man title is emphasized by its placement on either side of the sayings center, there is further strong evidence, that Mark has intentionally cast his recursive envelope in this form. Placed in such a way, the Son of Man title also provides a frame for the central bridegroom title and serves as a parallel structure between the two arms of this discursive envelope.

# HEALING MANY AS A RECURSION

    D    Healing Paralytic (Son of Man).
       E    Calling Levi (Sayings).
       E´   Fasting (Sayings).
    D´  Plucking Grain (Son of Man).

In answer to the question of whether this envelope has its own integrity displayed in its own definable shape, we may note that the extension of Jesus' ministry and the radical newness of his teaching continue to emerge as the dominant unifying themes. With the call of Levi, the scope of Jesus' ministry, sociologically and theologically, is considerably extended:

> As he was walking along, he saw Levi son of Alphaeus sitting at the tax booth, and he said to him, "Follow me." And he got up and followed him. And as he sat at dinner in Levi's house, many tax collectors and sinners were also sitting with Jesus and his disciples—for there were many who followed him. When the scribes of the Pharisees saw that he was eating with sinners and tax collectors, they said to his disciples, "Why does he eat with tax collectors and sinners?" When Jesus heard this, he said to them, "Those who are well have no need of a physician, but those who are sick; I have come to call not the righteous but sinners" (2:14-17).

The reader now steps into the center of Mark's recursion. The calling of Levi occurs at point C, the center. The first saying at the center of Mark's envelope, "Healing Many," is closely related to the doings of Jesus. As Lund observed, the Gospels' concentric constructions usually split off sayings from doings. Such splitting is easy enough when Jesus later speaks in parables and when his sayings are not directly related to the action of the story. But most often, Jesus' sayings do arise from the stories' actions, usually from some controversy scene. The Levi story, because it immediately provokes such a controversy, undergoes a welding of action and sayings. The doings (i.e., the action) really become a parable enclosed within the framework of a saying; as the eating with sinners and taxpayers becomes an example of the physicians' call to heal the sick.

As Jesus' ministry widens, the christology expressed in both Jesus' actions and in his words deepens in significance. We are not yet confronted with the Suffering Servant, but we approach that theme here as Jesus moves toward the outcasts of society. In other words, Jesus has not yet explicitly prophesied his rejection and suffering nor has he asked others to join him in that role. He is not far from it, however; for this movement toward the outcast is a further step toward the kind of renunciation Jesus will later demand when he speaks the words, "If any want to become my followers, let them deny themselves and take up their cross and follow me" (8:34). If the reader understands why Mark cannot yet have Jesus speak these words, then that reader understands the reason for the messianic secret as well as much about the unique nature of Mark as a religious text. Mark is walking the reader through the paces, the steps of mimesis, of *imitatio Christi*. The reader has more to learn about the nature of the Christ and of Christian discipleship, before Mark is ready to present Christ's essential demands. At this stage of his text, therefore, Mark is exhibiting his discipline and control as a religious artist. Sentimentality simply would not do at this or at any other point in the gospel. What is achieved must be achieved powerfully by understatement, and that is precisely how Mark proceeds. Jesus, the messenger of God, will not become a messianic king patterned after traditional notions of that figure; rather, the messenger of God involves himself in human disease, madness, and alienation. If Jesus is what we know of God, then we here observe God's involvement, through Jesus, with humanity. That encounter is what is understated in these stories gathered and arranged by the evangelist. It is the center of the recursion, then, which brings the reader back, in a non-chronological way, to the central ideas of Mark's gospel. The bridegroom prophecy, a foreshadowing of death, is not out of place in this sayings section.

In fact, Mark's entire gospel story, although organized into definable sections, is virtually a seamless garment depicting Jesus' progress toward the cross. He takes the first step when he stretches his hand—and God's—toward suffering and alienated humankind. Without this identification of Jesus with the outcast, the cross would appear to be an accidental and grotesque event incongruously ending the life of God's Son.

The powerful symbolism of the messianic banquet, also known as a "beggars banquet," seems to stand behind the meal with taxpayers and sinners. When God encountered humankind through Jesus and offered salvation, one of the first things God did, Mark is saying, was to identify with the outcasts of this world. "I have come not to call the example, the focus after the sayings is specifically upon Sabbath healings as illustrative of the themes of newness and power.

6. In all the envelopes, the sayings, including parables, are placed within the appropriate action context so that **both sayings and actions reinforce the unique theme of the envelope**. The wine and patch sayings, for instance, function in the context of Jesus' radical actions.

7. The **doublet material** itself — its sayings and actions — always states some aspect of each envelope's unique theme and thus **provides an effective thematic frame for the contents of each envelope**. In healing many, the form of the doublet recalls John's activity in the wilderness, thus establishing Jesus immediately as surpassing John's power and extent of influence. Such a thematic comparison enables the doublet to function as a powerful framework which both contains and comments upon the enclosed material. The christology is effectively developed against the similar activity of John, which now moves beyond the linear relationship of before-and-after into order to become a thematic fence interacting with the material it surrounds.

8. **Time**: Mark only sketches an outline of time. Time is of course important as an organizer to some extent. "Healing Many" occurs within the vague time frame of the early ministry. "The Twelve" represents some period of time between the choosing of the disciples and sending them out. "The Feedings" occurs after the death of John. "Healing the Blind" shows Jesus on the way to Jerusalem.

9. **Setting**: Many critics have pointed to geography (or topography) as markers of the boundaries between the different sections of the gospel, but geographical references in Mark can be notoriously vague and are not always of significance for determining the structure of the envelopes. The evangelist does, however, use settings symbolically within this envelope structure. For example, the epilogue tells of the baptism, the wilderness, and the shift of setting into Capernaum. In the first envelope, Jesus makes a point of moving away from Capernaum. The next envelopes portray Jesus crossing the sea on several occasions and often moving into the Decapolis or into the area of Tyre and Sidon. In the final envelope, Jesus is on the road nearing Jerusalem.

10. The basic shape of each envelope is created by the **dialectical interactions of a series of affirmations and negations**. Mark's method is a mill which grinds out fine christological statements about

Jesus. In "Healing Many," there is a negation of geographical space and of provincial theology. Jesus, interrupted by a chorus of awe and dissent, demonstrates his superiority to John the Baptist. Local triumphs in Capernaum do not hold him there, but he pushes on into a further series of conflicts with the establishment. Thus, the method of Mark gradually reveals the influence and power not only of Jesus of Nazareth in his historical mode but also of the risen Christ who still exists alongside human history. Much of our analysis of the next three envelopes will be under the aegis of this very important method.

11. Finally, each envelope will demonstrate its awareness of themes of the other envelopes, as **each envelope either resumes the theme of a preceding envelope or anticipates the theme of an envelope which will follow**, in addition to developing its own unique theme. While this may seem at first glance to mitigate against the unity of the individual envelopes, it does not; for each envelope has its own demonstrable thematic differences and emphases. We must not overlook, however, the fact that while Mark was motivated to cast his writing in this envelope form, he nonetheless presents the gospel story as one whole story. Segmentation of the story does not appear to be Mark's purpose. Probably for purposes of teaching and perhaps of liturgy, he has written in this envelope form, but he never forgets the powerful underlying unity of the gospel. "Healing Many" amplifies the theme of authority which was introduced in the epilogue. It also anticipates the themes of good response and good discipleship which shall find emphasis in the next envelope. The identity theme, which is now only establishing its presence, will come to the forefront in the next envelopes, especially in "Healing the Blind."

These, then, are the major organizational principles utilized by Mark in the organization of his gospel. Subject matter is not useful as an organizational principle, since it is not the topics, or ideas, which organize Mark's material, but the themes. Most early criticism unsuccessfully attempted to find order according to the topics of subject matter addressed by Jesus. The topical patterns which do exist, however, are scattered. Parables, for example, may be placed together and may refer to the kingdom or to good discipleship; several people in succession may be healed by Jesus, so that one conceivably could speak of a "healing section." If one applies only topical criteria, however, the envelopes would become invisible (that is what has happened), and the gospel of Mark would break up into random, brittle pieces which could never be seen as a unity except under the broadest of headings.

Topical patterns may be useful when the envelopes are established; for topics may be indicators of theme. It is not only the topic of kingdom which will be important, for instance, when Jesus' parables will later be gathered together. It will be the theme of kingdom which will become important as it moves across topical lines and establishes connections among apparently discordant materials. The seed of the parables moves thematically beyond an apparently moralistic topicality to the themes of the Suffering Servant and the acceptance or rejection of Christ. In fact, the prologue, the four separate envelopes, the Jerusalem section, and the epilogue are all interrelated through a process of thematic cross-referencing. In the next chapter, another theme will emerge within the borders of the next doublet: the choosing and sending of Jesus' disciples.

# 4
# The Twelve

A  **Choosing twelve** (3:13-19a).
   B  Beelzebul. **Rejection** by scribes from Jerusalem (3:19b-30).
     C  **Mother and brothers** (3:31-35).
        D  Faith and the kingdom (**parables** of seed and light) (sayings near center). Teachings concerning **right and wrong responses** to approaching kingdom (4:1-34).
           E  **Calming storm** (4:35-41).
                 ↕ (Two miracles at center)
           E´  **Gerasene demoniac** (5:1-20).
        D´  **Combined stories** of Jairus and woman suffering from bleeding. **Right response** to kingdom in both stories. Both stories are dramas confirming the parables (5:21-43).
     C´  **Combined stories** (5:21-43). Again, the right responses are confirmed. The **right response** of the woman touching Jesus' garment is contrasted with the **wrong response** of Jesus **mother**.
   B´  Nazareth. **Rejection** by the people of his hometown (6:1-6).
A´  **Sending twelve** (6:7-13).

For the doublet of his next envelope, Mark chooses passages about the calling and sending of Jesus' disciples:

> He went up on the mountain and called to him those whom he wanted; and they came to him. And he appointed twelve, whom he also named apostles, to be with him, and to be sent out to proclaim the message, and to have authority to cast out demons. So he appointed the twelve: Simon (to whom he gave the name Peter); James son of Zebedee and John the brother of James (to whom he gave the name

> Boanerges, that is, Sons of Thunder); and Andrew, and Philip, and Bartholomew, and Matthew, and Thomas, and James son of Alphaeus, and Thaddaeus, and Simon the Cananaean, and Judas Iscariot, who betrayed him (3:13-19a).
>
> He called the twelve and began to send them out two by two, and gave them authority over the unclean spirits. He ordered them to take nothing for their journey except a staff; no bread, no bag, no money in their belts; but to wear sandals and not to put on two tunics. He said to them, "Wherever you enter a house, stay there until you leave the place. If any place will not welcome you and they refuse to hear you, as you leave, shake off the dust that is on your feet as a testimony against them." So they went out and proclaimed that all men should repent. And they cast out many demons, and anointed with oil many who were sick and cured them (6:7-13).

This doublet is established by the basic parallels between the twelve, and by the similar activities of calling and sending. The first half of the doublet—the calling—contains dramatic tension even though it is a list: Judas is mentioned last as the betrayer, providing a bridge to the Beelzebul pericope. The second part of the doublet—Jesus' instructions to the twelve—is dramatized by Jesus' anticipation of what kind of reception his disciples will receive. This second half is not merely a formal repetition, but actually contributes to the plot of the gospel. Jesus shows his willingness to share his mission with the disciples. Thus, we see a progression, beginning with John the Baptist's work, then Jesus' activity in Galilee, and now the twelve who are empowered to do some of the same things which Jesus does. The symbolism of the word "twelve" also provides tension. Stock points out that in appointing the twelve, Jesus is recreating Israel.[95] A great responsibility, therefore, is placed upon the twelve, raising the dramatic question: "Are these men capable of contributing anything to Jesus' mission?"

The material enclosed within these doublets presents the most intense conflicts yet seen in the gospel. The confrontation with Satan appears first in the prologue, but Mark only makes brief reference to this conflict and then moves quickly on to the calling of the first disciples. Neither does Mark dwell upon the confrontation with the possessed man, but from there Mark passes quickly to the healings. The major confrontations in "Healing Many" begin with the affirmation/negation contrast between scenes A and B, as Jesus, after the affirmation of his power in the first half of the doublet, withdraws from Capernaum and announces his intention to extend his ministry. Then begins the series of debates with the Pharisees which reached a climax, at the end, where the Pharisees and Herodians were plotting to kill Jesus.

This new envelope begins, appropriately, where "Healing Many" ends, at a point of high tension. Interestingly, the last name given in the list of the twelve is the name of Judas Iscariot, "who betrayed him." This final reference forms a hook connecting the first doublet with the first episode in the envelope, for after choosing the twelve, Jesus goes home; and the crowd comes together, so that they can not even eat (3:19b-20).[96] The first of the two family references occurs at 3:21: "When his family heard it, they went out to restrain him, for people were saying, 'He has gone out of his mind.'" Once again, Mark uses the first scene following the doublet to introduce a basic conflict into the envelope. Mark's writing takes a considerably darker tone now; even though there was serious conflict before, the "Healing Many" section seems almost pastoral compared with this. For now Jesus' person, indeed his very sanity, is being attacked.[97]

In scenes A and B in "Healing Many," we saw that scene B immediately established a contrast with scene A. The first scene was the first half of the doublet, the picture of Jesus' day in Capernaum where he healed many people. In so portraying him, Mark affirmed his power and added to his portrait of the Christ. In the second scene, Jesus withdraws from Capernaum; and when the disciples seek him out, he tells them that he must go elsewhere. An apparent negation occurred, then, as Mark sought, not to qualify what happened at Capernaum, but to complement, or add significant elements to, his portrait of the Christ.

The same phenomenon occurs here, and Mark's method and intention again become apparent as he concludes the list of disciples with the name of Judas and then moves immediately into the Beelzebul scene. Jesus' choosing of the disciples affirms that he shared his mission with them, but we must remember that Jesus is not yet "magnified" by his disciples and that his essential *doxa*, or glory, exists independently of their recognition. The process of affirmation/negation/further affirmation repeats itself, therefore, in this envelope. Jesus' call to the disciples (and to us, or the initiates) is important, but responding to the call does not automatically transfer Jesus' divine status to the disciples, nor does the answering of the call fulfill the obligations of disciple to master. They must prove themselves to be worthy; above all, they must be faithful, and not betray him. The ending of the first half of the doublet, then, introduces the dark "hook" by giving notice that one of the disciples would betray Jesus. In the scenes that follow, Mark will demonstrate how not only Judas but even Jesus' family was capable of a destructive response to Jesus. Thus, the basic unity of the first scenes of the envelope is provided by the theme of wrong response.

The first scenes (3:13-25) contain a twelve-family-scribes constellation which is sinister. Judas is mentioned as one of the twelve; the family is associated with the question of Jesus' stability; and the scribes carry forward the hostility of the previous section. Quite possibly, this is an old text or one which retrieves an old tradition, for the realism of psychological concern and the involvement of family indicate, it seems to me, the kind of hostile rumor that would circulate during the life of Jesus of Nazareth or soon thereafter. The scribes heighten the notion of emotional instability by accusing Jesus of being possessed, not just by some minor demon but by Beelzebul, the "ruler of the demons" (3:22).

This intense conflict encourages us first to look at what is happening on the level of plot. In Mark's cosmology, the presence of the Christ produces a reaction from evil which will lead inevitably, step by step, to the crucifixion. This is the basic tragic progression of plot which we shall trace as it shapes Mark's story. Jesus, the protagonist, stimulates opposition from his antagonists, including some members of his own family in addition to those of the religious establishment. These all represent the growing opposition to Jesus, and the demons represent it at its supernatural level.

In the Beelzebul scene, the scribes, instead of conceiving of themselves as evil, neatly perform an act of projection: they project the evil onto Jesus. As it usually is, this projection is extreme, identifying the recipient as a scapegoat, one identified with the essence of evil. After assigning this scapegoat role to Jesus, they attack the credibility of God's messenger. The one who violates Sabbath law and associates with outcasts is now a madman possessed by Beelzebul. One wonders whether this entire section in Mark was not formed, originally, as an answer to the vicious charges made against Jesus' character during his lifetime, that is to say, a dialogue determined by the most forceful arguments brought against Christianity.

The house-divided saying which perhaps has basically a biographical and apologetic function, also assumes a catechetic role. What is being taught here is the reliability of Jesus of Nazareth. Furthermore, Mark will give this text its christological cast primarily by the statement: "But no one can enter a strong man's house and plunder his property, without first tying up the strong man; then indeed the house can be plundered" (3:27). This christological tone is heightened by Jesus' further comments: "Truly I tell you, people will be forgiven for their sins and whatever blasphemies they utter; but whoever blasphemes against the Holy Spirit can never have forgiveness, but is guilty of an eternal sin"—for they had said, "He has an unclean spirit" (3:28-30).

We find here a good example of the interrelationships between plot and character. Mark presents Jesus' character through a series of conflicts. The nature of Mark's text (and the tradition's story) is determined by the remembrance of this conflict through the lens of the resurrection; that is to say, Mark and his traditions have interpreted Jesus of Nazareth in the light of the risen Christ, who is contemporaneous with Mark's readers and who remains in conflict with those who opposed him in his role as Jesus of Nazareth.

Here, Jesus wins his argument in the sense that he walks away unscathed, after having the last word. This is, I think, not arrogance, but catechism. Jesus' life, in the cast of plot and character given by Mark, is intended to illustrate the ideas the initiates will need to become Christians and to grow as Christians. Mark transcends the family struggle by his giving it a christological shape:

> Then his mother and his brothers came; and standing outside, they sent to him and called him. And a crowd was sitting around him; and they said to him, "Your mother and your brothers and sisters are outside, asking for you." And he replied, "Who are my mother and my brothers?" And looking at those who sat around him, he said, "Here are my mother and my brothers! Whoever does the will of God is my brother and sister and mother."

Jesus speaks of himself here self-consciously as the Christ, and there is no reason to doubt that it was the historical Jesus who gave this saying its christological cast, just as he did in thinly-veiled references in many of the parables.[98] Mark, in presenting this saying, is already beginning to present the proclaimer as the one proclaimed.

The scenes dramatizing Jesus' harsh conflicts with establishment and with his family are followed immediately by the parables of seed and light. There is an obvious transition here provided by the very contrast involved. The bad soil, the improper response to Jesus, is dramatized as background for the introduction of the teachings of Jesus. These teachings have been delayed by Mark in order to dramatize first how they must be received. Before the parables section in chapter four, we know very little from Mark concerning the content of Jesus' teaching. What we get, instead, is the presentation of his actions with a focus, verbally, on the short sayings which develop christology: he refers to himself as Son of Man or bridegroom; he stresses the newness of his mission, or he emphasizes the importance of faith. Reading Mark is almost like watching a movie which begins as a silent film, with sound gradually added. There is a crescendo of speech during the conflicts in Jerusalem; and there are the eerie silences, punctuated by mockery, which accompany the crucifixion and burial.

Here, with the parables of seed and light, we begin to hear the teaching of Jesus which Mark chooses for the initiate to hear. Even though Mark has relented from his silence, he does not become talkative. He proves, in fact, to be highly selective. What teachings he does include are skillfully interwoven with narrative: are not merely decorative and moralistic. Recent criticism has certainly demonstrated that the parables section of Mark moves beyond pietistic instruction. It is probably owing to the simplistic commentary given after the parable of the sower (4:13-20) that these parables have been interpreted in a simplistic way. As James Williams convincingly demonstrates,[99] the parables of chapter four are organically united with Mark's story. To put it another way, the sayings of Jesus of this section are reflected in the doings of Jesus, the disciples, and others in gospel which precedes this section and in the gospel which follows. A thoughtful rereading of the familiar parable of the sower reveals its unifying contribution to the gospel:

> "Listen! A sower went out to sow. And as he sowed, some seed fell on the path, and the birds came and ate it up. Other seed fell on rocky ground, where it did not have much soil, and it sprang up quickly, since it had no depth of soil. And when the sun rose it was scorched, and since it had no root, it withered away. Other seed fell among thorns, and the thorns grew up and choked it, and it yielded no grain. Other seed fell into good soil and brought forth grain, growing up and increasing and yielding thirty and sixty and a hundredfold." And he said, "Let anyone with ears to hear listen!" (4:3-9).

This parable is an amplification of a theme just presented in the Beelzebul section: one must respond to Jesus with faith, for he is sound and his spirit is sound. Jesus, the messenger, finds his mothers and brothers and sisters only among those who accept him and who do the will of God. Being the good soil and receiving the seed present the way of receiving Jesus and his message. To say this seems, perhaps, to simply restate the parable of the sower in another moralistic fashion. But something else is here, and using the terminology of literary critics, we can state it this way: the alert reader can see from the context of plot that Jesus' third-person teachings begin to take on their first-person quality in these parables.

To be sure, Jesus still teaches at this point in the grammatical third person. The first summary of his message (1:14-15) is a third-person message, for example, delivered by a messenger pointing not to himself, but to events occurring independently of him. But since that time, in example after example in the context of the plot, Jesus shows that he himself must be accepted. Faith in him is necessary for healings, demons recognize the importance of his person, and the titles he applies to himself (bridegroom and Son of Man) acquire a personal edge. By his humble identification with outcasts, he includes his person in his message. In other words, the plot of the gospel is already showing the first-person character of the messenger. In that sense, for dramatic reasons, Mark advances the plot ahead of the teachings. Mark only gradually moves the proclaimer into the position of the message that is proclaimed: grammatical first person dominates in Jesus' self references during the trials, and the distance will be completely closed with resurrection and pentecost.

The technique of changing the focus to first person is actually a technique used by Mark to reflect Jesus' transcendence of history. The third-person seed will become the first-person cross. The cross will grow from these seeds of narrative and parable. The believer must receive Jesus into his or her life with faith just as did the man lowered through the roof. Unless there is a suspension of disbelief and mistrust, only a sour negativism will remain, as is demonstrated in the behavior of the scribes, or there will be only a panic, a fear such as that revealed in the behavior of Jesus' family. In this envelope, as well, the proper response to Jesus' teaching continues to be emphasized; the parable of sower, though third-person, is thematically related to the acceptance, by the believer, not only of seed as word, but of Jesus himself.

In regard to the parable of the sower, Williams writes that the "important thing here is the way in which Mark works the parable into his plot. For him it contains the mystery of the kingdom, the activity and presence of God. Jesus says to the disciples, 'Do you not understand this parable? And how then will you fathom all the parables?' (4:13). What one must possess and be possessed by is that secret if one is to serve Jesus in the kingdom. This concealed truth is the key to all the other dominical teachings."[100] For Williams, then, the basic mystery in Mark is the "sacrificial suffering of the Son of Man." He argues convincingly that the Son of Man, Suffering Servant, and seed imagery are all related in the Hebrew traditions. Mark, therefore, alludes to these interwoven traditions when he uses the symbol of the seed to refer to the Suffering Servant. Williams reaches much the same conclusion that I do, that Mark's gospel as a whole is devoted to the paradoxical development of the Christ as Suffering Servant.

Williams establishes a convincing relationship between seed symbol and the Suffering Servant theme. Jesus' sacrificial suffering is related to the dawn of the kingdom: as Mark writes that "the Son of Man came not to be served but to serve, and to give his life a ransom for many" (10:45). Here, Williams believes Mark is alluding to Isa 53:10, which reads as follows:

> And it pleased Yahweh to crush him with sickness. If you make his life (*napšô*) an offering for sin, he shall yet see his offspring (*zera'*), he shall prolong his days, and the will of Yahweh shall prosper through him.

Williams discusses how the Septuagint reads somewhat differently:

> And the Lord is pleased to purge him of his plague. If you give an offering for sin, your soul (*psuche*) shall see long-lived offspring (*sperma*).[101]

Concerning these differences, Williams says it "appears that the Greek translators took *nepeš*, soul, life, appetite, as the subject of the following verb, and 'cleaned up' the assertion that the Lord causes sickness. The switch to second person plural in the LXX ('If you give ...') reads like a parenthetical aside to the hearer within the narrative or to the reader. At Mark 10:45, he believes, the Greek is much nearer the Hebrew, because Jesus refers to the Son of Man giving his psyche (his soul) as a ransom. What is more important, according to Williams, "the passage in Isaiah, with which Mark is clearly familiar, indicates that the servant will eventually see the growth and extension of his seed." He points out that in "the Hebrew Scriptures *zera'* very frequently carries the secondary meaning of both children and male semen; in an extension of the former sense it denotes also the holy people who are charged with the special responsibility of maintaining their identity in the postexilic tradition (Ezra 9:2; Neh 9:2; cf. Isa 6:13 and 62:12)."[102] He then makes the following observation about the possible relationship between Mark's text and the "servant poem of Isaiah":

> It may be that for Mark the servant poem of Isaiah is in the background of the parable of the sower and Jesus' reference to the mystery of the kingdom of God. *In that case, what is sown is the sacrifice of the Son of Man, which will break the hold of the worldly quest for security for those who are able to see. The seed, the "offspring" or growth of this "planting" will be the community of those who understand that the way of the Suffering Servant is the way of their lord that they also will follow.* Thus the seed that is planted and the seed that grows are distinct but inseparable in the organic imagery of life, death, and the new life.[103]

For Williams, it "is the sower who sows the seed, but the word in its deepest dimension is the sacrifice of the sower himself and the fruits of this sacrifice, the posterity of the sower, namely the community of the kingdom."[104] Williams is careful not to restrict the meaning of this parable to any one interpretation, for he sees the strength of parable as consisting in its ability to contain multiple meanings. His point is that even if the popular, moralistic interpretation of the parable be a correct reading, it would be incredible if it were the only reading.[105]

His argument that Jesus can be identified with the seed seems to me to be a well-founded interpretation which can be supported by a careful examination of Mark's basic method. After all, Mark is concerned primarily with the emergence of the Suffering Servant theme. The messianic secret has served, as Wrede long ago observed, to repress that theme until Mark is fully ready to reveal it. Mark's presentation of the parable of the sower, then, according to our interpretation of the gospel so far, can be seen as another step in the revelation of the Suffering Servant. The Isaiah background given by Williams lends support to this idea: "There is a sense in which the sower becomes the seed, he is the one planted, the one who must 'fall into the earth', so to speak—that is, into the good soil. The disciples are to be the good soil, but they are also the further growth, the issue of the mysteriously working seed. Therefore in a deeper sense the 'seed' is both sower and fruit, master and disciples." [106]

When Jesus interprets the parables for the disciples, some might see a problem in the statements about the hiddenness of the kingdom: "To you has been given the secret of the kingdom of God, but for those outside everything comes in parables; in order that 'they may indeed look, but not perceive, and may indeed listen but not understand; so that they may not turn again and be forgiven" (Mark 4:10-13 from Isa 6:9-10). In God's instructions to Isaiah about his mission, there is this ironic refrain that occurs again and again: "lest they turn and repent." I don't find any harsh predestinarian meaning either in Isaiah or Mark. Isaiah's refrain is ironic; God, the speaker, intends the irony. To interpret Mark's passage as meaning that Jesus deliberately excluded many from the kingdom by making his teaching esoteric is to miss the central meaning of the gospel. Such an interpretation goes so much against the grain of this text that we must dismiss it. Jesus, aware of the ironies in the rejections of his message, reminds the listener that this hardness of heart is not new, not at all. Thus, his response is thematically connected with the repeated statements about rejecting the prophets. Any Jew in touch with the living heritage of Judaism, Jesus seems to me to say, cannot miss the meaning of Jesus' life and message.

To be adequately understood, the parable of the sower must, like everything else in Mark, be interpreted to some extent in the light of crucifixion and resurrection. This is also true of the other parables in this section. Consider, for example, the parable of the lamp:

> And he said to them, "Is a lamp brought in to be put under the bushel basket, or under the bed, and not on the lampstand? For there is nothing hidden, except to be disclosed; nor is anything secret, except to come to light. Let anyone with ears to hear listen!" (4:21-23).

Just as the parable of the sower can be best interpreted in the light of Mark's special placement and usage, so can this small parable, this metaphor of light, be best interpreted. We can perhaps discern Mark's intentions, keeping in mind the entire gospel as we read each of its parts. Christ's words to the disciples often have a powerful dramatic and tragic irony instilled by our knowledge of later events. The bridegroom reference is an early example; later, in the prophecies and in remarks made to James and John, Jesus supplies this kind of irony. This tragic irony is similar to that given by Sophocles in *Oedipus the King*, where the protagonist's words gain their force from the audience's knowledge of his fate. Christ's teachings, as remembered and preserved by the first Christians, resonate with ironies given by the fateful cross. Here, in the context of what is to happen later in Jerusalem, the reader must remember the cost of revelation. What will the revelation of light cost the disciples? What will it cost the Christians in Rome? What will it cost the Christ in Jerusalem?

This parable section is pregnant with such ironies, for the revelation of the light will cost many of the disciples their lives, just as Jesus' revelations will cost him his life. The real tragedy of hiddenness is the later cost of revelation. Those who attempt to sentimentalize the Christian experience or to emphasize the economic and psychological benefits it can bring indeed invent some other kind of religion. Christian experience involves real sacrifice and for some tragedy and suffering. Make no mistake about it, for Mark the Christian life is, in many ways, a tragic experience. A first-century person hearing Mark's story surely would have caught the connotations of tragedy: the involvement of a person with the net of his fate.

Those participating in the life and experience of Jesus Christ must expect persecution, moreover, because they are involved in the unfolding of a mystery. This inevitable, necessary unfolding brings a temporary nemesis. Unfortunately, that temporary time of retribution involves the entire span of the lives of Mark's audience. They may, some of them, not taste death until they see the kingdom come, but in the meantime, to walk the *hodos*, the way, of the Christ is to follow a tragic flow of action. The revelation of their belief, their allowing the light to shine, will probably bring persecution, but only along this path can one find the way to the new order which is to come. As Jesus said in another gospel:

> Enter through the narrow gate; for the gate is wide and the road is easy that leads to destruction, and there are many who take it. For the gate is narrow and the road is hard that leads to life, and there are few who find it (Matt 7:13).

Thus, in these parables, is not only moralistic instruction, or the promise of kingdom, but a forthright and unflinching statement of the double-edged quality of the Christian life. As we shall see, the seed that perishes is not the only seed to suffer; the act of Christian growth expressed in the flourishing seed—that growth will bring a nemesis (which Mark's audience may already have seen in action in Rome). The lamp which reveals its light calls attention to itself, as well. Mark attains this double edge chiefly by his juxtaposition of these parables with the Beelzebul conflicts which preceded them, and by the storm and demoniac which follow them. In a dark, hostile world, an unashamed revelation of Jesus' light was to be the task of the readers of Mark.

When first century Christians heard the lines "Take up your cross and follow me," at the center of Mark's gospel, they would have seen the relationship of that call to this earlier imprecation, in this chapter, not to hide one's light. Matthew would say "Let your light shine before others" (Matt 5:16). The Greek word for apocalypse means to come forth from hiddenness, and Mark's story is apocalyptic not only in its visions (chapter thirteen) of the end of the world, but Jesus' life, at every point, is a light which reveals God, bringing him forth from hiddenness. The cost of this revealed good news will be high, because of the misidentification of Jesus by both opponents and friends. Mark's artistic shaping of this religious work never ceases to remind us that the light of Jesus will indeed be made manifest, but only in spite of the disciples' misunderstanding, and only at great cost to them all. Receiving the good seed, too, would be interpreted as having all the implications associated with suffering. Mark intends both seed and light to be read as a part of the same gospel which presents the Suffering Servant. Suffering and growth cannot be separated.

In these few parables, we should overlook neither the sense of personal call nor Jesus' intent to show the inevitability of kingdom. This is highlighted in the parable of the growing seed.

> He also said, "The kingdom of God is as if someone would scatter seed on the ground, and would sleep and rise night and day and the seed would sprout and grow, he does not know how. The earth produces of itself, first the blade, then the head, then the full grain in the head. But when the grain is ripe, at once he goes in with his sickle, because the harvest has come" (4:26-29).

It is inevitable that light will shine without hindrance; it is inevitable that the seeds will grow (or perish); it is inevitable that the kingdom will come. Jesus himself probably gave this emphasis to his parables; their meaning will inevitably be demonstrated as the kingdom approaches. The harsh language of John the Baptist in the Q tradition, when he speaks of sickle and fire, is muted in Mark (cf. Matt 3:11-12 and Luke 3:9, 17), but the implications of judgment are surely present in Mark's presentation of these sayings, as well. They all are connected by the theme of the inevitable, certain approach of the kingdom of God.

One insight offered from the method of literary criticism is that all these parables are unified by the approach of the kingdom as well as by the definitions given of good discipleship. In the same way, the parable of the mustard seed functions on both the levels of describing the nature of faith and of inevitability of the kingdom's approach:

> He also said, "With what can we compare the kingdom of God, or what parable will we use for it? It is like a mustard seed, which, when sown upon the ground, is the smallest of all the seeds on earth; yet when it is sown it grows up and

becomes the greatest of all shrubs, and puts forth large branches, so that the birds of the air can make nests in its shade" (4:30-32).

The historical Jesus obviously spoke these parables with prophetic intent, but they took a deeper significance in the light of Jesus' crucifixion and resurrection and the experiences of the early church. The basic success of Mark's gospel is its ability to fuse all those experiences into one, ongoing Christian experience.

Mark follows the parables with a miracle story: the calming of the storm. The one who has called them to effective faith and discipleship, the one who speaks of the inevitability of God's kingdom, now again demonstrates the power of that kingdom and affirms, as well, his own essential relationship to the coming age. Here is the first instance of several occurrences:

> On that day, when evening had come, he said to them, "Let us go across to the other side." And leaving the crowd behind, they took him with them in the boat, just as he was. Other boats were with him. A great windstorm arose, and the waves beat into the boat, so that the boat was already being swamped. But he was in the stern, asleep on the cushion; and they woke him up and said to him, "Teacher, do you not care that we are perishing?" He woke up and rebuked the wind, and said to the sea, "Peace! Be still!" And the wind ceased, and there was a dead calm. He said to them, "Why are you afraid? Have you still no faith?" And they were filled with great awe, and said to one another, "Who then is this, that even wind and sea obey him?" (4:35-41).

From the point of view taken by literary criticism, we can see several things happening here. Not only is there a symbolic signal of movement toward gentile regions in "the other side," but this is another of the christological scenes, this time involving a nature miracle which reintroduces the theme of power. The disciples, furthermore, by asking the question Mark uses to end the pericope, heighten the identity theme which will increasingly be magnified as the gospel story continues. Most importantly, Mark underscores a theme introduced in the parable section: the theme of faith.

Mark reintroduces the power theme in the calming-the-storm episode in order to emphasize the christological element of power. These expressions of Jesus' power also defend him against the attacks against him earlier in this envelope. The parables were appropriately placed to refute the accusation that Jesus was in league with Beelzebul. Those parables relating to the kingdom show Jesus not allied with demons, but opposing them. Calming the storm also relates to the negativism of the earlier accusations. In this scene Mark reaffirms the *dynamis*, or the power of the Christ who is Lord of all, including the demonic powers which rule nature. Mark's focus, which began in the broad strokes of myth, has moved furiously downward through the world and into the very psyche of Jesus, revealing by implication some pain inherent in conflicts with his family. Now the upward movement begins again, in the presentation of Jesus as Lord. Double exposure, then, is not a static, not a still picture of Jesus, but grows as in a film, giving a moving picture of the dynamic interaction caused by God's confrontation with humankind.

Jesus' confrontation is not with some abstract power, but with the power of evil. The theme of confrontation with evil is thus dramatized this time not as a possessed person in the throes of exorcism. But nature itself is in turmoil. Nature is controlled by the same demons who control humans. One wonders if Mark is not close to Paul's conception of nature as longing for release (Rom 8:20-22). Jesus the Messiah is now, as *kurios* or Lord, set above all principalities and powers, and that is essentially what is revealed by the doubly-exposed photograph of the calming of the storm.

Confrontation with still another type of power may be mirrored in this story. If this gospel were written across the Mediterranean sea in Rome, the church there could not miss the symbolic use of the sea of Galilee; for Mark uses that sea to suggest the Mediterranean and the later movement of the gospel of the apostles across that sea to Rome. In this content, their pathetic cry for help takes on a special significance for the initiate, who received the message through the influence and martyrdom of those apostles.

Again, it must be emphasized that this story is not an allegory, but contains a rich allusiveness that characterizes the synoptics. The allusiveness that allows midrash from Judaism allows as well symbols from the traditions of the Gentiles, who have been told other stories about the powers of the gods. Mark knows full well that he is addressing a multicultural audience, and the rich symbolic quality of his presentation of Jesus Christ arises from the attempt to convince that audience of the divinity of Jesus. The sower is the initial mask provided, but Jesus Incognito is no mere moralist. He is the powerful Christ.

In addition to the theme of power, Mark also keeps alive the theme of faith. When Jesus asks the disciples, "Why are you afraid? Have you no faith?" he is returning to that parabolic theme of faith and growth. In the healings recounted thus far, faith is demonstrated in the proper response to Jesus. In regard to the parables of seed and light, faith is also the proper response to the approaching kingdom. Mark thus forms an equation in which faith in Jesus and in the kingdom are essentially the same. In the calming of the sea, the Lord displays the power which can proceed from his own faith. Mark, moving from seed to storm, reminds us that only from the seed of faith can grow the majesty of the kingdom, and that even nature's turmoil is calmed in the context of faith. Jesus' great power, furthermore, should encourage faith in those who wait for the kingdom. Once we grasp these central threads in each of Mark's envelopes, we can find a way through a labyrinth of text.

This theme of the good faithful response to Christ as Lord, so carefully created in the parables of seed and light, are dramatized in the Gerasene demoniac, Jairus's daughter, and the woman who touched Jesus' garment. In the story of the Gerasene demoniac, the audience once again confronts the dark power dramatized in the temptation by Satan, in the Capernaum synagogue, in the plots of the Pharisees, in the Beelzebul episode, and in the storms as convulsions of nature.

> They came to the other side of the sea, to the country of the Gerasenes. And when he had stepped out of the boat, immediately a man out of the tombs with an unclean spirit met him. He lived among the tombs; and no one could restrain him any more, even with a chain; for he had often been restrained with shackles and chains, but the chains he wrenched apart, and the shackles he broke in pieces; and no one had the strength to subdue him. Night and day among the tombs and on the mountains he was always howling and bruising himself with stones (5:1–5).

So begins one of the best stories in the New Testament. This is, in effect, a confrontation with a giant monster. A Greek audience would recognize all the allusions which Mark supplied to emphasize the power of Jesus. Dionysius could calm the sea, for instance, and Odysseus had to struggle, in Homer's story, with the wrath of the sea god. That same hero confronted the Cyclops, the one-eyed giant. Hercules was constantly, it seems, in a contest with a strong opponent. He had to struggle, for example, with Antaeus, who drew his strength from the earth. Only by lifting him up from the earth was Hercules able to vanquish him. Jesus in the preceding scene himself has conquered the rulers of the sea, and this Gerasene demoniac suggests the spirit of convulsed earth. Furthermore, the allusion to the Legion is unmistakable, not to be missed by anyone in the first century. Mark has already dramatized the powers of nature; now we meet the powers which rule the earth. Significantly, too, we have our structural signal again — *eis to peran*: to the other side.

In the very first verse of the calming-of-the-sea pericope, Jesus refers to the other side. Indeed, the reference is emphasized by its placement at the beginning of the scene. Mark is, in effect, introducing a gentile section of "The Twelve" envelope in Gerasa, a city of the Decapolis.[107] In "Healing Many," Mark presents a view of faith within the Jewish community. A good case can be made that "the other side of the sea" in Mark is symbolic of the gentile community, and that the phrase *eis to peran*, "to the other side" is a structural signal used consistently by Mark to call attention to his method.[108] The allusions to the Mediterranean and the struggles of the apostles' early missions would certainly appeal to Mark's Roman audience. Those allusions, in the first century, would not be seen as falsifications of the record, but they would be understood as true references, which happened to be foreshadowed by the struggles of Jesus near another sea, the Sea of Galilee.

Thus, on the level of plot, Mark extends Jesus' sphere of influence geographically at the same time that he extends it theologically. It is interesting to see how Mark expands the scope of his theme by using some of the same basic underlying formulas. Here, for instance, Jesus heals another afflicted human being, but Mark's theme is extended considerably by the Decapolis setting, by the connotative force of the word "Legion," and by the larger-than-life portrayal of the man among the tombs.

Something else may be observed, too. For the first time, the crowd-chorus (the herdsmen) responds fearfully to Jesus. There has been awe before, both from the crowd and from the disciples: What kind of man is this? But here the herdsmen are so frightened that they ask Jesus to leave the country! At the levels of double exposure, we again meet the awesome power of the Christ. The audience at the beginning of the story fears the madman, but the chorus at the conclusion of the story, fears Jesus. The poor victim of madness, after the fearful demon is expelled, feels no fear but now sits "clothed and in his right mind" (5:15). He has been given back to himself—as the Capernaum madman was, as were Peter's mother-in-law, the leper, the paralytic, and the man with the withered hand.

In the next scene, the transition from gentile to Jewish country is underlined, once again, by *eis to peran*. Jesus now journeys across the lake back to the Jewish regions and, appropriately, confronts "one of the rulers of the synagogue named Jairus" (5:22). Jairus's story, as most commentators observe, is opened for the insertion of another story so that we learn the conclusion of Jairus's story only after completing the story of the woman who touched Jesus' garment. The insertion of the story is in no way an intrusion, since the themes of the story overlap.

Notice the effectiveness of the transition. Jairus says, "My little daughter is at the point of death. Come and *lay your hands on her*, so that she may be made well, and live" (5:23). It is at this point that the woman comes forward and is healed by *touching* Jesus. Afterward, when standing beside the dead girl, Jesus *takes her hand*. Those who argue for Mark's clumsy transitions should wonder, at least, at Mark's skill here. Perhaps he did inherit the material and was an editor of lesser talent than the original composers, but it seems more likely that much of Mark's gospel, especially in the abrupt juxtapositions of scenes, is a deliberate archaizing of the Jesus material, a style assumed in order to repeat the form and style of the teaching books of the earliest mission.

Jesus again refers to faith—to the proper and correct response to his presence—as a prerequisite for healing. "Daughter, your faith has made you well; go in peace, and be healed of your disease" (5:34). The story of Jairus's daughter contains a contrast to the faith of the woman and to the faith of Jairus; for some of the bystanders laugh at Jesus, when he says "The child is not dead, but sleeping" (5:39). No one will again laugh at Jesus until the trial scenes when he is mocked and scourged. I interpret this story as a resurrection account and believe it to have been lovingly preserved as a statement of the early church's faith. Even if one believed the girl to be comatose, rather than dead, the symbolism should be compelling. This, in a way, is Mark's Lazarus story. Here both mockery and resurrection are foreshadowed; and although these two little stories may first appear anticlimactic when placed after the dramatic scene with the dangerous demoniac, the Jairus story at least, as a resurrection story, is the most awe-inspiring of all the miracles that Mark relates. Jesus' actions remind the reader to remember the future.

After journeying to the country of the Gerasenes, Jesus returns to the other side and then moves to his hometown, Nazareth. One might find here an example of Mark's clumsy editing, for praise of Jesus seems unaccountably to turn to hostility and disbelief in verses 2 though 6 of chapter 6. This apparently unmotivated shift in attitude may, however, be exactly what Mark intends to convey. We have already encountered the attitudes of awe, anger, and fear inspired by Jesus; and these are usually located, as we have observed, in the "choric sections" of various pericopes. Here, the mood swing is abrupt. Whereas Luke provides a motive for the anger of the people in that he tells of Jesus reading a messianic definition of himself from Isaiah (Luke 4:16-19), Mark simply and abruptly changes the tone:

> On the Sabbath he began to teach in the synagogue, and many who heard him were astounded. They said, "Where did this man get all this? What is the wisdom that has been given to him? What deeds of power are being done by his hands! Is this not the carpenter, the son of Mary and brother of James and Joses and Judas and Simon, and are not his sisters here with us?" And they took offense at him (6:2-3).

Once again Mark calls attention to the faith theme: "And he could do no deed of power there, except that he laid his hands upon a few sick people and cured them. And he was amazed at their unbelief." There is, perhaps, a recapitulation here of the movement away from Capernaum: "And he went about among the villages teaching" (v. 6b). Mark has his own way of dramatizing the fact that "the Son of Man has nowhere to lay his head" (Matt 8:20; see also Luke 9:58). Jesus is always on the move, generating turbulence, and then, in turn, apparently swept along by it. This is the pattern of the gospel plot. Jesus is an archetypal wanderer, not one so much who seeks the truth (though, as a human being, he does), but one whose very journey presents the pattern of eternal truth. Thus, the pattern of Mark's story perhaps both evolves from and contributes to a pattern for mimesis and ritual in the early church.

This scene of the rejection at Nazareth is best read in light of the sower parable, becuase that parable indicates the proper response to Jesus' message and is presented as both counterpoint and fugue to help thematically organize this envelope of "The Twelve." Jesus, at the beginning of this envelope, chooses the disciples to become his fellow teachers who would share his mission. Perhaps, in light of what is to follow, we might put it another way: Jesus, in choosing the twelve, is choosing his students—choosing stand-ins for the initiate, foils to demonstrate the difficulty and importance of understanding Jesus' message aright. And immediately, in the first half of the doublet, Judas, the bad seed, is introduced. He serves as a negative "hook," a transition into the Beelzebul pericope. That scene shows how the Pharisees as well as Jesus' family are not good soil for the seed of Jesus' message. Jesus' mother and siblings show their limitations as well. Paradoxically, it is the madman among the tombs who responds positively. What a strange place to find good soil!

The other parables of the mustard seed, of the seed that grows, and of light—these are all recalled, as well, whenever a response is made in faith to Jesus. Clothed and in his right mind, the healed man wants to follow Jesus. Told instead to tell how much has been done for him, he does not keep his light under a bushel. And in him one can discern that growth of kingdom will arise from proper reception of the good news. Just as the mustard seed, the seed that grows, and the light parables complement the sower parable by providing new metaphors for growth and productivity, so the faith of Jairus and the woman with the issue of blood complement the negative examples of Pharisees and family. Rejection at Nazareth provides the final counterpoint, dramatizing the bad soil in Jesus' own country. The pitiful shriveled reaction of Jesus' townspeople is symptomatic of their lack of faith.

After the rejection at Nazareth and with the second half of "The Twelve" doublet, this section ends. For Mark, this is the close of another teaching book, whose dominant themes—stated in teaching and action—are receptivity and growth. "Healing Many" introduced this theme under the umbrella of the theme of newness; here, in the envelope of "The Twelve," the theme of the good response to Jesus is developed on both sides of Mark's symbolic sea: the area of the

Gentiles and the area of the Jews. Against this background, we have the Janus-like conclusion to this section in the sending out of the twelve. Jesus' mission expands even further—now against the background of how people react to his message. The teaching function of this form is increasingly clear: the initiate is literally being led along the way of Jesus. Coming into the new church, still a revolutionary organization, the initiate is not only being trained in the way of the Master, is learning a proper response which applies to the present reality of the risen Christ.

An effective way to summarize the envelope might be to consider whether it, like the previous envelope, displays a recursive rhythm. In fact, there are some striking topical parallels (refer to diagram on page 77). This is especially so between B and B´, both of which present the theme of rejection. Furthermore, the mother without faith in C is contrasted with the woman of faith in C´. Jairus, also in C´, is a man of faith; and Jesus rewards him with a resurrection miracle greater than the nature miracle in D. Calming the storm (E), moreover, is set in relation to healing the Gerasene demoniac (E´), as Jesus heals both human beings and nature. A perfect construction, of course, would require the dismantling of the two healing stories (C´ and D´) which Mark has combined into one; also, a smaller construction would probably not contrast a sayings section with a doings section D and D´. We have already stated, however, that it is a mistake to apply criteria too rigorously, especially to these longer constructions, since many ancient writers, including many of the writers of Hebrew Scripture, did not always apply them rigorously, but seemed content, rather, with recursive constructions as defined in this book. Such a rhythm is here found again in Mark.

The sayings consist of parables which on one level represent Jesus' response to attacks made upon him and at another level develop the christology of Mark's gospel. These teachings, though not at the mathematical center of the recursion, do perform the task given to sayings in all the envelopes; they provide commentary upon the doings of Jesus. The detractors, in B and C, find their contrasts in the healing stories of faithful response found in D´ and C´. The Beelzebul controversy (B) is paralleled in a recursive manner with the rejection at Nazareth (B´), back across the construction, as it were, as once again Jesus' family is mentioned as opposition now comes from the people of his home town. Thus, once again, as in "Healing Many," this envelope, "The Twelve," displays a recursive rhythm.

There are other patterns as well. The scenes before the sayings present a Jesus who comes under serious attack from the establishment, family, and friends. By way of contrast, the parables section demonstrates the proper response to be made to the approach of the kingdom. After the verbal definition of the proper response to kingdom, in which Jesus' teachings are contrasted to the attitudes of the preceding scenes, Jesus speaks of transcendence (in regard to future kingdom) and demonstrates the transcendent power of the risen Christ (seen and retrospectively dramatized through the lens of memory of the early church). In calming the storm, for instance, he again shows his mastery over the powers which rule the world, and in the confrontation with the Gerasene demoniac, he demonstrates his superiority to the political powers which rule this world. The two faithful responses (of Jairus and the woman) are placed before the initiate soon after the parables and are therefore naturally associated with the response made by the good and bad soils to the seeds. Mark skillfully, therefore, in this envelope, dramatizes and illustrates the sayings of Jesus by showing their truth in the actions of the characters. He did the same in the "Healing Many" envelope when he illustrated the newness of Jesus' message and mission by showing the radical actions transgressing Sabbath traditions.

The basic unity of this envelope—its structural integrity—is achieved by Mark's unifying theme of the proper response to Jesus' message and mission. Because Mark shows the intensity and personal nature of the attacks mounted against Jesus, this envelope hits harder than "Healing Many." The first envelope established the newness of Jesus, and the chorus there regarded him with awe and wonder. In this envelope, the chorus, in the person of Pharisees and family, turns almost bitterly paranoid, indulging in vitriolic attacks against the person of Jesus. The proper responses to Christ and the kingdom, then, are demonstrated by action and parable.

How not to respond is demonstrated in the uglier scenes. In these negative scenes, Mark uses his themes for christological purposes. For example, one should not think of Jesus in only human terms, in a limiting way (as the people of his own country or as his family thought of him). Because this limited view ignores the blending of the spiritual with the temporal and with humanity, it forces one to think of humankind in an either/or way, as radically separate from God and God's kingdom and thus to miss the message of Jesus' teachings and person. These people reject Jesus because he is a man and has a family whom they know! The scandal thus becomes a scandal of particularity. Jesus' identity and efficacy as the risen Christ, however, are rooted in the faith of those others who do the will of God as Jesus' true brothers and sisters. Thus there is a shift into a transcendent key. The correct and faithful response to Jesus must be a response to the transcendent identity which the townspeople and family cannot see.

It may at first seem odd that Mark would choose passages about the twelve as doublets which would serve as frame for this material. In "Healing Many," we saw how the doublet functioned to frame the portrait of Christ within his qualities of compassionate healing. Once we analyze the construction of this envelope, we begin to see how the doublet here, as well, provides a thematic frame which is organic with the portrait which it encloses. The twelve, for Mark, are symbols of human fallibility characterized by the bad soil of the parable of the sower. At least this is so in the sense that one of them will betray him (a foreshadowing placed in the first half of the doublet) and in their fear and lack of faith during the storm at sea. This association of the disciples with human fallibility is just touched upon here, but will be amply demonstrated in the next two envelopes. In effect, what we have in the doublet frame is the sharing of Jesus' mission with fallible persons, thus framing his story within the context of misunderstanding, fear, hostility, and lack of faith.

The fallibility of the disciples, demonstrated again and again in Mark's plot, is also a positive and encouraging quality. The new believers, who are fallible human beings themselves, would likely see Mark's theological point that God's approach was toward flesh and blood and that his promises were made to fallible human beings. Through the doublet-panels, Mark emphasizes what he has stressed in the words of the parables and in the activity of plot: the kingdom of God is presented in the context of human choice and response. Anyone who approaches Christ must do so in the context of faith as good soil. God's offer, in the person of Jesus, is presented to humanity in such a way that a transformation of human attitude is necessary even to receive the seed!

Thus, the real significance of repentance (from the Greek *metanoia*, meaning a "turning about") can now be understood. Mark's conception of repentance is no sentimental one of a sinner simply declaring sorrow on account of offense committed. *Metanoia* involves a change of mind and heart—a thorough transformation. The message and person of Jesus thus involves personal struggle. Like the twelve, the initiate joining the church would struggle bitterly at times with the identity of Jesus. To accept the seed is accept the fate of Christ as one's own fate. The twelve can answer the riddle of the Christ only when they realize that they are called upon to be the riddle.

## Principles of Organization

1. **Theme**: Acceptance and rejection of Jesus and the kingdom constitute the basic organizing principle for this envelope.

2. **A/B Relationship**: The Beelzebul scene is a negative assault upon the first scene, which affirms Jesus' sharing of his mission with his disciples.

3. **Christological Assertions against Negation**:

3a. **Assertion by Healing**: Before the healings cease with the arrival in Jerusalem, it might appear that they could be interchanged with one another among the different sections or be placed just about anywhere in the first half of the gospel. This is not the case. Just as the Sabbath miracles were especially suited to the themes of controversy and newness in the first envelope, the healings in this second envelope are especially suited to their context of faith. Mark has achieved this unity himself, evidently, with the redactive references to faith which occur in the calming storm scene as well as in the Jairus/woman scene. This is an envelope containing violent, extreme reactions as well as release of strong natural powers opposed to Jesus. Those fearing Jesus after the healing of the demoniac are like the Pharisees and family. After the healing of the possessed man, even the powerful goodness in Jesus frightens and evokes hostility. Human emotional reactions are reflected in nature's reactions, as Jesus heals both human beings and nature, asserting the dominance of his power and promising the appearance of the source of that power: the approaching kingdom.

3b. **Assertion by Miracle**: When Jesus calms the storm, he is reasserting authority over against the accusations of the Pharisees.

3c. **Assertion by Sayings and Parables**: The parables of seed and light imply a right response to Jesus himself as well as to his message. Message and messenger fuse into the same entity in Mark.

3d. **Symbolic Narrative**: In this envelope, narrative symbolism basically involves the response of others to Jesus. There is a strong symbolism of resurrection, as well, in the healing of Jairus's daughter. Although this scene is conceivably Elijah midrash, it looks forward to the future of Mark's story and to the future of the faithful. Mark, again and again, employs the powerful technique of combining the backward look of midrash with the forward look of Jesus' message. This method is overlooked by those reductionist critics who wish to prove that the gospel is essentially only midrash and therefore a fiction.[109]

3e. **Assertion by Titles**: During the storm, Jesus is addressed as teacher (4:38). Jesus is a teacher who not only speaks in parables, but also acts them out. The teacher's actions demonstrate the powerful kingdom proclaimed in his teachings. The demonic legion refers to Jesus as "Son of the Most High God" (5:7). In Nazareth, Jesus refers to himself as prophet (6:4). All these titles are assertions against the attacks made upon his character, authority, and power.

4. **Negative Assertions** against the envelope's theme: Discussed in #10 below.

5. **Recursive Rhythms**: Discussed in #10 below.

6. **Relation of Sayings to Action Context**: This relationship is more profound here than anywhere else in the gospel, except perhaps in the final envelope concerning the healing of the blind. Jesus' person and mission are communicated through metaphors of seed and light in such a way that the significance of his activity is related strongly and inevitably with response to him. This, of course, is the theological significance of the proclaimer becoming the proclaimed or, to put it another way, of the giver becoming the one who must be received. The parables transcend ethics and move into a religious dimension.

7. **Doublets as Thematic Frame**: Choosing and sending disciples provides a focus for the response theme. Discipleship is defined to some extent in this envelope as making the proper response and then growing in faith toward the kingdom. It is, therefore, appropriate for Mark to organize his materials creatively within the framework of material about the disciples. It is interesting that Jesus warns them

that they may not themselves receive a good response from those encountered (6:11).

8. **Chronological Frame**: Mark implies only an indefinite period from choosing to sending disciples. What Mark wants to emphasize within this rather vague time frame is the struggle with rejection and the assertions of Jesus' power.

9. **Setting**: The symbolic movement continues outward from Capernaum, with Nazareth serving as a marker at the outer limits of Jesus' initial extension of activity. After Nazareth, the geographical sphere widens with continual references to the other side of the sea, and then to the journey toward Jerusalem.

10. **Dialectical Growth of Christological Assertions**: The affirmations of the first half of the doublet, "Choosing Twelve," are immediately assaulted by the Beelzebul and family negations. This conflict, in effect, generates the assertions of the parable section. Following upon hostile and fearful reactions to Jesus, the proper response is indicated by metaphors of seed and light. The power of the kingdom which is accepted in the seed is demonstrated by the miracle and healing that follow. The calming of the storm reintroduces Jesus at the powerful level of *kurios*, lord of all powers and principalities. The Gerasene demoniac scene shows both the improper and proper responses to Jesus' power.

Recursive contrasts occur in the scenes that follow the Gerasene demoniac, which stands near the center of this envelope. In contrast to the response of the family and the hostile Pharisees, the faith of Jairus and the woman are presented in a single powerful pericope. Mark caps this violent envelope with the rejection at Nazareth, which stands parallel—across a recursive structure—to the Beelzebul scene. When Jesus sends the twelve, in the second half of the doublet, he is in effect sowing seeds, so that the final frame is enriched by the material it encloses.

11. **Relationship to Other Envelopes**: On the level of plot, there is continuing movement outward toward Nazareth and toward the areas into which the disciples are sent. In other words, the action of envelope one is allowed to flow freely into envelope two. A unity with the first envelope exists in the continuance of healing activity, but the healings in this second envelope are related more specifically to the theme of faith. There is, as well, a progression from the displays of newness and power in the first envelope toward growing hostility and fearful opposition in this envelope. As a result of these negations,

# THE TWELVE

Mark parabolically defines kingdom as being necessarily related to human response. This is a critical theological issue, and he is extremely careful to lay the groundwork for it. There is further connection between the first two envelopes in the continuing flow of the demonic, a theme which will grow in intensity as Jesus approaches Jerusalem and the cross. Jesus' sphere of influence expands even further in the next envelope, which is enclosed by the feeding of the five thousand and the four thousand.

# 5
# The Feedings

Outer frame: **The old**: Death of John the Baptist (6:14-29).
  A    **Feeding** 5000 (6:30-44).
      B    **Walking on water** (6:45-52); miracle + hardness of heart saying (6:52).
         C    **Healings** in Gennesaret (6:53-56); **Jewish healings**.
            D    **The old**: Traditions of elders (7:1-23); sayings center.
         C´    **Healing** gentile woman (7:24-30); **gentile healing**.
      B´    **Healing** the deaf (7:31-37); healing miracle + opening of hearing; zealous acceptance.
  A´    **Feeding** 4000 (8:1-10).
Outer frame: **The old**: Demand for a sign; Pharisees and Herod (8:11-21).

Each of the preceding envelopes has found its unity in its own unique theme. In "Healing Many," the theme of newness was developed, and conflict with the authorities began. In "The Twelve," the theme of the good response to Jesus was developed in what will prove to be the most violent section of the gospel before the trial and crucifixion. Thus, the envelopes are, in a sense, set pieces with their own themes, but they also form a dynamic progression and blend into the larger plot as Jesus moves closer toward the gentile regions and toward the theology of the early gentile church.

In addition, both "Healing Many" and "The Twelve" consist of individual pericopes which carry the thematic stamp and dominant tone of the envelopes which enclose them. In "Healing Many" the calling of Levi, the controversy over fasting, and the Sabbath healings seem inextricably connected with the theme of the newness of Jesus' teachings. Thus, while these pericopes may have been detachable and reattachable units of traditions when Mark found them, he melds them together into envelopes which acquire their own structural integrity. In the envelope of "The Twelve," the Beelzebul scene, the calming of the storm, the Gerasene demoniac, and the rejection at Nazareth all belong to an envelope with a very different atmosphere, an atmosphere of intensified conflict and cosmic symbolism.

Now in "The Feedings," Mark creates another unique section of his gospel, a section which could be read and studied separately as an introduction to the new faith and which could be also read as part of the dynamic flow of action from the wilderness to Jerusalem. Mark's gospel is proving to be a coat of many colors, a series of interrelated materials woven into a larger unity.

Between the sending of the twelve and the feeding of the five thousand, Mark places the story of John's death (6:14–29). In this position, the story provides a transition between "The Twelve" and "The Feedings" envelopes and is part of a larger frame which encloses all of "The Feedings." The conflicts with the political and religious establishments, which appear in the story of John's death, are matched later by the second half of that outer frame: Jesus' conflicts with the Pharisees and with his own disciples after the feeding of the four thousand (8:11–21). Later in this chapter, when we examine the recursive form of the envelope, we will look more closely at this outer frame. For now, the feeding doublet introduces us to the basic structure of this envelope.

In "The Feedings," Mark brings his gospel even closer to the Gentiles. It could be argued that the first feeding, as the first half of a doublet, concerns Jews in their country, while the second feeding is for Gentiles in their territory. Mark further underscores the Jewish/Gentile contrast by placing Jesus' controversy with the elders at the center of the envelope.[110] After the disciples return to Jesus from their first mission, they go apart to a "lonely place" in order to rest, but people learn of their whereabouts and hurry there from all the towns, arriving ahead of them (6:31–33). Thus, the circle of the narrative continues to widen, moving away from its center at Capernaum. Even in that town, the crowds pressed against the door; now they have become multitudes. Jesus' attitude toward them is the same: "As he went ashore he saw a great crowd, and he had compassion for them because they were like sheep without a shepherd; and he began to teach them many things" (v. 34). We are no longer surprised that Mark does not give the content of Jesus' teaching, for the evangelist's method is now transparent to us, what Jesus does is what is important; thus, actions form the first half of the doublet:

> When it grew late, his disciples came to him and said, "This is a deserted place, and the hour is now very late; send them away so that they may go into the surrounding country and villages and buy something for themselves to eat." But he answered them, "You give them something to eat." (6:35-37).

The envelope is introduced by Mark's signaling that he is still educating the disciples (and the reader). They have just returned from teaching, but now they must be taught more themselves. Thus the question arises from their anguish of not understanding: "Are we to go and buy two hundred denarii worth of bread, and give it to them to eat?" And he said to them, "How many loaves have you? Go and see." And when they had found out, they said, "Five, and two fish" (6:38). That this teaching theme is important in this doublet is indicated by Jesus' question—especially sharp and challenging—to the disciples after the second feeding about whether they still do not understand about the loaves. In this, Mark calls attention to an important symbol in his riddle of the Christ. The reader, identifying with the disciples, is learning to pay close attention; for something of the identity of Christ is to be revealed within the symbolism of this section:

> Then he ordered them to get all the people to sit down in groups on the green grass. So they sat down in groups of hundreds and of fifties. Taking the five loaves and the two fish, he looked up to heaven, and blessed and broke the loaves, and gave them to his disciples to set before the people; and he divided the two fish among them all. And all ate and were filled; and they took up twelve baskets full of broken pieces and of the fish. Those who had eaten the loaves numbered five thousand men (6:39-44).

There are twelve baskets of fragments, and after the feeding of the four thousand, there will be seven baskets of fragments left over (8:1-10). Mark intended these numbers to be significant and he expected their significance to be understood by his audience, though it is not entirely clear to modern readers and critics are divided as to the meaning. The numbers may refer, respectively, to the twelve disciples associated with the Jewish ministry of the earthly Jesus and the seven mentioned in Acts (Acts 6:1-7).

This numerological interpretation, with its equation of early disciples and later apostles, gives credence to the possibility that the feeding doublet alludes to a resurrection appearance of Jesus. Imagery here resembles that in the appearances of Jesus especially as described in Luke and John, where the risen Christ is associated with meals. But it is more likely that in Mark's double-exposure, he presents Jesus in terms of the Eucharist, which incorporates themes from Exodus and from Kings (among others). The basic symbolism obviously comes from the Elijah-Elisha cycle (2 Kgs 4:42-44) where we read of Elisha's miraculous feeding of one hundred:

> A man came from Baalshalishah, bringing food from the first fruits to the man of God: twenty loaves of barley, and fresh ears of grain in his sack. Elisha said, "Give it to the people and let them eat." But his servant said, "How can I set this before a hundred people?" So he repeated, "Give it to the people and let them eat, for thus says the Lord, 'They shall eat and have some left.'" He set it before them, they ate, and had some left, according to the word of the Lord (2 Kgs 4:42-44).

In regard to the Elijah theme, we have already observed how Mark both affirms and negates the Elijah symbol. John the Baptist was strongly identified with Elijah; but as John recedes into the background, Jesus himself appears in the wilderness, reminding us of Elijah, as he does later when he heals Jairus's daughter, just as Elijah, at the imprecation of a parent, healed a child (1 Kgs 17:17-24). But as the symbolism of the Suffering Servant emerges, the Elijah theme subsides. Mark is in the process of affirming the Elijah prophetic tradition, but is also distinguishing Jesus from Elijah. It is interesting that feedings similar to the one performed by Elisha should follow immediately after the story of the death of John the Baptist. In a symphonic way, the Elijah/Elisha theme reemerges, as if intended to be a dirge for John the Baptist. Jesus is now identified with the Elisha theme of feeding. Elisha inherited the mantle of Elijah, and Jesus inherited—and transcended—the role of John.

While the Elijah parallel is important, especially in the traditions which Mark inherited, Mark uses this material, as he did the John the Baptist traditions, as foundation for a larger christology. Mark knew that in this story, the audience would recognize the risen Christ. He was able, therefore, to synthesize the traditions of the Hebrew Bible, perhaps some biographical material, and the appearances tradition. Though not strictly allegorical in nature, the scene alludes to the future activities of the disciples/apostles who take the food from Jesus and distribute it to the people. What we have, if these allusions are indeed present, is a story which includes highly compressed layers of meaning resulting in a symbol of extraordinary power.

We remember how Luke, in his road-to-Emmaus story, uses double exposure to summarize the future experience of the church by relating it as the experience of the two people on the road: "Did not our hearts burn within us when he opened to us the Scriptures?" (Luke 24:32). Many critics have spoken of Luke's artistry in referring to the later experience of the church, which, reinterpreted the Scriptures under the influence of the Holy Spirit. Here, in "The Feedings" is the picture of the later apostles and their presentation of the Eucharist to the early church.

Mark's religious art (as Luke's) combines the life of Jesus of Nazareth with experiences associated with the resurrection on yet a third level—the sacraments of the early church. The mode of perceiving Jesus in sacraments, this memory of the future, becomes the mode of symbol-making for the evangelists. Jesus' story unites past and present; Jesus' past has become present ritual. Much the same happens, surely, in the baptism pericope, which has also been seen as alluding to the resurrection experiences.

Manna symbolism is also present. Stegner remarks how the feeding of the five thousand contains the manna symbol and he connects that symbol with both the Hebrew Scriptures and with the Eucharist:

> The sequence of thought from bread in the wilderness to eschatological manna to Eucharist implies a strong connection between the eucharistic bread and the manna of the new age. This close relationship, in turn, shows that the Eucharist was understood typologically (cf. 1 Cor 10:1-4) ... (many) contemporary scholars believe that the feeding of the five thousand was originally an anticipation of the

> messianic banquet ... According to the Jewish expectations of the time, the eschatological manna would be eaten at the messianic banquet. The manna of Jewish expectations was like the Eucharist, in that it pointed backward toward the past and forward to the consummation."[111]

The traditions are compressed into a complex multilayered symbol, a complicated midrash fusing past, present and future. In this compression of feeding multitudes with Eucharist and possibly with resurrection, Mark reveals his memory of the future. As noted in the introduction, the Christian remembers the future in the Holy Spirit as well as in the experience of faith. In other words, the God who will bring the kingdom gives the Christian a foretaste of the future. Mark's religious text uses symbolism to fuse the future with the present, just as living experience does. In fact, it is the function of religious text to stimulate and feed living experience. In the symbol of feeding, then, is a memory of future ritual and of the future banquet.

From the gentile Christian point of view, the messianic banquet would be presented upon a table open to Gentiles as well as Jews. Mark is probably demonstrating this extension of grace in his presentation of two feedings, one for five thousand and then the second feeding for four thousand. The distinctions between Jewish and gentile feedings are noticed by Stock. He sees the first feeding occurring in Jewish territory, but understands the second, for Gentiles, to take place in the Decapolis. The Gentiles are thus invited to participate in an early representation of the Eucharist and of the messianic banquet. Stock notes that the sayings grouped together in the tradition of the elders' section confirms explicitly what the feedings assert metaphorically: a Gentile can also be clean if he or she obeys the demand of conscience, and nothing can prevent a Gentile from taking the Eucharist if that person sees Jesus as the source of life.[112]

The portrait of Jesus is also becoming more complex. Williams, in noting the connection between the feedings and the Eucharist, calls attention to the Suffering Servant concept that Mark is now bringing forward. He writes that "in Mark's plot the bread broken in the wilderness is a manifestation of divinely given life and redemptions. But that life and that redemption come about only through this breaking, viz. the suffering of the Son of Man." Jesus is, he says, "the One-Who-Shares-Bread" (p. 123). This metaphor is found early in Mark, according to Williams, in 2:26, when Jesus refers to David giving "the bread of the Presence to those who were 'with him.'" Jesus shares his presence with those he feeds in the wilderness. "This bread, the 'bread of the setting before' (so the Greek; literally 'bread of the face' in Hebrew), is really the bread of Jesus as the Son of Man. It is his insofar as the giving of life and the power of sacrifice are at work in him."[113]

If Williams is correct—and I believe he is—then we are moving now, even in this feeding section, toward the Suffering Servant theme. The bridegroom reference (2:19) foreshadowed the death and suffering of Jesus and in the feedings we see the future: the sacrificial and giving quality of Jesus' passion. Mark, as religious art, synthesizes the manna, the bread of presence, and the Elisha miracle of the Hebrew Scriptures with the Last Supper's establishment of the New Covenant. The feedings, historically, may well have been Jesus of Nazareth's reenactment of the Elisha miracle, his own symbolic presentation of himself to the crowds in the wilderness. I have already suggested that the imagery of the resurrection appearances often includes the eating of food.

Before we analyze the interior of Mark's recursion, a look here at the second half of the doublet (8:1-10) will help us better to understand the frame of the envelope. The similarities are extremely close: 1) a large crowd is present in both; 2) in the first feeding, there was "no leisure even to eat," and in the second, the crowd has nothing to eat; 3) in both, Jesus displays compassion for the crowd; 4) in the first, the disciples suggest sending the crowd away so that they can find food in surrounding villages, and in the second Jesus does not want to send them away to their homes because they might grow weak and faint on the way; 5) the disciples object in both that there is no way to feed such a crowd in the wilderness; in the first scene, their objection is to Jesus' explicit instructions, "You give them something to eat"; both objections are expressed in the form of questions; 6) Jesus asks how many loaves they have; in the first they respond that they have five, and two fish, and in the second, seven, and a "few fish"; 7) the crowd is commanded to sit down; 8) in the first, Jesus looks up to heaven, blesses the loaves, breaks them, and gives them to his disciples to distribute, and then divides the two fish among them, and in the second, Jesus takes the loaves, gives thanks, breaks them and gives them to his disciples and then also blesses the fish; 9) in the first, "all ate and were filled," and in the second, "they ate and were filled"; 10) after the first, twelve baskets of broken pieces and of fish remain; after the second, seven baskets of broken pieces are left over; and 11) in the first, five thousand are fed; in the second, four thousand.

These doublet halves encompass the two symbolic territories, making a symbolic set of bookends for Mark's theology. We can infer that the first feeding is identified as in a Jewish area, on the west side of the sea, because immediately afterward Jesus makes his disciples get into the boat and go before him to Bethsaida on the other side (6:45). The second feeding is probably set in gentile territory, since the preceding two scenes occurred in the region of Tyre (7:24), and then apparently in the Decapolis (7:31).

Immediately after the first feeding Jesus' crossing over to Gennesaret is the occasion for the scene showing him walking on water. This "to the other side" of the sea (6:45) is once again an important structural signal which gives some clues concerning Mark's editorial and compositional concerns. This movement, which shows Jesus extending his ministry to gentile areas once again makes of the Sea of Galilee a symbolic Mediterranean. As Stock observes, the crossings of the sea are an important symbol for Mark. He recounts, by way of summary, Mark's use of this symbol. After teaching in parables, Jesus makes his first crossing from "west to east." Then they "land in the country of the Gerasenes [in the Decapolis, a predominantly gentile area] ... Next, after the first miracle of the loaves, Jesus makes the disciples get into the boat and tells them to cross, west to east, to Bethsaida. On the way the wind was against them, and Jesus came to them, walking on the sea. The disciples were astounded, "for they did not understand about the loaves" (6:45-52). Then, after coming to land in Gennesaret, "Jesus heals a great number of sick people." Stock believes, as I do, that these "two crossings establish a pattern: Jesus and the disciples start out across the sea, a significant event occurs midway, the disciples fail to understand its significance, and when they come to land again Jesus heals someone." There will also be the argument on another crossing about the significance of the loaves. "What the disciples cannot understand is the point that Jesus is making about the gentile worlds and their own future orientation and mission."[114]

Kingsbury also notices this symbolic crossing. He believes that in compelling the disciples to sail to Bethsaida, Jesus is entrusting them with a mission into gentile territory. Kingsbury also understands the second feeding to take place in gentile regions. He believes that Jesus wants his disciples to understand that the feeding of the five thousand signalled the continuance of their mission to the Jews, whereas in the feeding of the four thousand, they were seeing the beginnings of their mission to the Gentiles.[115] Kingsbury's interpretation has the virtue of removing much of the awkwardness of these passages which arises from an apparently pointless repetition.

Kingsbury is certainly not suggesting, nor am I, that Mark's gospel is a formal allegory. I continue to emphasize this point, because any strict allegorical reading of the gospel would be destructive. Formal allegories, like Spenser's *Faerie Queene* or Bunyan's *Pilgrim's Progress* require the reader to follow, point by point, another level (or more) of meaning continuous with the primary story. Mark's gospel is not written in that way. To make the gospel or any of its sections allegorical would trivialize it, causing extensive damage to the theological content. Mark does not want to reduce the meaning of Jesus' activity by allegorizing it; he wants to extend the meaning of Jesus' activity by making it richly allusive (as in midrash), freighted with ideas important to his first-century church. In other words, Jesus is not allegorically moving to Rome as he would later as the risen Christ so that all succeeding episodes can be read as happening in Rome in any strict allegorical sense. But there is no doubt that Mark invites the reader to see, once again, the doubly-exposed photograph.

In addition, Jesus, when crossing the sea of Galilee, has, as in the feedings, an apparent connection to the appearances tradition, and here it is all right, I believe, for the modern believer to see the activity of the risen Christ, just as one may see the Eucharist activity in the feedings:

> Immediately he made his disciples get into the boat and go on ahead to the other side, to Bethsaida, while he dismissed the crowd. After saying farewell to them, he went up on the mountain to pray. When evening came, the boat was out on the sea, and he was alone on the land. When he saw that they were straining at the oars against an adverse wind, he came towards them early in the morning, walking on the sea. He intended to pass them by. But when they saw him walking on the sea, they thought it was a ghost and cried out; for they all saw him and were terrified. But immediately he spoke to them and said, "Take heart, it is I; do not be afraid." Then he got into the boat with them and the wind

ceased. And they were utterly astounded, for they did not understand about the loaves, but their hearts were hardened (6:45-53).

Mark has placed two large and symbolic scenes from Jesus' life alongside one another—the feeding of five thousand and the walking-on-water scene. By this he intends to intensify his symbolism in this envelope. One of the first things we notice is the reemergence of the *kurios* figure, the Christ. In both the first feeding and in the walking across the sea, Jesus dramatically foreshadows the Christ who will rise from the dead and cross the Mediterranean Sea. Augustine Stock incisively interprets Jesus' previous miraculous activity. Referring to the miracles in 4:35 - 5:43 ("The Twelve"), he observes how Jesus' miracles "continue the preparation of the disciples for their missionary apostolate. Jesus shows them that their mission is rooted in his power over the elements, over demons, and over death. And by an initial and symbolic action, the mission is also spread into pagan territory beyond the frontiers of Israel." Stock reminds us as well that the calming of the stormy sea is a sign, in Hebrew Scripture, of the power of God (Job 7:12; Pss 74:13; 89:8-9; 95:3-4; Isa 52:9-10). In Ps 107:23-32, the storm is also the setting from which God, because of his love and care, saves humankind.[116] When we see how the symbols of sea, demons, and death are interrelated, we cannot miss the symbolic unity provided by these miracles: exorcisms are calmings of chaos, a brave walking across its waters. Walking across waters and calming them are really exorcisms of the convulsive evil which possesses this age. Healing the sick is essentially the same process, it seems, as is exorcism and nature miracle, for Jesus confronts the demonic world in all three activities.

As Kelber has noticed, Mark is depicting a power struggle between two kingdoms. He understands that the basic purpose of exorcism is to wage battle on behalf of the kingdom.[117] Stock has noticed, too, that in demons, the raging sea, and the wilderness, one can see the chaos which can only be controlled by God or by his Son.[118] The approach, according to Stock, of Jesus and his disciples toward the sea is a movement into a symbolic region which reveals its essence in storms, as is twice reported by Mark (4:27-28; 6:47). This movement toward the sea, like the travels into the wilderness, involves an entrance into a dominion of forces hostile to God. Jesus, Stock believes, while confronting these forces simultaneously renews the determination to do God's will.[119] The symbolism of Jesus in conflict with the powers is seen also by Williams who writes that in the first half of this gospel, God's presence among humans is dramatized using the symbol of the sea. Mark associates the Sea of Galilee, Williams says, with the mission of Jesus and his disciples, and with faith and power. Jesus calming the sea becomes an expression of divine power. For example, when Jesus walks by the sea, he calls four to become fishers of people, to forsake their own boat to enter a boat of faith that can cross between their land and the other side. The first teachings of Jesus took place near the sea, as was the call of the tax collector, Levi. After the conflicts with opponents, Jesus and his disciples withdraw to the sea (3:7), where God's numinous presence and power will be revealed in Jesus.[120] In such passages, the sea configures metaphorically the mission of Jesus, who becomes the powerful voice of God, which "makes a way in the sea, a path in the mighty waters" (Isa 43:16). Williams's interpretation is very helpful to our interpretation, for he rightly sees the symbolic power of Mark's topography:

> Jesus as Son of Man and Son of God is the focal point of the Presence that moves between life and death, that leads into insecure waters and foreign territory—but the waters and the foreign land are simultaneously presented as the context of assurance and healing, if only the disciples could perceive it. The Greek *to peran*, "the other side," is derived from *peras*, "end, limit, conclusion." In the first half of the gospel Jesus is the one who comes from and goes to the "end," "the other side." He is sent by the Other, he is the manifestation of the divine reality, that which is not of the ordinary world and in which the ordinary world has its being. It is the reality disclosed away from ... the reality disclosed in the depths and extremes of the human condition. "The other side" is therefore a signal of meaning complementary to "beside the sea" and "a lonely place" ... In terms of narrative images, the crossing of the sea into foreign territory is a kind of prefiguration of the crucifixion and resurrection. As Jesus crosses the deep and troubled waters into foreign territory and returns then to Galilee, so also he endures suffering and death on the cross to rise and return to Galilee.

Williams makes the interesting observation that the boat symbol is the gospel text itself, the vessel that can carry the disciples to the other side. Furthermore, the boat symbol is missing from the second half of the gospel. Once ashore in Jerusalem, they are no longer sailing with Jesus but become competitive with one another; they are, temporarily at least, no longer buoyed up by the teachings and spirit of the gospel text.[121]

There is even more to the lake symbol, for these crossings also develop the theme of the way of Jesus, the *hodos* (see 4:35; 5:2, 21; 6:45; 8:13; cf. 6:53). This theme of the way will find its fullest development in the next envelope, "The Healing of the Blind" (8:22 - 10:52), but it is interesting to see how the theme has already begun its development in the sea symbol. Just as the way on the land provides a test for the disciples, so the way at sea challenges them and helps to define the demands of discipleship. The disciples are "unable to comprehend and believe God's governance of chaos, which is disclosed in his chosen one. The boat is an image of those who travel in intimate fellowship with Jesus, separated from other followers and the masses who stand on the security of the shore. In crossing in this boat the disciples encounter the strange outcome that the identity of Jesus is recognized in foreign territory by the one possessed by many demons (5:7)."[122]

It is noteworthy that Mark refers to the feeding of the five-thousand here, and it is clear that the disciples do not understand either event. As Williams says, they do not "understand the connection of these displays of power with the loaves that fed the multitudes (6:52). A hard connection it is to relate overwhelming displays of power and authority to the bread that feeds the hungry!"[123] For Mark, it is very important that the initiate make the connection between the exorcisms, healings, feedings, and the sea miracles. As we are discovering, only in discerning the unity that unites these symbols can we find Mark's answer to the riddle of the Christ. The reference to hardness of heart also emphasizes the unity of this gospel, for at once we recall the parables which delineate the right responses to Jesus and his message. It seems that the disciples and Jesus are more alienated from one another than ever before during this scene, or at least that is my interpretation of "he meant to pass by them" (6:48). But they call out to him, even if in confusion and fear, and as he always has and always will, he responds to their cries for help.

There is an interesting insertion by Mark at this point of a summary-scene of the kind we encountered in the description of John's ministry and in the healing-many doublet:

> When they had crossed over, they came to land at Gennesaret and moored the boat. When they got out of the boat, people at once recognized him, and rushed about the whole region and began to bring the sick on mats to wherever they heard he was. And wherever he went, into villages, cities, or farms, they laid the sick in the marketplaces, and begged him that they might touch even the fringe of his cloak; and all who touched it were healed (6:53–56).

This brief summary is little more than a transition to this envelope's central sayings section, which includes the controversy with the elders. Structurally, Mark indicates by this that we have returned to the Jewish side, and now we can expect more controversy between Jesus and the conservatives. But there is also an affirmation of the Jews' faith in Jesus here, and this should not be overlooked. Mark is sensitive concerning the conflicts within the new religion, but he is not anti-Jewish. He underscores their faith with this brief scene; and, as we shall soon see, an incident that will occur in the region of Tyre and Sidon will provide a recursive echo.

In the preceding envelopes, Mark had prepared us for what we now encounter in the sayings section of "The Feedings." Once again, he underscores the theme of teaching by inserting appropriate sayings of Jesus. These insertions occur near the center, though not always exactly at the center. For example, the parables section of "The Twelve" is not centrally placed and is "central" only because of its dominical quality and its function as a hinge of the recursion. Here, near the center of this envelope, the sayings of Jesus are placed in the context of the tradition of the elders, which according to Stock, was "the unwritten tradition of legal interpretations handed down by generations of leading rabbis and regarded by the Pharisees to be as binding as the written Torah."

> It constituted the oral law, the most important part of which was the halakah, which showed how a Jew was to live ... These interpretations, transmitted orally in the rabbinical schools, were fixed in writing during the second century of

our era in the Mishnah and Talmud. By the time of Jesus the prescriptions were already so numerous that the observance of the Torah, written and oral, was a heavy burden. This was especially true for the "people of the land," those living outside Jerusalem. In Jerusalem the necessary cleansings after violations were ready at hand and there were legal experts who were able to indicate how and when the laws applied and when they did not.[124]

Mark chooses this point (7:1-23) near the center of his recursion, to focus on those traditions which he feels actually blind people in regard to their spiritual lives and their true religious duties. These controversies are fused in several ways with the material in "The Feedings" envelope. Most obvious of all is that two of three parts of this section are related to food. The washing-before-meals section (7:1-8) concludes with a generalization concerning religious attitudes:

> He said to them, "Isaiah prophesied rightly about you hypocrites, as it is written,
> > 'This people honors me with their lips,
> > but their hearts are far from me;
> > in vain do they worship me,
> > teaching human precepts as doctrines.'
> You abandon the commandment of God and hold to human tradition" (7:6-8).

The corban section which follows serves to provide an example of this general point. "You have a fine way of rejecting the commandment of God in order to keep your tradition!" (v. 7). Mark then returns to the topic of food with the sayings about defilement (7:14-23). The material is organized climactically with the strongest sayings and the catalog of evil things placed at the end.

Up to this point in each of his envelopes Mark has emphasized guiding metaphors which dominate his presentation. For each section, he establishes a major theme, and under the aegis of that theme, develops fugues and counterpoints which provide for the movement of the plot. He has, in addition, taken much care to assure the catechetical nature of the text, never once forgetting that this is a teaching book which invites the initiate to share the basic Christian experience. This appears to be the bottom line; everything is

# THE FEEDINGS

subordinated to the purpose of presenting for mimesis the way of the Christ. The ethos of the teachings continues to be less important for Mark than the person of Jesus as expressed in symbolic action. In this feedings section, Mark underscores Jesus' conflict with tradition and further reveals the powers of the Christ. These conflicts are strongly related to the theme of identity, as Mark continues to look backward to the Old Testament and forward to the resurrection. The dominant metaphor, which serves to synthesize past and present, is the metaphor of food (which combines several levels of meaning and tradition in the manna/bread/body symbol).

Mark wants to emphasize the universality of the Christian message, and its ever-widening circle of influence, and to demonstrate how faithful response to Jesus is superior to quibbling about the law. In "Healing Many," Jesus shows the new way to be one of adventure, not of stagnation in the old traditions. In "The Twelve," he shows the initiate the true nature of discipleship and teaches about the true family of Jesus. In the parables of seed and light, Jesus teaches the relationship of the heart to kingdom and of the dangers of hardness of heart. And now in the envelope, "The Feedings," the initiate observes Jesus moving even further toward the center stage of the universe, as one who dominates the powers of nature both in his multiplication of food and in his power over chaos itself. The traditions theme is again central, just as in "Healing Many," but the setting has been enlarged by the repetition of powerful symbols.

In this section about defilement and corban, Mark again attacks, through Jesus' words, the traditions of the elders. To use a military metaphor, this is a *Schwerpunkt*, a point against which Mark will direct most of his forces. If Mark truly represents a gospel developed in the context of a church community, we obviously learn much here about that community's conflicts and fears. Traditionalism was seen to be a major enemy of the developing gentile church. But it is the way which Mark uses his reserve forces which determines the quality of his gospel, which is much more than a Jeremiad against tradition. His reserves are invariably the stories about Jesus' healings and exorcisms, at least in this first half of the gospel. After the breakthroughs against tradition, Mark wants to establish the nature of the Christ. Tradition is to be replaced by a new identity. That is why that theme, present since the beginning of the gospel, will, in the next envelope concerning blindness and sight, assert itself as the dominant theme of Mark's story.

There is an apparent narrowing of focus in this controversy section, a narrowing-down to small specific laws. The Sabbath controversies concerned a large issue of obvious importance. By taking on other elements of the traditions, such as washing before meals and withholding money from parents, we meet issues in this section which, though still important, considerably narrow the scope of the argument. A lesser writer might have lost his sense of proportion here, and destroyed this gospel by turning it into a catalog of traditions honored by the Jews and a Jeremiad against those traditions. But Mark keeps his balance, for his very point is that there can be a grotesque warping of religious faith when the believer is hypnotized by traditions. The new faith is to be different in its traditions and in its attitudes toward its new traditions. Mark, in other words, does not allow propaganda to distort the gospel, any more than he allows the tone of diatribe to dominate. Jesus' concern is with the internalization of the law, and his constant emphasis is upon the primacy of the human soul—this concern shines in the concluding comment: "All these evil things come from within, and they defile a person" (7:23).

So far in our analysis, we have paused at each sayings section to consider whether or not it represents the emphatic center of a recursive structure. Proceeding inductively, we decided to allow Mark to tell us what kind of recursive structure he was using, if any. We have also been careful not to proceed merely from deduction in regard to concentric constructions. A careful analysis of "The Feedings" envelope (see the diagram on p. 105) does, in fact, reveal a recursive structure.

Especially interesting here are the "extra" verses on either side of the envelope. Just before the first feeding, Mark reports the death of John the Baptist (6:14-29). At the end of the section, the Pharisees ask for a sign, and then a strange discussion between Jesus and his uncomprehending disciples ensues concerning the two feedings (8:11-21). By establishing the symbol of John the Baptist in the first half of the outer frame, Mark establishes a parallel with the latter half of the frame when Jesus confronts the Pharisees. John the Baptist, for instance, loses his life to those offended by his message, and Jesus, in his confrontation concerning a sign, also stands before hostile detractors. In other words, both John and Jesus offend the religious and social establishments, and the resulting similar conflicts are what Mark is recalling in this outer frame occurring on either side of the doublets.

Moreover, each half of this frame is logically related to context, however abrupt the scenes may appear to one who seeks smooth narrative flow. For example, the story of John's death is reported immediately following the return of the disciples, whom Jesus invites into the wilderness to rest. This sequence recalls a similar sequence at the beginning of the gospel: after John's imprisonment, Jesus' mission begins. Mark has thus thematically established a relationship between John's decline and Jesus' new beginnings; this connection is not only foreshadowed in John's own words but also in the formal composition of the gospel.

The second part of the outer frame is characterized, in addition, by the strange confrontation of Jesus with his disciples over the loaves. This scene has given critics much trouble. Whatever form of this story he inherited, the issue here for Mark is obviously a symbolic one. Only on a symbolic level is there a road between the second feeding, the Pharisees' request for a sign, and the discussion with the disciples. The original road of continuity was washed out, for the modern reader, by the numerological significance of the numbers twelve and seven, but a thematic continuity remains in the themes of hardness of heart and of identity.

Because of their hardness of heart, the Pharisees cannot comprehend the significance of the feeding of the four thousand (8:1-10). Now this feeding, as we have noted, encompasses not only the manna of the Old Testament but also the Eucharist of the New. Symbolically, the Pharisees represent those people who cannot understand the essential identity of the Christ. They want a sign. For Mark, who is anxious to use the historical life of Jesus to represent christological qualities of the Lord's person, the request for a sign amounts to a rejection of Jesus' essential person and of his mission. The demand for a sign, therefore, provides a negative mirror to the misunderstanding of John by Herod in the other half of this outer frame. Like Peter on the mount of transfiguration, the Pharisees want to touch the kingdom now. Just touch it for a little while in this sphere of the five senses. Peter wants to build tents for Jesus, Moses, and Elijah. The Pharisees want a sign from heaven. In other words, they want empirical verification of spiritual truth. Dominated by such an attitude, they stand from the beginning to the end of the story as opponents of Jesus.

This hardness of heart causes these Pharisees who search for a sign, to be just as blind as those elders with whom Jesus argues at the center of the recursion. Stereotypical notions prevent them from seeing and responding to the Christ. For Mark, the kingdom is now, but not yet. For the initiate, surely this point is beginning to be grasped. The giving of the bread and fish is the giving of God's grace-filled manna intervention; for the Christ who gives the food of himself to his people is the Son of God. The man who heals storms of madness and storms upon the sea, the man who demonstrates his power over all nature—this same man represents in his person the graceful intervention of God into the helpless plight of humankind. Mark, in his nature miracles, does not establish the power of Jesus in the triumphalist sense of earthly Messiah; rather, he establishes the power of Jesus to demonstrate the efficacy of God's intervention. It is in the two feedings that the strands of previous nature miracles join to help delineate the face of Jesus, to add the necessary christological threads to his developing portrait.

Mark's recursion is here primarily topical, and the basic meaning of the text does not derive as extensively as in the two preceding envelopes from any specific comparison between terms. Still, some striking comparisons reveal themselves. Consider the healing of the woman's daughter:

> From there he set out and went away to the region of Tyre. He entered a house and did not want anyone to know he was there. Yet he could not escape notice, but a woman whose little daughter had an unclean spirit immediately heard about him, and she came and bowed down at his feet. Now the woman was a Gentile, of Syro-phoenician origin. She begged him to cast the demon out of her daughter. He said to her, "Let the children be fed first, for it is not fair to take the children's food and throw it to the dogs." But she answered him, "Sir, even the dogs under the table eat the children's crumbs." Then he said to her, "For saying that, you may go—the demon has left your daughter." So she went home, found the child lying in bed, and the demon gone (7:24–30).

The parallels of this C´ scene with C, the Gennesaret healings, consist in 1) the recognition of Jesus, 2) the approach made toward him, and 3) the demonstration of his power. These elements are repeated immediately after the sayings section; their relationship is contrapuntal, and their contrast makes a theological point. This is what we find in all Mark's recursive constructions. The sayings section, furthermore, has prepared this turn in the opposite direction toward Gentiles by Jesus' attack against Jewish traditions, buttressed by the quotation from Isaiah. Here too, interestingly enough, the bread theme from feeding five thousand appears in a bread metaphor related to the feeding of children and dogs. In his first response to the suppliant, Jesus himself is made to speak just like one of the elders with whom he has been arguing! In a novel or romance, Jesus' comment, in light of the Marcan background, would be out of character. Evidently, the first-century Gentile converts to Christianity were not so much offended at the metaphor of feeding dogs as they were impressed by the crumbs under the table. Jesus was speaking, after all, as a devout first-century Jew might speak. But this provides the needed background to establish the theological contrast, expressed in Jesus' assertion that faith is the avenue of salvation which has been opened to the Gentiles. Again and again, in the nature miracles and healing miracles, we see this emphasis upon faith, both in Jewish and in gentile territory.

The second half of this recursion continues its emphasis upon gentile salvation in the region of the Decapolis. We have already briefly discussed the story of the deaf and dumb man in regard to its place in the recursion. While this story also, implicitly, shows the faith of the Gentiles in Jesus, the primary emphasis here — and the primary counterpoint — is the contrast between the Pharisees and these "outlanders" who approach Jesus in faith, praise him, and cause his fame to spread.

> Then he returned from the region of Tyre, and went by way of Sidon towards the Sea of Galilee, in the region of the Decapolis. They brought to him a deaf man who had an impediment in his speech; and they begged him to lay his hand on him. He took him aside in private, away from the crowd, and put his fingers into his ears, and he spat and touched his tongue. Then looking up to heaven, he sighed, and said to him, "Ephphatha," that is, "Be opened." And immediately his ears were opened, his tongue was released, and he spoke plainly. Then Jesus ordered them to tell no one; but the more he ordered them, the more zealously they proclaimed it. They were astounded beyond measure,

saying, "He has done everything well; he even makes the deaf to hear and the mute to speak" (7:31-37).

Mark's recursion invites a backward look to see how walking on water (B) is related specifically to this healing the deaf and dumb man (B´). Only two general similarities appear: 1) under the large topical heading of miracle and 2) within the continuing themes of faith and good response. Mark establishes a thematic contrast by closing (B) with a comment on hardness of heart and (B´) with the comment that the people respond zealously to Jesus.

Jesus looks up to the heavens shortly before he says "Be opened," with specific regard to the man's hearing. This is quite probably intentional on Mark's part. Having Jesus glance upward while he speaks to the afflicted man creates an association between the opening of the heavens at the outset of the gospel and the reception of Jesus' message to the Gentiles portrayed in this pericope. The first opening of the heavens, at the baptism of Jesus, was for all people. In the immediate context of John's baptism and of Hebrew Scriptures, however, the radical nature of that metaphysical and theological breach could not be fully presented. Mark's method has been to widen gradually the scope of Jesus' ministry and at the same time to widen the scope of Markan theology. A central theological concept which is emerging from Mark's special retelling of the gospel drama is that in the person of Jesus Christ, access to God is provided for all humanity.

Such comparisons as Mark does make between B and B´ are far too general for a small formal chiasmus. In this envelope Mark once again proves himself to be a master of the larger form, the recursion, by working primarily with those larger contrasts between the two arms of the recursion. It is precisely the large themes he wishes to compare and contrast; and in this envelope, he especially wants to juxtapose the two arms of the mission—Jew and Gentile—along the two arms of the recursion. The placement of these two arms on either side of the sayings center shows that he once again wishes to form another recursive envelope within the doublets.

Because the feeding of the four thousand occurs immediately after the healing of the deaf man in the Decapolis (7:31),[125] the feeding of the four thousand appears to be a gentile miracle. Nineham writes that it has been "suggested at least as early as the fourth century that St. Mark may have intended the feeding of the five thousand to symbolize the giving of the Bread of Life to the Jews, and the feeding of the four thousand the giving of the Bread of Life to the Gentiles." He quotes A. Richardson as follows:

> The scene of the Feeding of the Five Thousand suggests a Galilean (i.e., Jewish) crowd; that of the Feeding of the Four Thousand suggests a crowd drawn from the neighbourhood of the Decapolis ... on the south-eastern side of the Sea of Galilee, i.e., a Gentile crowd. The Five Thousand receive the five loaves (possibly a reminiscence of the Five Books of the Law); the Four Thousand receive seven loaves (... the Septuagint, the Seven Deacons of Acts 6:3 ...). At the former miracle twelve baskets are taken up, representing the Twelve Tribes of Israel ... at the latter, seven baskets remain.[126]

Nineham comments that given the "ancients" love of allusiveness and symbolism, there is probably something in this theory.

With the second half of a doublet, Mark ends this third envelope. Because of the eucharistic overtones of his symbolism, the evangelist has moved us closer to Jesus' person. In giving the bread, in feeding the multitudes of Jews and Gentiles, Jesus has given of himself. Person is more important to Mark than verbal teachings, especially as Jesus moves closer to the ultimate personal sacrifice.

## Principles of Organization

1. **Theme**: Manna and Eucharist, and mission to the Gentiles are the basic themes and organizing principles.

2. **Negation of A**: In summarizing this chapter, we can enumerate the same essential principles which Mark has applied to his organization of the other envelopes. The structure of this section, however, is complicated by the existence of an outer frame which encloses the doublets themselves: John the Baptist's death at the beginning (6:14-29), and Jesus' conflicts with the Pharisees and Herod and his warnings against them, at the end (8:11 - 8:21). This outer frame does not consist of doublets, but is topically related by references to Herod and thematically unified by parallel notices of Jesus' conflicts with authority. The usual beginning is also disrupted by the fact that the scene following the feedings—walking on water— is not a negation of the feedings; rather, it is actually an assertion by

miracle. The usual A/B, affirmation/negation, is therefore not present in this envelope. We shall summarize, in #10 below, how negation has operated in this section.

3. **Christological Assertions against Negation**: See #10.

3a. **Assertion by Miracle**: Feeding the multitudes is not only a miracle which is presented to affirm Christ's power; it is rich in theological implications from Hebrew Scriptures and from the Eucharist. The doublet in this section, then, is created by the doubling of a feeding miracle. Furthermore, the first feeding miracle is followed immediately by another miracle: walking on water. We discovered that this miracle asserts that Jesus' power continues to operate and also acclaims the universality of the Christ who moves to "the other side," the side of the sea where the Gentiles live.

3b. **Assertion by Healing**: The healings in this envelope continue to acclaim the power of Christ. The healing of the woman in the area of Tyre and Sidon as well as the healing of the afflicted man establish a recursive contrast with the material presented before the sayings section. Activity in Jewish territory is followed by sayings which present Jesus' conflict with tradition; and following the sayings section, Jesus moves into gentile territory. Once again, theology travels with geography.

3c. **Assertion by Saying**: Jesus' dispensation of manna and Eucharist bring him into conflict with authorities; therefore, the central sayings of this envelope are constituted by Jesus' answers to their specific objections. Because of their specificity they seem less universal and powerful statements regarding Jesus' mission and person than the sayings of the first two envelopes.

The parables section of the second envelope could be termed Mark's Sermon on the Mount. These parables define the basic response which should be made to Jesus and demonstrate the interrelationship of kingdom with those who are waiting for its appearance. The sayings in "The Feedings," bound by the theme of defilement from within, rather than from without, seem rather disappointing in contrast. But the theme of defilement gives some force to the sayings, since Jesus implies much here about the nature of the approaching kingdom and who will be accepted into it and who will not be prepared.

Here Mark makes a basic point: this kingdom will immediately know its own (as in the Sermon on the Mount in Matthew and the Sermon on the Plain in Luke). What is uttered in secret will be shouted from rooftops; what has been interior and subjective will be known. The kingdom will thus be a great reversal; it will bring to light those things which are now in darkness.

Since the sayings section occurs at the recursive turning point between Jew and Gentile, Mark sharpens the emphasis by referring to specific conflict between Jesus and the elders, the representatives of Jewish tradition. Jesus does not turn away from tradition for trivial reasons, but the entire emphasis of his message is different from theirs, a point Mark has affirmed ever since the wine and garment parables. Thus, specific arguments about ritual purity are stress lines that point to deeper fractures, just as the Sabbath controversies highlighted great differences in theology and attitude. Jesus' next healings will be in gentile areas, as indicated by the location of the second half of the doublet (the feeding of the four thousand).

3d. **Symbolic Narrative**: As seen in the body of the chapter and as already emphasized in this summary, Jesus' activities are more formally symbolic here than in any of the other envelopes. Now the doubly-exposed photograph clearly reveals the image of the risen Christ behind and above the earthly Jesus.

3e. **Titles**: No explicit titles are given to Jesus in this envelope. However, the walking on water scene reveals the transcendent Jesus. Significantly, this transcendence is the very quality which enables him to reach across the sea and into the regions of the Gentiles.

4. **Reassertion of Negatives against the Basic Envelope's Theme**: See the discussion in #10 below.

5. **Recursive Comparisons and Contrasts, Before and After the Sayings**: Discussed in #10

6. **Relationship of Sayings to Context of Action**: See 3c. above.

7. **Relationship of Thematic Frame to Enclosed Material**: We already noted (see pp. 109-110) that Mark's feeding frame displays transcendent action by Jesus and that Jesus' transcendence displayed during these feedings involves the identical transcendent power which enables him to cross the sea to the Gentiles or to move into other areas where they live. Here is a good example of how Mark uses the envelope form. The doublets can function to connect apparently disparate materials into thematically related units. The power of theme to organize is similar to the power of a magnet placed under a sheet of paper covered with iron filings. The presence of the magnet causes the scattered filings to jump into the shape given by the magnetic field. In the preceding envelope, we observed

how the symbols of seed, light, kingdom, discipleship, family, Beelzebul, etc. were all interconnected by Mark's theme. The material in this envelope would probably appear somewhat random, lacking any effective organization were it not for the feeding doublet, which reveals the material in its thematic network.

8. **Chronology** is significant in this envelope only in the general context of gospel time that moves from baptism through Capernaum and Nazareth and into Jerusalem. Time is basically present only in the theological contrast of the earliest mission exclusively to the Jews and the later mission predominately to the Gentiles.

9. **Geography** is practically synonymous with ideas in the sense that place is symbolic of theological concepts which occur in dramatic sequences.

10. **Dialectical Growth from the Affirmation/Negation Series**: The theme of the first envelope — newness in conflict with authority — is strongly renewed and developed in "The Feedings." The scope of the theme is considerably extended as Jesus becomes the provider of manna and Eucharist and as he moves toward the Gentiles. The negative series, which develops christology, begins outside the doublet frame, in the John the Baptist story. The arrest and execution of this prophet offers a strong introductory negation, building a dark bridge between the sending of the disciples and "The Feedings" envelope, in which the strong affirmations of Jesus' nature are asserted by the miracles of feeding and walking on water. Then, after the negations by the elders at the sayings center, Jesus heals in the gentile areas, the faith found in those regions forming a strong contrast to the attitude of the elders.

After the feeding of the four thousand in gentile territory, the final half of the outer frame provides the final negation. The Pharisees demand a sign, and Jesus reprimands his disciples for their lack of understanding concerning the significance of the feedings. The envelope itself is therefore contained within a darker wrapping. Ignorance concerning Jesus' identity, even among the disciples, causes a black border to encircle all the actions and teachings of Jesus. God's confrontation with humankind, through Jesus, will bring an offer of salvation. But Mark's negations remind us that this confrontation, in its historical mode, was embroiled in tragedy.

11. **Relationship to Other Envelopes**: On the level of plot, the intensifying conflict with the establishment continues. This envelope reminds us of all the conflicts that have gone before. At the same

time, Jesus is now well on the road toward crucifixion; and the stage is already set for the appearance, in the next envelope, of the Suffering Servant. The Janus symbol of the bread, with its double reference to manna and Eucharist, is a strong link between Galilee and Jerusalem. In the next envelope, Mark highlights the theme of identity, and in so doing brings us closer to the answer to the riddle of the Christ.

# 6
# Healing the Blind

A    **Healing blind man** (8:22-26). **Partial vision**; 2 healing attempts.
    B    **Peter's confession** (8:27-30). Partial affirmation. Theme of **messianic power.**
        C    **First prophecy** (9:31-32a) + **Peter's caution** (32b-33). **Suffering Servant** sayings (8:34-38).
           D    **Transfiguration** (9:1-8) + **disciples' confusion** coming down mountain (9:9-13).
           D´   **Second prophecy** (9:30-32) + **disciples' inability** to heal boy (9:14-29). Imitation of the **Suffering Servant**—sayings (33-35). Child sayings (36-37) + Discourse on sin, divorce, etc. (9:38 - 10:16).
        C´   **Rich man's caution** (10:17-27). Parallels with Peter's caution at C. + **Suffering Servant** sayings—Sacrifices for the kingdom (10:28-31). **Third prophecy** (10:32-34).
    B´   **Request of James and John** (10:35-45). Ironic comparison with Peter's confession at B. Theme of **messianic power** contrasted with humility of **servant.**
A´   **Healing blind man** (10:46-52). **Partial vision** of son of David.

With "Healing the Blind," we come to the last portion of Mark (8:22 - 10:52) which can be identified as an envelope. Even though discursive rhythms, as well as other patterns we have analyzed, are present in the Jerusalem section of the gospel, the formal envelope patterns, at least those established by easily identifiable doublets, ends with "Healing the Blind." It is fitting, then, that this envelope is the climax of the first part of the gospel, bringing the identity theme to it farthest point before the highest points of crucifixion and resurrection—the central events necessary to answer fully the riddle of the Christ. But presented abruptly without introduction, these central events might confuse the initiate. Thus, this introduction, consisting of a prologue and four envelopes, is necessary background without which it would be virtually impossible to understand the sacrifice of Jesus and his renunciation of earthly glory. Against the background of Greek myth only, Jesus would either be understood in a triumphalist way, at best as a Promethean[127] figure or—most probably—rejected as a shameful failure. Mark's introduction is concerned with the paradox of Jesus' identity; and in this envelope, he brings forward, in its full force, the theme of the Suffering Servant. It is this theme which merges with the identity theme to present the new Christian with the portrait of the Christ who entered Jerusalem. The blank canvas introduced by John the Baptist in the beginning is not yet complete, for only the cross and the resurrection can complete the portrait.

The Suffering Servant is a bridge theme binding the first half of the gospel with the second half and preparing the initiate for commitment to Christ and to imitation of his example. The identity theme, which has so often been expressed by exclamations of demons and choruses of awed bystanders or by hostile observers, now is released through the powerful polarities of the blindness/sight symbol. The two blind men who approach Jesus reflect within themselves all the "blind" incomprehension of the disciples and of Mark's readers and listeners. Troubling questions have been constantly generated by Jesus' words and behavior. Through the dramatic mediation of the blind men and of the disciples, the initiate is pulled onstage, as it were, and shares the agony of the questions posed by Jesus. Mark knows what he is doing; a dry, objective documentary about the journey into Jerusalem would lose this sharp and intense focus.

The conflicts preceding this first scene depicting a blind man indicate how difficult it is to understand Christ; some miracle of grace is necessary if anyone is to receive sight. Understanding is not enhanced by intellect or special revelation. We learn in chapter four that the parables of Jesus do not reveal secret doctrine. The mystery of the kingdom involves faith and willingness to accept this word and to grow. We can trivialize Mark and the Christian gospel itself, if we do not fully grasp that the ability to understand the identity of Christ is given by the grace of God. All that one can do is to approach the Christ with an attitude of faithful expectancy—as so many do in the first half of this gospel. To receive the bread can bring a sense of fulfillment, so that all are satisfied, but that fulfillment is a gift from God. The blind seekers can fall on their knees and open their hearts, but the miracle of sight and understanding is a gift from God. Certain conditions of behavior and especially of attitude may be required before this gift is offered, but in no way whatsoever can this gift be earned, as we shall see in the story about the rich man. Human beings must be helped by God's grace shining through the person, teachings and examples of Christ. Perhaps Paul says this better than any New Testament writer:

> For it is the God who said, "Let light shine out of darkness," who has shone in our hearts to give the light of the knowledge of the glory of God in the face of Christ (2 Cor 4:6).[128]

The good news is not the oral or written word alone; it is not some objective set of symbols existing independently of human beings. The good news requires a receiver of the news in order to define itself. The gospel, whatever other forms it may take or however people are pleased to define it, is fully experienced only when it becomes a life-changing event within the human heart. Borrowing Heidegger's creative syntax in his description of the human as a "being-toward-death," we could say that gospel is news-toward-changing-lives. No definition of Christianity is complete without the inclusion of grace. This grace precedes or accompanies the good news and functions as its catalyst. In Mark's theology, the openness of faith is necessary for the reception of grace. Here in this story, these two blind men, who stumble into the path of the Christ, are open to the miracle of sight and are healed. And now at this point, a more complete christology is possible, for faith in Christ is the catalyst not only for those diseased or possessed, but for all the blind who recognize their blindness and who approach him with humility.

While the historical Jesus may have healed the blind, for the early church blindness was a transcendent symbol of the state of unenlightened humankind. Thus, for Mark, the blind man—as well as the paralytics, the leper, and the demented—is Everyman. These characters are not presented in a neat, allegorical way, such as those in *Pilgrim's Progress*, which presents a parallel plot in which a character, action, or idea always represents some corresponding allegorical action or idea. Those healed by Jesus, in contrast, are presented as concrete examples with which the seeker must identify if he or she is to receive the miracle of grace. These blind men seek the seed from the parable of the sower, the light which must shine before humankind, the grain which must grow (miraculously, we know not how). As believers begin to glimpse the true identity of Jesus Christ and to anticipate the grace of God both in their attitudes and in his response, they move near the heart of the Christian mystery.

We must emphasize that one is not healed by knowledge itself. Intellectual knowledge, taken alone, can not achieve grace. Such a belief would indeed be gnostic. Intellectual knowledge of the divine nature of Christ was given even to demons! Conversion requires a new heart, not merely some new idea. The two, of course, should work together; knowledge can and should feed faith.

Mark, from beginning to end of his gospel, clearly intends for the believer to identify with and thus interiorize Christ's own heart and attitudes. He implies that if one would be a disciple of Christ and follow him, one must understand the Suffering Servant. One may be healed without this full knowledge of Jesus' identity, but one cannot fully understand Jesus or effectively follow him without this knowledge. The paralytic, the man with the withered hand, and the Syro-phoenecian woman, for example, are not required to know intellectually the identity of Jesus; their faithful response to God's offer make possible their healing. Faith is a helper of grace. The same is true of the two blind men; they are not required intellectually to know Jesus. Their stories could have been placed in any one of the earlier envelopes, but they are particularly suited to this envelope because of their blindness and its thematic relation to understanding Christ. What has changed in this section is that healing begins to symbolize more than it did in the earlier examples. At this point, Mark is particularly urgent to explore the meaning of the cross, so that he presents Jesus now as the Suffering Servant.

A faithful and humble approach to Christ enables healing. Discipleship requires, however, that one understand that he who heals is also the one who died for humankind. Discipleship requires heart knowledge, just as healing requires heart knowledge. The heart knowledge required for the disciple is the understanding that the power of the one who heals derives from the power of the cross. This is the theological view of Mark which informs his story.

This section is concerned with the healing of the understanding, so that when Jesus heals someone within the context of this envelope, the healing must be understood differently than if it were placed within some other envelope. Mark is attempting here a wedding of form and content, in that the theme of each envelope helps the reader to understand the contents of the envelope, and vice versa. In other words, by virtue of their own unique themes, these envelopes define the pericopes they contain. For example, placing the story of the first blind man in "Healing Many" would substantially change its meaning. His exclamation, "I see people . . . like trees walking" (8:24), would then be only a strange saying because Mark has not yet developed his identity theme. In the context of this envelope, however, his statement is thematically related to that identity theme with all its theological implications. In such a way, then, the hermeneutic circle of interpretation is established by "Healing the Blind."

There is yet another element of Mark's art which enhances his gospel, and that is his understated style. This mystery of Christ's identity is not served by sentimentalism. The two kinds of sentimentalism which Mark avoids are 1) facile avoidance of suffering and 2) a gushing overemphasis upon suffering. In regard to the first, we have seen how Mark insists upon keeping ever before the initiate the harsh realities of the prototypical Christian life. In regard to the second, Mark has nothing to do with emotional overstatement, whether of gushing sentiment or of masochistic, pointless suffering. He avoids both kinds of sentiment by understatement. Later, in his powerful portrayal of the suffering and death of Jesus, he will say simply, "They crucified him" (15:24), and ". . . [he] breathed his last" (15:37). While the mockers jeer from the background, we hear only the simple assertion of the gentile centurion, "Truly this man was God's Son!" (v. 39). Thus, even though he obviously wants the reader to identify intensely with the disciples and with Jesus himself, Mark never indulges in sentiment in order to force the identification. If Mark has his way, the reader becomes a member of the audience who moves up on the stage of an understated drama. The emotions will be there, certainly; but they will be the inner emotions stirred by the gospel as the participants struggle to understand in mind and in heart the significance of the story they watch and relive. Through the lens of Mark's powerful understatement, then, the reader will struggle with Jesus' three prophecies of death and will attempt to learn from the blind who move out from the crowds to fall at Jesus' feet. Even the transfiguration will be only a brief scene, with only a few powerful references to the transformed appearance of Jesus.

Mark's avoidance of sentiment is helped by the fact that the Christian story he tells is not intrinsically a sentimental one. Jesus' life was difficult and his sacrifice painfully real; and likewise the initiate will be called to sacrifice. Thus, according to Mark, illumination in Christianity is always accompanied by a cross. The mystery will present itself as an offered illumination to the humble seeker, but the seeker, at that point, must walk along the way of Christ. This is the polarity of Christian experience as it is presented by Mark.

Mark's stage for the presentation of this final envelope is enclosed by the doublet of the blind men who come forward on separate occasions to be healed by the Christ.

> They came to Bethsaida. Some people brought a blind man to him and begged him to touch him. He took the blind man by the hand and led him out of the village; and when he had put saliva on his eyes and laid his hands upon him, he asked him, "Can you see anything?" And the man looked up and said, "I can see people, but they look like trees, walking." Then Jesus laid his hands upon his eyes again; and he looked intently and his sight was restored, and he saw everything clearly. Then he sent him away to his home, saying, "Do not even go into the village" (8:22-26).

> They came to Jericho. As he and his disciples and a large crowd were leaving Jericho, Bartimaeus son of Timaeus, a blind beggar, was sitting by the roadside. When he heard that it was Jesus of Nazareth, he began to shout out and say, Jesus, Son of David, have mercy on me!" Many sternly ordered him to be quiet, but he cried out even more loudly, "Son of David, have mercy on me!" Jesus stood still and said, "Call him here." And they called the blind man, saying to him, "Take heart; get up, he is calling you." So throwing off his cloak, he sprang up and came to Jesus. Then Jesus said to him, "What do you want me to do for you?" The blind man said to him, "My teacher, let me see again." Jesus said to him, "Go, your faith has made you well." Immediately he regained his sight and followed him on his way (10:46-52).

Stock, quoting Van Iersel, points out the doublet frame here: "The way, the center section of Van Iersel's five-part structure ... is framed by two cures of blind men—that at Bethsaida and that of Bartimaeus."[129] In the first blindness episode (8:22-26), Mark graphically describes Jesus' healing techniques (v. 23). This first story contains an unusual phrase which provides the best statement in Mark of the theme of recognition. The partially healed man describes what he sees: "I can see people; but they look like trees, walking." Mark also tells us something else in this first half of the doublet; it requires multiple healings to cure this man. How similar this is to the multiple healings which must be attempted upon the understanding of Peter, James and John in this section as they attempt to comprehend the identity of the Christ. The second episode (10:46-52) differs from the first in that the blind man is given a name—Bartimaeus—and it is a faith story in the sense that Jesus once again announces that the faith of the afflicted has effected the cure (v. 52). This second scene, as well, shows many rebuking the blind man, "telling him to be silent" (v. 46). Further distinguishing this scene is the fact that Bartimaeus refers to Jesus as "Son of David" (v. 47).

In this envelope, physical blindness becomes a symbol for the spiritual blindness of the disciples and others (like the rich man) who try to identify Jesus and to understand his message. "I see people; but they look like trees, walking," is a sentence which could stand as an epigraph for Mark's gospel. The unfolding identity of Jesus is the dynamic energy driving Mark's story as the evangelist tries to clarify the image of Jesus for the reader. From the baptism, through the awed responses of the chorus, through the hostile reactions of enemies, through the miraculous acts, the initiate is given a drama which, step-by-step, defines the essential nature of the risen Christ. The life of the earthly Jesus is the material used to draw this portrait, and in this blindness/sight envelope, that portrait will literally be transfigured.

This first blindness episode is a bookend made of reflecting crystal, anticipating the underlying theme of the envelope and reflecting its plot. For example, in the first pericope following the healing of the blind man at Bethsaida, Peter (both in his confessions and in his later caution) is remarkably like the blind man. And as a result of his incomplete vision, Peter, too, will need multiple healings. It is significant that Mark again confronts the Elijah theme at this critical point in the search for Jesus' identity. Elijah was important as a harbinger who metaphorically reappeared in the person of John the Baptist; and Jesus himself, as Mark has been careful to dramatize, shares several similarities with Elijah. He has the same affinity with the wilderness, has raised a child from the dead as Elijah did, and is himself a sign of the end time.

But Jesus is not John—not Elijah. The process of affirmation and negation continues.

> "Who do people say that I am?"
> And they answered him, "John the Baptist;
> and others, Elijah;
> and still others, One of the prophets."
> He asked them, "But who do you say that I am?"
> Peter answered him, "You are the Messiah" (8:27-30).

Peter's affirmation, "You are the Messiah," is not incorrect; it is incomplete. This confession belongs back with John the Baptist's affirmation. Much has happened in the gospel since that time and thus Peter's confession is anachronistic and immediately falls short, so that Jesus must correct Peter by introducing the theme of the Suffering Servant, for this is essentially what the three prophecies of Jesus' death are all about. Once again, what is earlier stated is not repudiated or even denied; it is merely declared as insufficient. Stock reaches the same conclusion: "Peter's confession is correct but insufficient to the extent that it does not mesh with the total understanding of Jesus that Mark projects in his story."[130]

With the first prophecy of Jesus' death, the tone of the whole gospel darkens: "Then he began to teach them that the Son of Man must undergo great suffering, and be rejected by the elders, the chief priests, and the scribes, and be killed, and after three days rise again" (8:31-33). Mark's dramatic economy combines prophecy with healing, for Jesus is making a first attempt here to heal Peter's "eyes." The healing will be incomplete; and two more applications, or prophecies, must be "applied."

Peter resists Jesus' first application of the healing lesson by taking Jesus aside and rebuking him (8:32). Most surprising is the severity of Jesus' rebuke of Peter: "Get behind me, Satan! For you are setting your mind not on divine things but on human things" (33). In the Greek, the passage implies wrongness of attitude; for *phroneo*, translated as "setting your mind on," connotes a way of conceiving or thinking of something.[131] In effect, Jesus seems to be saying, "You are not thinking the thoughts of God, but looking at life and at my mission from a human point of view."

In the first two envelopes, the second (B) negated the first A pericope. One might argue that C negates A in this envelope; for the progression of scenes could be interpreted as:

    A   Healing the blind man
    B   Peter's confession
    C   Peter's caution

C and B are so closely related, however, they are virtually the same scene. At any rate, near the beginning of this envelope, Mark once again uses negation to fuel the plot and bring themes into dramatic juxtaposition. He chooses, at this place of Peter's stumbling into a dramatic confrontation, to introduce Jesus' central teachings.

We have already identified the teaching function provided by negation. Many of the most dramatic negations in Mark—Jesus' decision to move beyond Capernaum, his own acted-out rebellion in eating with sinners, his constant negations of triumphalisms established by miracle—take the form of conversations with spiritual pride. Mark has chosen this method of telling Jesus' story, not just as story, but as itself containing examples designed to combat the dangerous pride which can fill Christians when they first sense Christ's power. Perhaps he is not as severe as Bunyan, who placed a road to hell near the gate of heaven. But that image captures Mark's basic idea. Peter wants to avoid Jerusalem for the same reasons he wanted to remain in Capernaum and for the same reasons he wanted to build the three dwellings on the mount of transfiguration. Few things are more thoroughly destructive than spiritual pride.

Now, for the first time, in dramatic negation of the disciple's attitudes, we hear of the cost of discipleship. If Jesus spoke this way to the four or to the twelve when he called them, we were not told about it. Something decisive is happening. The third-person prophecy of death, which Jesus has just spoken, now becomes a dark, first-person command. The way Mark tells the story of Jesus, Jesus' actions, and now his words, call for mimesis, for imitation by the disciples and by all Christians.

> If any want to become my followers, let them deny themselves and take up their cross and follow me. For those

> who want to save their life will lose it, and those who lose
> their life for my sake, and for the sake of the gospel, will
> save it. For what will it profit them to gain the whole world
> and forfeit their life? Indeed, what can they give in return
> for their life? Those who are ashamed of me and of my
> words in this adulterous and sinful generation, of them the
> Son of Man will also be ashamed when he comes in the
> glory of his Father with the holy angels (8:34-38).

The Suffering Servant demands are now extended to the followers of Jesus—and to the initiate standing rather uncomfortably on the stage of Mark's gospel. This new perception of Jesus is certainly lacking from the outline given by John the Baptist and by the voice at the baptism. Tragic life experiences have become necessary, and will be necessary again and again, to comprehend Jesus and the nature of the Christian experience which he has initiated.

Jesus himself was certainly familiar with Isaiah 53 where we hear of the "man of suffering" who is "acquainted with infirmity" with whose "bruises we are healed" (vv. 3-5). Nineham points out that it was not the Isaiah passage alone that inspired the Suffering Servant theme, but also such passages as 2 Macc 7:37-38, 4 Macc 6:27 and 17:32, and he adds that "in view of the remarkably few references to the Isaiah passage in the Gospels, it is probably better to think of a general background of ideas than of direct influence from that particular passage." Nineham's comments reveal the state of mind of Mark's readers and perhaps give a strong hint concerning Jesus' view of himself:

> Neither here nor elsewhere in Mark is any theory offered as
> to why it should be God's will that the Messiah and his
> disciples should suffer, but in this connexion we need to
> remind ourselves of the eschatological mould in which the
> thought of the early Christians was cast ... For them God's
> reality in heaven entirely conformed to God's holiness, and
> stood in the sharpest contrast to this age or world ruled by
> forces of evil ... One day God would judge this world and
> bring this age to an end, transforming whatever in it was
> capable of being transformed, and transferring it to the
> conditions of his realm. But meanwhile, so long as the world
> lasted, anyone in it who represented God's realm and its

values must look for misunderstanding and persecution from the evil powers and the human beings under their sway.[132]

Cranfield suggests that Jesus may have cast himself in a role which would have been readily recognized: "The common assumption that Jesus was the first to associate suffering with messiahship is questionable ... Evidence for suffering Messiah in Judaism exists ... and its rareness is probably the result of anti-Christian polemic."[133]

Our basic point here is that Mark has chosen the center of his gospel to introduce the Suffering Servant theme and its central teachings. For Mark, these obviously are the central teachings of the new faith. It seems that Mark may have inherited many of them in the form of a list of sayings, and then arranged them into a connected series. Consider how easily they separate:

> If any want to become my followers, let them deny themselves and take up their cross and follow me.
>
> For those who want to save their life will lose it, [and]
>
> Those who lose their life for my sake, and for the sake of the gospel, will save it.
>
> For what will it profit them, to gain the whole world and forfeit their life?
>
> For what can they give in return for their life?
>
> Those who are ashamed of me and of my words in this adulterous and sinful generation, of them the Son of Man will also be ashamed, when he comes in the glory of his Father with the holy angels (8:34-38).[134]

Mark has put these sayings together to emphasize the Suffering Servant theme in Jesus' teachings, and has saved them for inclusion in this climactic section of the gospel, placed between Peter's confession and the transfiguration. For in Mark's view, Jesus' discovery of his own role as Suffering Servant typified the discovery of the role necessary for anyone who wishes to inherit the kingdom. Mark uses the teachings which he has interpreted so far primarily to demonstrate the nature of Jesus' mission and the kind of response necessary from the believer. On several occasions, the theme of the Suffering Servant has been anticipated especially in the healing activity of Jesus; it was implied as well in the bridegroom prophecy and in the parables of seed and light. In contrast, the christology of the miracles has been a triumphant one, emphasizing the power of the Christ.

The first strong symbolic hint of the approach of the Suffering Servant theme, as we previously noted (see p. 110-111), came in the feeding doublet. Now, Mark tells the initiate plainly what the cost of discipleship is. In a sense, then, he has intentionally repressed and delayed the center of Jesus' message until after Peter's confession, indicating that his gospel is a selective, dramatic portrayal of the historical Jesus. Mark's organization also reveals a possible motive: to heighten the Jesus plot which was mimetically to serve as gospel. If Mark knew the Q traditions, he quite radically jettisoned most of them. In doing so, he made a practical religious decision as well as a theological one. He wished to preserve and perhaps improve the oral traditions' presentation of Jesus' life by focusing on his doings as redemptive example (which is, after all, what the gospel essentially is). Thus, he postpones the central teachings, except for the parables, until the actions of Jesus have reached the critical point.

Mark's presentation of basic teachings, then, coincides with the dramatic revelation of Jesus' character. Now, after Peter's confession (8:27), we can detect certain changes in Mark's presentation. Stock agrees with Quesnell's conclusions that after 8:27 (Peter's confession), certain changes "in the presentation of the figure of Christ can be detected. Mark begins to present Christ as a figure of destiny whose fate is entirely marked out for him ... And this destiny becomes the basis of exhortation to the disciples." Had Mark's gospel "stopped at 8:26, Jesus would be a great prophet, teacher, healer, but he would not have been the crucified Messiah ... the most significant difference after 8:27 is the extraordinary extent to which Jesus' universal moral directives have been gathered into this one part of the gospel."[135]

Now, at this highest point of teaching and action, Mark is ready to relate the story of the transfiguration (9:2-13). As Nineham suggests,[136] Mark may have been setting the stage for this scene in Jesus' prophecy (9:1) that "there are some standing here who will not taste death until they see that the kingdom of God has come with power."

> Six days later, Jesus took with him Peter and James and John, and led them up a high mountain apart, by themselves. And he was transfigured before them, and his clothes became dazzling white, such as no one on earth could bleach them. And there appeared to them Elijah with Moses, who were talking with Jesus. Then Peter said to Jesus, "Rabbi, it is good for us to be here; let us make three dwellings, one for you, one for Moses, and one for Elijah." He did not know what to say, for they were terrified. Then a cloud overshadowed them, and from the cloud there came a voice, "This is my Son, the Beloved, listen to him!" Suddenly when they looked around, they saw no one with them any more, but only Jesus (9:2-8).

However else one interprets the transfiguration, Mark conceivably uses it here to portray the kingdom-as-presence which the disciples recognized in Jesus of Nazareth before his resurrection. In this experience, Jesus transcends all time to become the memory of the future. The disciples remember the future resurrection and also the transcendent Christ who will be present with the new church. The transfiguration can be seen as an intentionally misplaced post-resurrection account, an appearance pericope rearranged by Mark. An excellent case can be made for this, especially in the light of the anti-triumphalist concerns which probably guided Mark's editing. If, for instance, in parts of the oral tradition, the gospel ended with the triumphant shining appearance of the risen Christ, Mark is concerned to emphasize the theology of the cross instead, replacing the appearance account in the middle and thus changing the theological emphasis from the power of Jesus after his resurrection to the powerful incarnative presence of the Christ in human life.[137]

Our primary concern in this study, however, is to discover Mark's patterns of composition in order to shed light on his theology. In that context, we can see, against the background of our previous analysis, that Mark is again bringing forward the Elijah and Moses themes with the appearance of those figures on the mountain with Jesus. He presents the Jesus-Moses-Elijah triangle affirmatively, in the symbolism associated with theophany. Here Mark essentially repeats the divine commission given to Ezekiel and Isaiah, for instance; and in so doing he draws on the symbols associated with theophany in the Hebrew Scriptures and in intertestamental writings.

These two types are "negated," in the sense that they are presented as subordinate to Jesus.[138] Elijah is only the harbinger of the Messiah, and Moses only foreshadows Jesus, who is the new Moses on a new mountain with a new covenant. Thus, the newness theme from the "Healing Many" envelope has moved once again to center stage, merging now with the theme of identity.

So, as we have seen with Mark's affirmation/negation process from the beginning of the gospel, what Mark gives with one hand, he takes away with the other. He constantly creates vacuums which he, in turn, will fill again.[139] The affirmation of Jesus' identity occurred first at Jesus' baptism; now, in the transfiguration, it occurs again. Mark once more "lays hands" on the initiate's eyes. One must look steadily and clearly at the gospel story and must see more than "people . . . like trees walking."

Peter's response to the transfiguration provides a key to understanding both its form and its meaning. In regard to form, we see this disciple presented again as a dramatic foil, as the confused disciple with whom the initiate is often able to identify. What Peter does not understand here is that humans cannot fully possess the kingdom here in this life and on this earth. This desire for glory is a basic theme of this blindness/sight envelope. In the ecstasy of divine revelation, Peter assumes that divinity can literally be "housed" upon this earth. "Rabbi," he says, "it is good for us to be here; let us make three dwellings, one for you, one for Moses, and one for Elijah" (v. 5). The concept of "Now, but not yet," is perhaps one of the most difficult concepts for the Christian. The presence of God may be experienced upon this earth, but that experience may not become permanent in the earthly context. Just as the Holy Spirit may present us today with a foretaste of the future experience of kingdom, so what Peter saw on the mount of transfiguration was a memory of the future. The future resurrection is certainly foreshadowed here, but so also is the proleptic consummation of the kingdom. As I understand Augustine, God is, after all, the future moving toward mankind. Whether or not, therefore, the transfiguration was originally an appearance scene, Peter, James, and John remember the future second-coming of Christ. Peter and the other disciples must now learn to live with this knowledge in a finite and dangerous world. Here, then, is a profound statement of the nature of discipleship. The

Christian does live on the earth as if it were the alien world; his homesickness is for heaven. Christians, in their deepest religious experiences, touch the substance of things hoped for, and thus, even in the present, they remember the future.

Peter does not understand. Nor is there any time to begin the building of dwellings; for they are greeted—for the second time and now at the center of the gospel—with the divine voice: "This is my Son, the Beloved; listen to him" (9:8). The admonition to listen is new; otherwise the voice repeats the same message as at Jesus' baptism (1:11). The added commandment to listen is especially appropriate for this blindness/sight envelope, where the quest for Jesus' identity is at its most intense.

Peter, James, and John discover that the experience is at an end, for suddenly when they look around they see no one but Jesus. If there is any statement that Mark intends to dramatize in his gospel it is this one—that we are to see Jesus only. This picks up the important point made at Jesus' baptism, where we are also left, essentially, with Jesus only—not with John the Baptist or the prophets he quotes. No matter how much Mark may emphasize the past prophecies and promises, Jesus essentially transcends the past: he is always completely new and full of one surprise after another, as Mark has been careful to dramatize.

Even though Mark's world is not so strange as to be called surreal, he nonetheless presents here strange and dangerous new concepts about the relationship of God to humankind and to the world. After almost every scene in this gospel, we have been left with Jesus only. He has stood alone, time and again, as victor in contests with humans and with nature; in the awesome grandeur of one who makes such absolute claims and states such absolute conditions, he has stood alone. Even as the focus of intense hatred, he has stood alone.

Now, as first person replaces third, as Jesus replaces tradition, the disciples live on a stormy sea (a microcosm of the age); and their eternal future will depend upon their faith strengthened by the understanding of the Master who remains in dignified solitude even in crowds. It is as if he calls to people and then constantly recedes before every forward step they take. Such is the state of affairs as the disciples descend the mount of transfiguration, and such is the state of affairs today, according to the belief of many Christians. Matthew and Luke are somewhat easier on the new believer, because, no matter how harsh the Q tradition may be at times, an almost comfortable and even pastoral atmosphere at times shelters the reader. Not so with Mark. Stripped of most teachings, his story is an action gospel with a powerful unencumbered plot. Mark allows the character and christology of Jesus to grow from that plot, perhaps as it had already done in the oral tradition.

So that we do not become too negative in our attitude toward the disciples, it is important to keep reminding ourselves that Mark uses them as foils for teaching purposes; their lack of understanding provides a dramatic occasion for emphasis. Actually, Mark maintains the obvious respect for Peter, James, and John which evidently imbued the oral tradition. As Schnackenburg points out, these three were the ones chosen to witness

> the raising to life of the daughter of Jairus (5:37), the transfiguration, and the agony in the garden (14:33). These are mysteries of Jesus' earthly life and ministry which must not remain hidden after his resurrection, since they provide a key to the understanding of his person.[140]

The journey down the mountain provides an immediate and negative assault on the transfiguration experience. Once again, the disciples are confused:

> As they were coming down the mountain, he ordered them to tell no one about what they had seen, until after the Son of Man had risen from the dead. So they kept the matter to themselves, questioning what this rising from the dead could mean. Then they asked him, "Why do the scribes say that Elijah must come first?" He said to them, "Elijah is indeed coming first to restore all things. How then is it written about the Son of Man, that he is to go through many sufferings and be treated with contempt? But I tell you that Elijah has come, and they did to him whatever they pleased, as it is written about him" (9:9-13).

Mark's church evidently was preoccupied with the Elijah prophecies, for it seems to be very important for him to put them into what he considers their proper perspective. Perhaps Mark's audience, like Jesus' disciples, cannot transcend tradition. Perhaps they insist, as the disciples did, even after the transfiguration, upon seeing Jesus rooted in the past, in a tangle of prophecies. Jesus tells them here that John the Baptist was the returned Elijah, and thus invites them to look away from tradition just long enough to take a good look at their present experiences. Furthermore, by yoking the disciples' misunderstanding about resurrection with their confusion about Elijah, Mark himself, after a grudging acceptance, negates Elijah once again. It is more important, he implies, to understand these present revelations than to become obsessed with the past. For Mark, prophecy was an open door, not a room for confinement.

After Jesus descends the mountain, he finds the other disciples also lacking spiritual potency and faith. In the healing of the possessed boy (9:14-29), Mark seems to have composed or inherited a midrash reflecting the experience of Moses after he descended the mountain.[141] The parallelism with Sinai in the transfiguration pericope is very close. When Moses and Jesus descend the mountain, for instance, they both encounter a lack of faith. When Jesus comes down from the mount of transfiguration, he finds faithless and spiritually impotent disciples, just as Moses, whose face glowed when he was on the mountain, came down to confront Aaron and the faithless people who were worshiping the golden calf.

> Then Moses turned and went down from the mountain, carrying the two tablets of the covenant in his hands . . . The tablets were the work of God, and the writing was the writing of God, engraved upon the tablets . . . As soon as he came near the camp and saw the calf and the dancing, Moses' anger burned hot, and he threw the tablets from his hands and broke them at the foot of the mountain . . . Moses said to Aaron, "What did this people do to you that you have brought so great a sin upon them?" (Exod 32:15-21).

To be sure, the disciples are not worshiping a golden calf, but they still lack the power offered to them by Jesus. When Jesus learns of this inadequacy, he says, "You faithless generation, how much longer must I be among you? How much longer must I put up with you?" (9:19). Mark's placing of this pericope after the transfiguration further establishes a Jesus-Moses parallel and makes points about Jesus' teaching as a new covenant as well as about the initial misunderstandings of the disciples. In the scenes which are to follow, Mark continues using the disciples as foils so that he may elaborate upon the nature of the kingdom, of discipleship, and of Jesus' identity.

The basic problem presented by some material in this healing scene is new to us. For the first time, with the possible exception of reporting the death of John the Baptist, we have excess material which is not really necessary to the gospel. We must be extremely cautious in making this suggestion, especially since we do not know what topical concerns preoccupied Mark's church. What they recognized in this scene may be lost to us. But we see that Matthew and Luke seem to realize the excess and abbreviate this scene radically (cf. Matt 17:14-20; Luke 9:37-43a). Mark keeps many things he could have excised (certainly just as easily as he excised the Sermon on the Mount!): the details of the boy's seizure, reported in a "clinical" fashion; the dramatic description of the seizure; Jesus questioning the boy; Jesus' faith pronouncement; his ritual command to the spirit; the convulsions of the boy as the spirit leaves. Most, if not all, of this is extraneous to Mark's immediate purpose of making a christological statement in the context of the Moses theme. The final statement, furthermore, seems to be so didactically awkward as to seem tacked on: "This kind can come out only by prayer" (v. 29).

We have already noted Mark's respect for tradition, which may partially explain his retention of this material. His cautious retention demonstrates perhaps what Childs suggests—that Mark is aware of his participation in a canonization process.[142] He keeps everything he inherited, for he wants to preserve the integrity of the inherited pericopes. Even though he may have taken some liberties with the transfiguration in regard to its placement; and even though he may have added transitional phrases and other minor touches, Mark is concerned with the essential canonical integrity of the writing. He is aware that he is being selective in presenting his theology through the gospel story, but also that he must take care to preserve what he considers to be the important inherited traditions. The original didactic freight detected by form critics is brought along with the story and allowed to coexist, however uncomfortably, with those portions of the story which would function, in a modern historical narrative, to advance the plot and develop the themes. Up until now, the structure has been relatively rather tight. Now, a modern reader hears a rattle or two. Mark seems to be simultaneously deft and clumsy—and we see that there are reasons for this.

In spite of its awkward length and details, Mark does use this exorcism scene primarily to give structure to his story; for like many other ancient writers, he sees architectural patterns in writing. He juxtaposes this healing pericope with the transfiguration and thereby makes a comment in regard to Moses coming down the mountain.

Mark also reveals his structural pattern by placing Jesus' second prophecy of his death (9:30-32) near the center of his recursion.

> "The Son of Man is to be betrayed into human hands, and they will kill him, and three days after being killed, he will rise again." But they did not understand what he was saying and were afraid to ask him (9:30-32).

Later, he will repeat this prophecy for the third time (10:32-34) and thus complete his recursive triangle, with the first and third prophecies at C and C´ and the central second prophecy at D. Ancient writers, including Homer and Virgil, often repeat key verses or scenes, not only for emphasis but also to achieve esthetic balance.[143] By using this technique, Mark reveals his skill as an artful editor. He uses repetition to hammer again and again at the basic points he wishes to emphasize.

The first and third prophecies are longer, dwelling in more detail upon the rejection by chief priests and scribes. In this middle prophecy, Jesus focuses briefly and emphatically upon his ultimate sacrifice. Still, his disciples remain blind.

The process of affirmation/negation creates vacuum-like spaces within the narrative, little pockets of emptiness (e.g., after John's prophecies, after Jesus' leaving Capernaum, and also after his decision to go to Jerusalem). These spaces are intended by Mark; after raising questions he will bring forward answers to fill those gaps and create other questions! One can almost approach Mark's gospel as a motion study; in a slow-motion film of a person walking, the observer sees the walker move from temporary imbalance to balance and then imbalance again.

After the second prophecy, James and John step forward to show how little they have understood:

> Then they came to Capernaum; and when he was in the house he asked them, "What were you arguing about on the way?" But they were silent, for on the way they had argued

with one another who was the greatest. He sat down, called
the twelve, and said to them, "Whoever wants to be first
must be last of all and servant of all." Then he took a little
child and put it among them; and taking it in his arms, he
said to them, "Whoever welcomes one such child in my
name welcomes me, and whoever welcomes me welcomes
not me but the one who sent me" (9:33-37).

Although the Suffering Servant theme is not fully developed until the crucifixion and death of Jesus, here Jesus gives it full verbal expression, declaring explicitly that "whoever wants to be first must be last of all and servant of all." Such a statement provides a coloration that spreads backward along the pattern of actions through which Jesus has offered himself to humanity, reaching all the way back to the beginning of the gospel. It also spreads forward in its foreshadowing of Jesus' ultimate sacrifice.

What is particularly interesting in this section is the metaphor of the child, whose double appearance in this section, indicates that it is a powerful symbol. And in the progression of Jesus' teaching, the child symbol now takes its place within a powerful constellation of other symbols: disease, healing, storm, back-stabbing hatreds, transfiguration, and—very soon now—the cross. As the initiate's eyes moves across these symbols in catechism, an obvious invitation to meditation is given. This meditation will not be guided just by rote instruction, but also by the creative contrast of symbols. In this blindness/sight envelope, the child symbol takes meaning from and returns meaning to the other scenes, especially the preceding one portraying the disciples' prideful debate. As we have already seen, Mark has consciously constructed a hermeneutic circle. Just as each word in a sentence defines the meaning of the whole sentence, so does the whole sentence give meaning to each of the individual words. In this gospel, symbols are charged with meaning by an ever-expanding context; and this context is fed and fueled, in turn, by those same symbols. An awareness of this hermeneutic is a powerful tool for interpretation of the gospel.

Jesus does not mean for the disciple to become childish in the modern pejorative sense of that word. A child in the first century would age very quickly, by modern standards. Quickly placed in some sort of apprenticeship, the child would soon be seen and treated as an adult.[144] Nonetheless, however long or brief the period of childhood, the very young child has always been a symbol of innocence and humility—one who has not yet acquired the pride of the adult. The child is also a symbol of "being of no account" socially in the Roman world. And Jesus certainly would have had this attribute in mind as well. The juxtaposition with the first-and-last-saying also clarifies Jesus' meaning. Jesus, the messenger from God, is describing the posture to be taken before ultimate reality, the ground of being. The connections with the Suffering-Servant motif are virtually explicit, for Jesus' first response to the disciples' pride is "Whoever wants to be first, must be last of all and servant of all" (9:35). The attitude of prideful competition is not conducive to spiritual growth.

Up until now, the structure of Mark's gospel has been comparatively rather tight. Now, we can hear a rattle or two. From Mark 9:38 through 10:12 we find some "areas of turbulence" which challenge our hypothesis that this section, like the others, is a carefully constructed envelope. The sections which give trouble are the strange exorcist (9:38-41), the temptations to sin (9:42-50), and the teaching about divorce (10:1-12). They do form a kind of sayings section, but it is at first glance difficult to discern their connection with the surrounding material.

A careful reading, however, confirms a coherence within this section. We find certain parallels between this and the excess material in the story of the healing of the possessed boy. In that earlier pericope, we theorized that Mark had such respect for his inherited material that he refused to edit away those portions which were not thematically related to context. Thus, he included the clinical descriptions of the effects of the disease upon the boy, the statement by Jesus that only prayer could heal such a disease, etc. There are in that story no clues of form or language to help the critic, who thus has to remain in the realm of theory and hypothesis. In this section, however, linguistic clues do indicate that Mark saw the section as thematically related to its context. Consider, for example, the pericope that follows immediately after Jesus' discussion of the child:

> John said to him, "Teacher, we saw someone casting out demons in your name, and we tried to stop him, because he was not following us." But Jesus said, "Do not stop him; for no one who does a deed of power in my name will be able

soon afterward to speak evil of me. Whoever is not against us is for us. For truly I tell you, whoever gives you a cup of water to drink because you bear the name of Christ will by no means lose the reward" (9:38-41).

The three repetitions of "the name" provide hooks linking this section with the name reference in the last verse (v. 37) of the child section. Jesus says, "Whoever welcomes one such child *in my name* welcomes me." These repetitions indicate that Mark had inherited a "verse paragraph," a group of sayings saved in a thematic, or at least topical, bundle. Mark, the editor, has pulled up in his net a chain of sayings already assembled in the oral tradition. This chain was topically bound together by the *epi to onomati sou* ("in my name") theme[145] and was itself probably designed for catechesis: the catechumen thereby is challenged to see the connection between mimesis of Jesus and the power of the name of the risen Christ.

Mark can, as we have stated, seem to be simultaneously deft and clumsy — and we see that there are reasons for this. Mark's method here accounts for his apparent awkwardness of abrupt transition as it arises from his preservation of catechesis cast into narrative form while still expecting catechesis to form its function without interfering with smooth narrative progression. In fact, it has been Mark's challenge to create a written gospel from traditions which were not always narrative in form. Thus, Mark creates a new genre, because of his double purpose: 1) to write a gospel composed of bits of catechesis, and 2) to make certain that the redemptive outline and narrative flow of the gospel story are preserved in as coherent a manner as possible.

The sayings group which follows, the temptations to sin (9:42-50), does not fit smoothly into Mark's context, but even though the subject has shifted to sin, the repetition of the reference to the child provides the topical unity.

> If any of you put a stumbling block before one of these little ones who believe in me, it would be better for you if a great millstone were hung around your neck and you were thrown into the sea (9:42).

We can see a logical continuity — one who models his or her heart on the child's innocent heart cannot possibly commit a sin which corrupts the innocence of others. This inherited material thus reinforces, by way of negative warnings, what Jesus positively affirmed about the disciples attitude, which is critically important to recognizing and following the Christ.[146] They warn by showing the dangers of transgression. Similar warnings are also in the other hyperbolic material inherited by Mark:

> If your hand causes you to stumble, cut it off; it is better for you to enter life maimed than to have two hands and to go to hell, to the unquenchable fire. And if your foot causes you to stumble, cut it off; it is better for you to enter life lame than to have two feet and to be thrown into hell. And if your eye causes you to stumble, tear it out; it is better for you to enter the kingdom of God with one eye than to have two eyes and to be thrown into hell, where their worm never dies, and the fire is never quenched. For everyone will be salted with fire. Salt is good; but if salt has lost its saltiness, how can you season it? Have salt in yourselves, and be at peace with one another (9:43-50).

The question arises whether this material would not be more at home in Mark's chapter thirteen, in the material devoted to apocalypse? The harsh yoking together of images of child and hell jar the modern reader, whatever the response would have been from first-century Christians. The imagery of salt and fire seems also to be somewhat disconnected. The coherence is saved somewhat when Jesus closes with "have salt in yourselves, and be at peace with one another" (v. 50 b), for at least that recalls the child metaphor and the prideful competition of the disciples.

The divorce debate (10:2-12) can be topically related to a child-family complex. Mark has moved from 1) children, 2) sins against children, and now 3) marriage/family, and 4) sins against marriage/family.

> Some Pharisees came, and to test him they asked, "Is it lawful for a man to divorce his wife?" He answered them, "What did Moses command you?" They said, "Moses allowed a man to write a certificate of dismissal and to divorce her." But Jesus said to them, "Because of your hardness of heart he wrote this commandment for you. But from the beginning of creation, 'God made them male and

female.' 'For this reason a man shall leave his father and mother and be joined to his wife, and the two shall become one flesh.' So they are no longer two, but one flesh. Therefore what God has joined together, let no one separate." Then in the house the disciples asked him again about this matter. He said to them, "Whoever divorces his wife and marries another commits adultery against her; and if she divorces her husband and marries another, she commits adultery" (10:2-12).

This is basically didactic material designed to exhort and warn. Perhaps, like some of the recipients of Paul's letters, Mark's church (largely Gentile and perhaps in Rome) needs some lecturing about sexual morality and about proper attitudes towards marriage and family. Thus, he may here feel it necessary to address the special needs of those initiates who come forward with what we might today call an "attitude problem" toward marriage. If this section is the only place where Mark's text suffers because of his conservative retention of inherited sayings, then he is doing pretty well. Even Homer nods. Here Mark takes a rather lengthy nap and has a nightmare as well.

Thus, it is a relief to come to the second children section and to be once again on that thematic way that Mark has smoothed so skillfully and patiently since the beginning of the gospel. Here, he demonstrates his control over his material:

> People were bringing little children to him in order that he might touch them; and the disciples spoke sternly to them. But when Jesus saw this, he was indignant and said to them, "Let the little children come to me; do not stop them; for it is to such as these that the kingdom of God belongs. Truly I tell you, whoever does not receive the kingdom of God as a little child will never enter it." And he took them up in his arms, laid his hands on them, and blessed them (10:13-16).

Mark, the religious artist, recovers his balance here, working creatively again with his thematic comparisons by returning to the symbol of the child. The first children scene took its coloring from the adjacent "Who is Greatest?" pericope (9:33-37), and the metaphor was made complex by the welcome child/welcome Jesus/welcome God metaphor (9:37). In this second child passage, the tenor, or subject, of the metaphor is the reception of the kingdom. It is interesting how the equation presented in the first passage is extended in the second. In effect, Jesus has strongly implied that he is essentially the kingdom-presented-to-humankind. Through his sacrificial service, Jesus has become transparent to God. That is the central truth revealed by these quotations.

> Welcome child = Welcome Jesus (9:36-37).
>
> Welcome Jesus = Welcome God (9:37).
>
> Receive kingdom as child = To enter kingdom (10:13-16).

The second passage serves as a conclusion to the warnings about sin and divorce and also as an introduction to the rich man pericope which follows. Again, we see Mark using a passage to look backward and forward to comment on all surrounding passages in such a way as to splice together his material.

Up to this point, the linear relationships between Mark's scenes has been established in the envelopes. Having reached Jesus' confrontation with the rich man (10:17-27), we can pause for a moment, just past the center, to look backward and forward at Mark's organization of this envelope. In this envelope's recursion, for example, the transfiguration (9:1-8) and the sayings immediately preceding it (8:34-38) occur near the mathematical center of the gospel; as we might expect this same section forms a part of the center of the recursion. In addition, Mark molds the recursion around the three prophecies,[147] so that the second prophecy (9:31) also appears at the center of the recursion. Furthermore, the sayings which appear nearest the center (9:33 - 10:16) are those following that second prophecy (and thus include the sayings from the debate over who is greatest among the disciples—from 9:33 to 9:37). Many of these sayings, as we have already seen, affirm the central Suffering Servant theme as well as teach about the kingdom (9:36-37). This sayings section clearly underscores those same themes which clustered near the transfiguration and which are important to the entire envelope at the center of his larger story. These sayings, therefore, serve as the centerpiece of "Healing the Blind."

Whereas the first arm of this recursion presents the struggles of Peter and the disciples to understand Jesus' actions and sayings, the second arm contrasts with the first by introducing the symbol of the child and by illustrating the right attitude toward following Jesus and entering the kingdom. Mark thus underscores his linear and thematic gospel in this envelope by once again framing the plot and themes within doublets and by suggesting comparisons and contrasts on both sides of a sayings center.

In the diagram on page 131, for example, notice the rich comparisons between Peter's confession (B) and the request of James and John (B'). In both, the mistaken attitudes of the disciples grow from a materialist, triumphal conception of the Messiah and the approaching kingdom. We have already discussed Peter's attitude, and now we can see the parallels with that of James and John. Notice also that the first and third prophecies are aligned at C and C', with the resulting correspondence between Peter's caution and the rich man's caution; for essentially the same reasons, both men hesitate to follow Christ. As just noted, the transfiguration stands at the center, along with the disciples' inability to heal the boy and the second prophecy. If the first prophecy stands at C and the second prophecy at C', there is formal support for placing the second prophecy at the center of a symmetrical tripartite arrangement. The sayings from 9:33 through 10:16 also occur at the center, where they form the apex of a symmetrical sayings arrangement: The Suffering Servant sayings (in response to Peter's caution) appeared in C. On the other side of the center, at C', the Suffering Servant sayings occur again (in response to the rich man's caution). Mark probably intended, therefore, the following form for "Healing the Blind."

The rich man's caution (C') is placed as a contrast to the preceding child material, but it also serves as a rich commentary on Peter's caution (C), his attempt to dissuade Jesus from entering Jerusalem. Although Peter has identified Jesus as Messiah, he stumbled at a critical moment; once again, he is "driving with his brakes on," just as he did earlier when Jesus moved away from Capernaum. The basic pattern of the rich man pericope is similar. When he comes forward with his question, he affirms himself by affirming the law, but when asked to follow Jesus, he will not.

> And as he was setting out on a journey, a man ran up and knelt before him, and asked him, "Good Teacher, what must I do to inherit eternal life?" Jesus said to him, "Why do you call me good? No one is good but God alone. You know the commandments: 'You shall not murder; You shall not

commit adultery; You shall not steal; You shall not bear false witness; You shall not defraud; Honor your father and mother.'" He said to him, "Teacher, I have kept all these since my youth." Jesus, looking at him, loved him and said, "You lack one thing; go, sell what you own, and give the money to the poor, and you will have treasure in heaven; then come, follow me." When he heard this, he was shocked and went away grieving, for he had many possessions (10:17-22).

As in the case of Peter, Jesus attempts a multiple healing of spiritual vision, for the rich man does not see clearly but only sees "people ... like trees walking." Jesus thus repeats to the rich man the demands he made upon Peter and the other disciples, and all of these demands are made in conjunction with the three prophecies of Jesus' fate. The point Jesus is making is that to gain a vision of the kingdom, one must approach with the attitude of the child (9:36-37).

Mark may have intended that this rich man represent a typical first-century Jewish response to the Messiah. The man apparently sees Jesus, as an early Jewish Christian naturally would, as being the fulfillment of the law. His question implies just such a premise. Seeing both Jesus and himself in the light of the law, instead of the light on the mountain, he arrogantly assumes a potential equality with Christ. Jesus, of course, introduces the subject of the law, almost as one opens with a gambit in chess. The rich man takes the gambit pawn, affirms his excellence in regard to law, and then leaves himself wide open. Momentarily, at least, the rich man replaces Simon Peter as Mark's central foil to Jesus! Jesus attacks the rich man's weak position with the same demand he made of his disciples before and after the transfiguration: "Follow me." Neither the rich man nor Peter, at least not immediately, have the strength to do that. Peter does not want Jesus to go to Jerusalem, nor does he want any part of this newly-introduced Suffering Servant. The rich man approaches one whom he assumes is a traditional teacher only to discover, as Peter did, that Christ makes demands upon his disciples.

But to misidentify Jesus as merely teacher, exorcist, prophet, or miracle worker is to make a tragic mistake. To follow Jesus is to move into an adventure in which one's physical safety and comfort cannot be taken for granted. Mark's audience, if they were indeed a Roman church in the year 70 CE, would understand. This absolute requirement to follow Jesus is thus presented again and again to the initiate in this central part of Mark's gospel, not just in an abstract theological way, but in an intense dramatic fashion. At this point, we are truly near the center of Mark's teaching.

Mark's two methods of development nourish one another in an interesting way. Another key reference to children occurs at 10:13-16, just before the rich man's caution. Jesus says, "Truly I tell you, whoever does not receive the kingdom of God as a little child will never enter it" (vv. 10-15), thus setting the stage for the story of the rich man. But in attaching this saying to the rich man's caution at C´, Mark also allows the saying as well to be carried "backward" to C and thus to Peter's caution.

The sayings (10:23-31) which follow the rich man's caution, by virtue of their recursive position, are thus underlined by Mark as reinforcing parallels to the "Take up your cross" sayings (8:34-38) in section C, preceding the transfiguration. After the sorrowful departure of the rich man, Jesus says,

> "How hard it will be for those who have wealth to enter the kingdom of God!" And the disciples were perplexed at these words. But Jesus said to them again, "Children, how hard it is to enter the kingdom of God! It is easier for a camel to go through the eye of a needle than for someone who is rich to enter the kingdom of God" (10:23-25).

When Peter calls Jesus' attention to the sacrifices the disciples have already made for him, Jesus encourages them by assuring them they will be rewarded:

> Truly, I tell you, there is no one who has left house or brothers or sisters or mother or father or children or fields, for my sake and for the sake of the good news, who will not receive a hundredfold now in this age ... and in the age to come eternal life. But many who are first will be last, and the last will be first (10:29-31).[148]

The sayings preceding the transfiguration are, for the sake of convenience, quoted again. The parallels between C and C´ which Mark intends to underscore are obvious, in that they both present calls. Mark's recursion emphasizes that neither Peter, at that time at least, nor the rich man was able to take up the cross.

> If any want to become my followers, let them deny themselves and take up their cross and follow me. For those who want to save their life will lose it, and those who lose their life for my sake, and for the sake of the gospel, will save it. For what will it profit them to gain the whole world and forfeit their life? Indeed, what can they give in return for their life? Those who are ashamed of me and of my words in this adulterous and sinful generation, of them the Son of Man will also be ashamed when he comes in the glory of his Father with the holy angels (8:34-38).

Section C´, which contains the rich man's caution, also presents the third prophecy of Jesus concerning his fate in Jerusalem:

> See, we are going up to Jerusalem, and the Son of Man will be handed over to the chief priests and the scribes, and they will condemn him to death; then they will hand him over to the Gentiles: they will mock him, and spit upon him, and flog him, and kill him; and after three days he will rise again" (10:33-34).

The three prophecies form the basic hinge of the recursion, for here, equidistant from the central second prophecy, the first prophecy (C) is balanced over against the third prophecy (C´).[149] These three prophecies are three dramatically spaced statues in Mark's cathedral, around which are arranged the pericopes of this section. At the extreme ends of the section are the scenes picturing Jesus healing the blind men. This third prophecy (C´) stands in a balanced relationship with the first prophecy (C), and both the first and third provide symmetry for the second prophecy (D´) which is at home in the central position. The structure is thus reinforced by this triangle, which perhaps echoes an inherited formal chiasmus. Just as Luke intensifies Paul's Damascus experience during its third presentation (Acts 9:12-18), so Mark appropriately makes this third prophecy (10:32-34) a climactic one. In the last portrayal of Paul's experience, the light becomes more intense, and Jesus personally delivers Paul's commission.[150] Mark, in this third prophecy, makes it the climax of the three by adding "and they will mock him, and spit upon him, and flog him, and kill him" (10:34).

All three of these prophecies occur in the context of the most important sayings in this gospel. More importantly, however, there are thematic sayings attached to the second prophecy, or at least placed near it (9:33 - 10:16), which underscore the basic themes of this envelope. Thus it is here, at the sayings center of the envelope, that Mark has Jesus respond to the arguing disciples: "Whoever wants to be first must be last of all and servant of all" (9:35) and to identify himself with the child: "Whoever welcomes one such child in my name welcomes me, and whoever welcomes me welcomes not me but the one who sent me" (9:37). Mark indeed may have been saving this saying for inclusion in his centerpiece because of the explicit connection made between Jesus and God: the acceptance of Jesus is ultimately the acceptance of God.

The second story which Mark tells after the transfiguration is the request by James and John that they may share Jesus' power in the coming kingdom (B´).

> James and John, the sons of Zebedee, came forward to him, and said to him, "Teacher, we want you to do for us whatever we ask of you." And he said to them, "What is it you want me to do for you?" And they said to him, "Grant us to sit, one at your right hand and one at your left, in your glory." But Jesus said to them, "You do not know what you are asking. Are you able to drink the cup that I drink, or to be baptized with the baptism that I am baptized with?" They replied, "We are able." Then Jesus said to them, "The cup that I drink you will drink; and with the baptism with which I am baptized, you will be baptized; but to sit at my right hand or at my left is not mine to grant, but it is for those for whom it has been prepared." When the ten heard this, they began to be angry with James and John. So Jesus called them to him and said to them, "You know that among the Gentiles those whom they recognize as their rulers lord it over them, and their great ones are tyrants over them. But it is not so among you; but whoever wishes to become great among you must be your servant, and whoever wishes to be first among you must be slave of all. For the Son of Man came not to be served but to serve, and to give his life a ransom for many" (10:35-45).

At a basic level this reiteration of the earlier request provides emphasis. The focus here, however, is sharpened to center upon specific disciples, as once again Mark does not spare them, but uses them for his catechetical purposes. He does achieve something more as well. This is virtually a fourth prophecy, or at least an extension of the third, with the imagery of Eucharist and baptism now included. In response to the request by James and John that they be allowed "to sit, one at your right hand and one at your left, in your glory," Jesus counters by expanding his previous prophecies: "Are you able to drink the cup that I drink, or to be baptized with the baptism with which I am baptized?" (10:38). James and John must be set straight about the kingdom, for they are essentially making the response of Peter when he tempted Jesus to safeguard earthly glory and cautioned him not to enter Jerusalem. The approach to the kingdom requires risk, humility, and sacrifice.

James and John want to have, right now, the deeds of ownership of their dwellings in glory. Once again Jesus must attempt a multiple healing, for he is still working with the blind whose vision, though improving, remains distorted by half truths. People are like trees walking. So Mark, in the final logia, drives his point home again: "Whoever wishes to become great among you must be your servant, and whoever wishes to be first among you must be slave of all. For the Son of Man also came not to be served but to serve, and to give his life a ransom[151] for many" (10:45). If this is a reversal of modern western values, it was no less so in the value system of the first century, with its patronage, *personalismo*, and rigid social boundaries.[152]

The second healing of a blind man brings us to the end of the envelope.

> They came to Jericho. As he and his disciples and a large crowd were leaving Jericho, Bartimaeus son of Timaeus, a blind beggar, was sitting by the roadside. When he heard that it was Jesus of Nazareth, he began to shout out and say, "Jesus, Son of David, have mercy on me!" ... Jesus stood still and said, "Call him here." And they called the blind man, saying to him, "Take heart; get up, he is calling you." So throwing off his cloak, he sprang up and came to Jesus. Then Jesus said to him, "What do you want me to do for you?" The blind man said to him, "My teacher, let me see again." Jesus said to him, "Go; your faith has made you well." Immediately he regained his sight and followed him on the way (10:46–52).

This scene provides the ironic conclusion to all four envelopes. The irony consists in another incomplete identification of Jesus — the blind man's acclamation of him as the "Son of David." Seeing Jesus only as a messenger who displays messianic power, is tragically to misidentify him. This acclamation will be repeated by the Jerusalem crowds during the triumphal entry and is essentially repeated as accusation during Jesus' appearances before the Sanhedrin and before Pilate. This wrong answer to the riddle of the Christ will therefore contribute to the death of Jesus.

Blind Bartimaeus has certainly undergone a real healing; he can see. In no basic way does Mark denigrate the value of this experience, and Jesus does indeed say to him that his faith has made him well. Mark's inherited pericope, evidently, was primarily a healing miracle accompanied by a glorious title, and Mark obviously wants to convey the full positive impact of this scene. Mark's context, however, without detracting from glory, also highlights the negative ironies. The ironies derive from human failures, not God's. The disciples could not understand the significance of transfiguration. The same is true here. The blind man was truly and fully healed by a man he could not understand and whom he misidentified as earthly Messiah.

The multiple healings are again necessary, but Mark now moves away from the blindness symbol. In this last envelope, that symbol has completed its work by pointing ahead to the spiritual blindness that afflicts those who will now desert, mock, and kill Jesus. Multiple healings will still be necessary in Jerusalem. The second half of the doublet reveals a tragic darkness present among those who acclaim Jesus as Messiah as they attempt to usher him triumphally into Jerusalem. In the context of this gospel, of course, the real triumphant entry will be through the tomb. In Mark's gospel, there is very little to suggest that it is easy to be a Christian.

## Principles of Organization

1. **Theme**: Understanding Jesus (awareness of his true identity and understanding his teachings).

2. **The Negation of A**: The healing of the blind man seems at first to be affirmed by Peter's confession, but that confession is immediately followed by Peter's caution, so that he basically undermines his own affirmation. We could perhaps see this as an

A – B affirmation here which is negated by C, since we could view the caution as a separate pericope. At any rate, the negation comes quickly, as it does in most all the envelopes.

**3. Christological Assertions against Negation:**

**3a. Assertion by Miracle**: Unless the healings are classified as miraculous, there is really no miracle in this envelope; it would be a mistake to classify the transfiguration as one. That experience could be better defined as a revelation; together with the opening of the heavens during the baptism could be seen as an assertion by revelation. However one classifies the transfiguration, it does perform one function of the miracles, since it demonstrates the power of the transcendent Christ. That experience, like the feedings, looks backward to Hebrew Scripture and forward to the future. The transfiguration is the most beautiful example of a doubly-exposed photograph, for here, in the context of the teachings in this envelope, we can discern the figure within and behind Jesus of Nazareth with greater clarity than ever before.

**3b. Assertion by Healing**: The last two healings performed by Jesus are quite different from the healings to which we have become accustomed. While those earlier healings were symbolic, they retained something of a "documentary" quality, as if one were watching the historical Jesus performing actions which are first and foremost historical. The significance of the symbolism emerged as we considered context. In contrast, these healings of the blind call attention to themselves as symbols in a way that the earlier healings do not. The juxtaposition of blindness with Peter's struggle to understand, for instance, provides an unmistakable entry into Mark's basic theme of identity.

**3c. Assertion by Sayings**: Much of the body of this chapter is devoted to those sayings which are obviously the most important to Mark as he attempts to educate the initiate into the new faith. He highlights the servant sayings and those sayings concerning the child in such a way that they provide the most important commentary to be made upon the Christian life. What has preceded is important, to be sure; for instance, the parables make important statements about the kingdom. What follows – the Jerusalem controversies and the long apocalypse of chapter thirteen – is also important. But the gospel itself is recursive in that the most important sayings occur near the center of the gospel along with the transfiguration.

3d. **Symbolic Narrative**: The analysis of this envelope shows it to be the most powerfully symbolic of the envelopes, as the multiple healing attempts by Jesus provide a symbolic commentary on the nature of the Christian faith.

3e. **Titles**: The identity theme generates titles: John-Elijah-Prophet (8:27ff), Messiah (8:29), rabbi (9:5), Son of Man (8:31; 9:9; 9:12; 9:31; 10:32), Elijah (9:12), and teacher (9:17; 9:38; 10:20). Mark uses titles to highlight ambiguity, not certainty. In the strange dialectical flow of his narrative, he demonstrates the inadequacy of every title assigned to Jesus. To be sure, each title contains theological truth, but each title also obscures the knowledge necessary to enter into a truthful relationship with the risen Christ.

4. **Sayings in Appropriate Action Context**: In this relationship, Mark develops the theme of the Suffering Servant. Jesus' teachings are concerned with his death and with the necessary new attitudes which must be developed by those who would follow him. The actions of healing the blind and inviting the rich man to discipleship take on their true dimensions from the teachings in this envelope. Ironically, in the first envelope, which introduces the theme of the newness of Jesus' teaching, his opponents reacted against his Sabbath activity and association with outcasts and thus missed the real newness accompanying the messenger. The initiate must wait for this envelope concerned with blindness before being able to discern many of the true features of the Christ.

5. **Recursion**: The scenes after the central sayings provide parallels to the problems experienced by Peter.

6. **Thematic Relationship of Sayings to Actions**: Sayings and actions find their common denominator in the theme of multiple healings. Jesus makes multiple attempts to enlighten his disciples, just as he made multiple attempts to heal the first blind man. All the sayings are intensified by their placement within the context of the journey toward Jerusalem and the cross.

7. **Thematic Doublets**: Here more than in any other envelope, the doublets define the meaning of the material they enclose.

8. **Time**: This envelope encompasses the journey toward Jerusalem.

9. **Setting**: Geography itself becomes midrash when the mount of transfiguration is placed at the center of the gospel.

10. **Dialectical Series**: Mark reaches his apex as religious artist in this section in his symbolic alternation of scenes. Here, more than

anywhere else, we find a wedding of form and content as the form of the stories told becomes the meaning of those stories. The multiple attempts at physical and spiritual healing provide a basic introduction to the problems of being a Christian.

11. **References to Other Envelopes and to the Jerusalem Section**: Mark clearly has intended the themes of the envelopes to stand in a series:
- a. Newness and power ("Healing Many")
- b. Good response to that power ("The Twelve")
- c. The universal nourishment provided by that power ("The Feedings")
- d. Dynamic understanding of the power can be achieved through understanding the identity of Jesus

There has been a movement throughout toward the Suffering Servant theme, which will now find its dramatic expression on a universal stage in Jerusalem.

Only in Jerusalem can the gospel be concluded, as all the themes of the introductory envelopes are acted out on the historical stage. Mark has arranged the teachings of Jesus in such a way that only crucifixion and resurrection can complete the portrait of the Christ. He shows the limits of what the earthly Jesus can do; and behind the earthly portrait, as in a doubly exposed photograph, he portrays for us the risen Christ who will be experienced by the early church. Mark's constant damping down of giddy fires, his constant insistence upon secrecy—these all point toward the ultimate revelations (the ultimate healings) as coming only with the cross and the empty tomb, and some not until the consummation of time and the full arrival of the kingdom.

Jesus is a man of earth, and love calls him to things of this world. But in the constant metamorphosis of Jesus from pericope to pericope, we see him becoming the future. Mark would certainly agree with the writer of Hebrews: "Jesus Christ is the same yesterday, and today, and forever" (Heb 13:8). For in each scene in which he presents Jesus he surely intends us to glimpse the eternal, unchanging Christ.

But for Mark, this confluence of God and time brings a dynamic, changing turbulence—a crisis which will reach its zenith in the end time. In the meantime, we glimpse the eternal in the turbulence. The face of Jesus of Nazareth has the lineaments of the face of God. It is not easy to see that face or discern those lineaments. We must learn to see, however; for all we can know of God is given to us in Jesus. This struggle to teach and understand is Mark's drama.

Jesus himself attempts to relieve the ambiguities by providing a model for mimesis: "Take up your cross and follow me" (8:34). This is the great demand of the riddle of the Christ. Understanding with the mind, or even with the heart, is not enough. We must love God with the whole self, including the will. We must so surrender ourselves so as to become the riddle. That is the answer to the riddle of the Christ as dramatized by Mark. In this, it is similar to the riddle of the Sphinx. Any full answer to the riddle of the Sphinx requires that a person live through the rhythms of the riddle: the child, the person in the prime of life, and finally the feeble old person walking only with the aid of a cane. No intellectual answer can possibly satisfy; certainly no intellectual answer can substitute for the living of a life! The riddle of the Christ, as well, demands the entry into the life given by Christ. Only then is the *peirasmos* overcome. Only then does the coin show that it is not counterfeit, that it rings true.

Mark's gospel, therefore, has a special impact upon the initiate in or near the year 70 CE, Christ has now died and risen; the lesson is complete. There is no excuse for incomplete seeing. They have the advantage of being a later generation which learns from the mistakes of the earliest Christian generation. For an understanding of Mark's gospel, however, those early initiates and modern Christians must realize that even after the crucifixion and resurrection, many of the ambiguities about Christ remain. Surely Bartimaeus and Peter can be forgiven for seeing "people ... like trees walking." It is just as difficult now to understand the riddle by becoming the riddle as it was then. This is why Mark casts his traditions into the form resembling a Greek drama. He invites the audience upon the stage to overcome the same problems concerning Jesus as the disciples did. Mark's gospel remains a religious text characterized by an invitation into experience. After crucifixion and resurrection, his drama persists in the flow of time around the curve of ambiguous earth, where humanity can have the kingdom now, but not yet.

Many dark misunderstandings have functioned throughout the gospel so far to cause trouble for Jesus. The next section of the gospel will show the deepening of that darkness, for the Jerusalem section will be introduced by a replication of the blind man's error: the crowd which welcomes Jesus into Jerusalem greets him as the herald of "the kingdom of our father David" (11:10). So the end of this final envelope, the second half of its doublet, points toward the final section of Mark's gospel. And in a sense, Mark has indeed written a long introduction to the passion. After the prologue and the four envelopes, the reader is prepared for what the evangelist hopes will be a final and successful attempt to heal the understanding.

# 7
# Jerusalem

A The **King's triumphal entry** (11:1-10).
  B   **Curse** and cleanse: **Death** of temple and **fig tree** (11:12-26).
    C   **Authority questioned** (11:27-33).
      D   Parable of vineyard **(the son) logia from controversy & apocalypse.** (12:1 - 13:36).
        E   Plot to kill **(Judas and the authorities)** (14:1-2).
          F   Anointing at Bethany **(preparation for death)** (14:3-9).
            G   **Passover: The Last Supper** (14:12-31).
          F´   Gethsemane **(preparation for death)** (14:32-42).
        E´   Betrayal and arrest **(Judas and the authorities)** (14:43-52).
      D´   Before counsel: **logia of apocalypse.** (**The son.**) Peter's denials. (14:53-72).
    C´   **Authority question** by Pilate (15:1-5).
  B´   **Curse of the tree-cross**; Jesus sentenced to be **crucified** (15:6-15).
A´ The **King's exit** (15:16-20).


The major themes of the envelopes all reach their ultimate development in the Jerusalem section (11:1 - 15:20) of the gospel. Woven together in the Passion story are the themes of newness, discipleship, the demonic, Eucharist, and identity which have figured so prominently in the introductory envelopes as Mark has portrayed the movement of Jesus and his disciples toward Jerusalem. The theme of newness and its attendant controversy reach a high point in

Jerusalem, especially in the reactions to Jesus during the controversies and during the two trials. The theme of discipleship—a theme presenting the right response to Jesus—reaches a negative climax in these last chapters. The disciples, typified by Mark in the person of Simon Peter, all fail Jesus at the critical time. The theme of the demonic, so closely allied with the discipleship theme in "The Twelve," now issues in direct physical assaults upon Jesus. At this point in the story, the demons do not howl in the wilderness, but from the throats of the crowd when Pilate offers to release Jesus and from the throats of the religious and political establishment which Jesus has offended. The theme of Eucharist reappears in the Last Supper, where Jesus speaks in the first person: "Take; this is my body ... This is my blood ..." (14:22-24). The theme of multiple healings, from "Healing the Blind," continue as Jesus makes his last attempts to heal the understanding of the disciples and of others.

Each chapter summary has revealed that Mark's envelopes in some way connect to the envelopes which surround them. The unity provided by the interweaving of their themes reveals that these envelopes have indeed been written as a series of interconnected introductions to the Passion. No real organic break in plot or theme occurs as the story moves from the four envelopes into this Jerusalem section. Mark's *tour de force* in composing this religious text has been to combine into a coherent story those small detachable units which he rearranged into recursive groups enclosed in doublets. These units, or pericopes, probably were used separately in catechism before baptism and Eucharist and may have taken shape in a generation or more of church liturgy and instruction.[153]

The evangelist gives a basic thematic unity to his text by his careful negations of triumphalist Christianity. Probably composed for the membership of the persecuted church in Rome, the gospel is careful to demonstrate both the necessity for temporary suffering and the humility of the "non-triumphalist" Savior. Mark seems to address his writing to those who might fall away because of the bitter realization that not only the Savior himself but his followers must suffer and that there must be a period of darkness and of turmoil before the arrival of God's kingdom; for in this story, he highlights Jesus' sayings about suffering and good discipleship are highlighted at the obvious expense of triumphalist notions.

"Take up your cross and follow me." This statement would not represent only a theological proposition for the church at Rome; it would represent past experience and future possibility if they dared to imitate the life of Jesus and tried to practice his teachings. By constructing his written gospel from the traditions of the early church itself, Mark underscores the Suffering Servant and composes a remarkably unified portrait which is essentially a profound christology. Mark prepares carefully for the final theme of suffering by beginning with newness, moving through right response, to Jesus the giver of bread, healing, and nourishment, and then to the theme of identity which reveals the Suffering Servant. The four envelopes, then, are organically connected—not a tacked-on introduction—and each of them contributes to the final christological portrait.

Thus, as introduction to the Passion, the envelopes hand along the developed theme of suffering to the events in Jerusalem. The theme of misunderstanding from "Healing the Blind" is immediately taken up in the triumphal entry, when the welcoming crowd calls out to Jesus in a way which illustrates the theme of affirmation/negation. When they address Jesus as a Davidic Messiah, they are right, and they are wrong. He will bring deliverance, but not the kind they immediately expect.

> Hosanna!
> Blessed is the one who comes in the name of the Lord!
> Blessed is the coming kingdom of our ancestor David!
> Hosanna in the highest heaven! (11:9-10).

The Jesus we met at the beginning of the gospel, the Jesus who moves aggressively out of the wilderness to confront society's demons, this Jesus was extremely aggressive and fearless. Because his aggression took the form of healing and exorcism, it did not appear to be aggression at all, but it was. He has been engaged in a cosmic battle throughout this gospel. The envelopes have indeed focused upon different phases of the fight: the struggles with disease and madness, with hypocrisy and hatred, and with spiritual blindness. But Jesus has been so selfless that even though he has walked upon water and calmed storms, he gives the impression of one who is only meek and mild.[154] Both impressions, aggression and gentleness, are correct as Jesus carries the battle into enemy territory when he crosses the Jordan. When he enters Jerusalem, he has reached the enemy's command center and the final battle is soon to be fought.

Jesus' mind is set against Jerusalem from the time he enters the city. Although up to this point he has been a healer, a gentle person, upon entering Jerusalem from Bethany on his second day in that region, he curses the fig tree which bore no fruit. This is an unpleasant business which Mark will not allow the reader to forget. The Christian religion was born in the turmoil of the major shift from Jewish to Gentile dominance. In Jesus' cursing the fig tree, with its obvious traditional references to Israel,[155] can be seen the power of the Christ to alter the nature of humankind's relationship to God. The double exposure is informative here: Jesus, the historical figure, struggles with the Jerusalem establishment on a religious and political level; Jesus, the risen Christ, also encounters opposition from the Jewish establishment who rejected him. In the latter case, there was a mission away from Jews and toward Gentiles. Mark blends these two phenomena, making no distinction between them.

As a first-century Christian theologian, Mark is not constrained by any notion of biography or history beyond what he knows of their generic forms. It does not matter to Mark that some of his contemporaries might object that Jesus did not historically reject Judaism, but indeed fulfilled the law. Mark, on the other hand, is always guided by the synthesis, as he conceives it, of history and resurrection. The analysis of his religious text demonstrates that his very techniques of composition issue from that synthesis, resulting in the phenomenon called double-exposure.

The cursing of the fig tree by the gentle Messiah is another doubly-exposed photograph. Mark does not see it as a doctored photograph, not at all; rather, he presents it as an improved photograph, intended to give a consistent picture of the historical Jesus as the early tradition wanted him to be remembered. For Mark, as well as for his congregation and for many modern Christians, there is no way to separate the life of Jesus from the life made available to the Christian. Mark's text presents an invitation to the reader to immerse himself or herself in the story, to be baptized into the story of the miracle of God's continuing encounter with mankind. There is no desire to mislead or to falsify. Faith found much of its communicative technique, as we have observed, in midrash. Symbolism was second nature to the early Jewish Christians; their Hebrew past was saturated with it, especially the history and literature of intertestamental times.

This acted-out parable of the fig tree has a strange connection with the parables of chapter four. The promised kingdom, potentially present to humankind in the person of the messenger, was presented in that earlier chapter under the organic metaphors of mustard seed and growing grain. In those parables, the disciple is given powerful, positive metaphors. In the fig tree scene, however, the organic metaphor darkens. Lack of reception of seed and lack of growth now become the failure of Judaism to accept Jesus! This analysis has emphasized the synthesis of parables (or sayings) with actions or "doings." Now, in effect, the parables of chapter four comment on the action as Jesus enters Jerusalem. The very thing he warned against—rejection of the seed—has happened. We now can look back and realize that Jesus was speaking of himself, even in those early parables. He now presents himself as the seed as he enters Jerusalem in an atmosphere ranging from benevolent misunderstanding by his "followers" to murderous hostility on the part of the religious establishment.

The Jesus who enters Jerusalem is above all the aggressive Messiah who will strike three powerful blows against the opposition. John the Baptist speaks of the fire of the Messiah, and no portrait of the Christ is complete without this element. The first blow is the cursing of the fig tree; in its theological symbolism lies a powerful assertion about the uniqueness of Christianity. The second blow will be the cleansing of the temple, by which Jesus demonstrates that he came to Jerusalem to do battle. The third blow will be the attack upon nature itself in chapter thirteen, Mark's "little apocalypse." The Messiah brings violent change which was prefigured in confrontations with Pharisees, Herodians, demons, and in storms at sea. All the Gospels attest to this aggressive nature of Jesus, and as he enters Jerusalem, he expresses that nature to its fullest extent.

The Suffering Servant motif is not disrupted by the theme of the fiery Messiah, however. In fact, the two roles are intimately connected in the full, emerging portrait of the Christ. Undoubtedly, Jesus of Nazareth was a complex person combining within himself these passive and aggressive qualities. As Mark's christology develops, these qualities are seen as two faces of the same coin. The offer of salvation—the offer of seeds for growth—does indeed bring humanity under crisis and judgment.

The cleansing of the temple is one in a continuing line of controversies extending from the wilderness to Jerusalem. In it we find the same shape of material identified by Dewey in "Healing Many." Jesus enters; the opposition plots or tests; Jesus performs the healing (here he heals the temple itself!); Jesus then makes a pronouncement which is followed by a choric statement from the crowd. As often is the case, the crowd's reaction is hostile.

> Then they came to Jerusalem. And he entered the temple and began to drive out those who were selling and those who were buying in the temple, and he overturned the tables of the money changers and the seats of those who sold doves; and he would not allow anyone to carry anything through the temple. He was teaching and saying, "Is it not written, 'My house shall be called a house of prayer for all the nations'? But you have made it a den of robbers." And when the chief priests and the scribes heard it, they kept looking for a way to kill him; for they were afraid of him, because the whole crowd was spellbound by his teaching (11:15-18).

Although Mark never makes an explicit connection between the temple cleansing and the charges brought against Jesus, the implications are very strong that this aggressive action provided the goad that prompted his opponents into action. Jesus is not far from death at this point. Mark's literary construction here indicates the serious nature of the temple incident. The two frame passages concerning the fig tree form a little chiasmus or concentric construction, with the temple cleansing at the center:

A   Cursing of fig tree.
   B   Cleansing of temple.
A´  Withering of fig tree.

This may be a package inherited from tradition, or it could well be Mark's own construction. Whatever the case, the second fig tree passage (A´) obviously functions as the second half of the negative frame enclosing the temple incident. The strange comments on faith in this second passage seem somehow out of place in Mark as if they have been added by some later editor or awkwardly retained by Mark out of his respect for tradition:

> In the morning as they passed by, they saw the fig tree withered away to its roots. Then Peter remembered and said to him, "Rabbi, look! The fig tree that you cursed has withered." Jesus answered them, "Have faith in God. Truly I tell you, if you say to this mountain, 'Be taken up and thrown into the sea,' and if you do not doubt in your heart, but believe that what you say will come to pass, it will be done for you. So I tell you, whatever you ask for in prayer, believe that you have received it, and it will be yours. Whenever you stand praying, forgive, if you have anything against anyone; so that your Father in heaven may also forgive you your trespasses" (11:20-26).

Here is another example of a discordant inclusion. In "Healing the Blind," we were able to speculate, with some justification, concerning Mark's possible retention of tradition in regard to his inclusion of apparently unrelated sayings. This passage, however, is so manifestly out of place here that it would be surprising if it were anything but a later redaction.[156] The basic point of this little "envelope" is obviously Mark's literally damning commentary on the Jerusalem establishment which was responsible for the execution of Jesus. The envelope form, so carefully constructed to provide emphasis at its center, cannot be defused by the faith comment added later at the end. The contextual material here is angry in tone; Mark is angry here; his story is angry. The temple incident has intensified the forces which are already moving Jesus and his disciples toward trouble with the authorities.

As we have seen happen so often in the envelopes, Jesus' authority is questioned by the authorities. Now, however, the doubters are the chief priests, scribes, and elders, the very people referred to in Jesus' prophecies concerning his death. Moving now to center stage, they ask Jesus, "By what authority are you doing these things? Who gave you this authority to do them?" (11:28). Jesus responds, "I will ask you one question; answer me, and I will tell you by what authority I do these things. Did the baptism of John come from heaven or was if of human origin?" (v. 30).

With this particular dispute, Mark is interested in dramatizing what has been prophesied: the rejection of Jesus in Jerusalem. The John the Baptist material which he chose from Jesus' sayings is certainly appropriate in several respects and fits effectively into its context. John had been in conflict with the Jerusalem establishment (according to Matthew and Luke), so that the mention of his name is appropriate at this point when Jesus moves toward intense conflict with the same people.

But there is also another function which his particular passage performs. Immediately following this exchange with the authorities, Jesus will tell the parable of the vineyard about the rejection, wounding, and murder of those sent by the owner of a vineyard to collect the produce which was his due. At least one of these references seems to refer to John. One slave was "beat over the head," and another was killed (12:2-5).

After these two slaves were rejected, the owner sent his son, for he was certain "They will respect my son" (v. 6). But "those tenants said to one another, 'This is the heir; come let us kill him, and the inheritance will be ours.' And they took him and killed him, and threw him out of the vineyard" (vv. 7-8). Jesus closes the parable by indicating the consequence of this rejection: "What will the owner of the vineyard do? He will come and destroy the tenants, and give the vineyard to others. Have you not read the scripture:

> The stone that the builders rejected
>   has become the cornerstone;
> this was the Lord's doing;
>   and it is amazing in our eyes" (Ps 118:22-23).

Jesus uses the parable of the vineyard to build upon the three prophecies of Jesus which refer to his rejection. Notice that this parable is itself a prophecy, one which closes in such a way as to reveal why Mark relates the temple cleansing to the cursing of the fig tree. The vineyard will be given to others. There is a thematic hook here which catches up those pericopes and sayings which refer to the salvation of the Gentiles.

With this parable, Mark also retrieves the organic imagery of the parables of the sower, mustard seed, and the grain which grows mysteriously. Following Williams, I suggested in chapter four (see p. 83) that Jesus was himself the seed of which he spoke. Here, Jesus places an obvious reference to himself within the parable of the tenants, which is dominated by the organic metaphor of the vineyard. The fig tree episode, an acted parable, was also organic. Thus, we begin to see the common denominator guiding Mark's editorial choices as he composes this section of this gospel.

In the course of this analysis, we have often remarked how Jesus' controversies tend to involve specific, sometimes small subjects, which though appearing to be merely topically distributed and organized, in nearly all cases so far, function—with varying degrees of coherence—within the larger thematic patterns of the four envelopes and of the gospel as a whole. Also in this Jerusalem section the controversies, even though seemingly only topical, continue to emphasize Jesus' radical newness and above all, the necessity to internalize the law. Just as in the debate over washing before meals, all of these controversies stress the spiritual aspect of Jesus' teachings as opposed to the legal or strictly messianic interpretations frequently embraced by his opponents.

These controversies represent the penultimate stage in the progression of debates beginning in Capernaum and leading to the ultimate high point in the two trials of Jesus. Their position at this point in the story causes them to function as a summarizing of Jesus' attitude. Once again the Greek word *phroneo* comes to mind, the word Jesus used to criticize Peter after the confession. Spiritual attitude—the stance that one takes before God and the approaching kingdom—is quintessentially important to the understanding of Jesus. The unifying theme which underlies these controversies, then, is Jesus' insistence, in nearly everything he says, on maintaining the right stance in the face of the coming *peirasmos* and the ensuing kingdom.

Even the first topic of debate, concerning payment of taxes (12:13-17), is basically a statement of proper attitude. Deflecting the political issue which motivated a hostile question, Jesus answers "Give to the emperor the things that are the emperor's, and to God the things that are God's" (v. 17). A basic theological point seems to underlie this statement: God's kingdom is essentially of another dimension than the one in which the politics of the present age exist. Whenever Mark presents the political leaders of Jesus' time to us, they invariably range from the slightly sinister to the demonic. They are, in other words, of this world and age, not of the age to come. One's spiritual attitudes are always more important to Jesus because they provide the detachment necessary for spiritual growth, for the right reception of the seed.

I would not suggest that detachment in early Christianity is identical to that concept in Buddhism, but any comparative study would affirm some critical resemblances between the attitude of Jesus and the attitudes of the Buddha concerning detachment.[157] Of course, there would be fundamental differences. But Jesus' Sermon on the Mount in the Q tradition, as well as in the teachings given by Mark, demonstrate at least that Jesus believed the kingdom was not of this world. Above all, in Mark, the believer should be detached from any worldly concern which would distract from receiving the seed and growing. Activism against Caesar is not what Jesus taught. Even though his actions did bring him into conflict with Rome, what Jesus did was always under the aegis of the approaching new age of which he saw himself as messenger. The debate about taxes, therefore, is actually a statement about spiritual attitude and detachment. Thus, when we identify the underlying theme, we can see that even here in this section, Mark's method of organization is not basically topical, but thematic.

The Sadducees' question about the resurrection is itself primarily a political question reflecting the religious politics of the questioners (12:18-27).[158] They present a hypothetical case in which a woman has a series of husbands, all of whom have died, and then ask whose wife she will be after the resurrection. Jesus' answer illustrates the attitude which has dominated all his teachings:

> Jesus said to them, "Is not this the reason you are wrong, that you know neither the scriptures nor the power of God? For when they rise from the dead, they neither marry nor are given in marriage, but are like angels in heaven. And as for the dead being raised, have you not read in the book of Moses, in the story about the bush, how God said to him, 'I am the God of Abraham, the God of Isaac, and the God of Jacob'? He is God not of the dead, but of the living; you are quite wrong" (12:24-27).

Here is another example of Mark's using recursive rhythms to emphasize his points:

A   Is not this the reason **you are wrong**,
   B   that you know neither the **Scriptures**
      C   nor the power of **God**?
         D   For when they **rise from the dead**, they neither marry nor are given in marriage, but are like angels in heaven.
         D´   And as for the **dead being raised**,
      C´   have you not read in the book of Moses, in the story about the bush, how **God** said to him,
   B´   [Quotes **Scripture**] "I am the God of Abraham, the God of Isaac, and the God of Jacob"? He is God not of the dead, but of the living;
A´   **you are** quite **wrong**.

Mark uses the debate which follows, concerning the greatest commandment as an exclamation point to highlight the theme of this entire controversy section. Jesus' own interpretation of Scripture is given here, and Mark uses it to emphasize the attitudes so strongly advocated in the four envelopes: one must meet the coming kingdom with the right stance—not with posturing, but with a strength capable of maintaining integrity even when the ego is selflessly disciplined. When asked which of the commandments is the greatest, Jesus responds:

> The first is, "Hear, O Israel: The Lord our God, the Lord is one; you shall love the Lord your God with all your heart, and with all your soul, and with all your mind, and with all your strength." The second is this, "You shall love your neighbor as yourself." There is no other commandment greater than these (12:29-31).

When the scribe who asked the question also agrees with the answer, adding that these commandments are "much more than all whole burnt offerings and sacrifices" (12:33-34), Jesus tells him, "You are not far from the kingdom of God." If Jesus ever speaks plainly and not in parables, this is it. Mark, in the epilogue and four envelopes, states and dramatizes for the initiate what is important for the acceptance and practice of this new religion. Here he highlights, much as he did in the envelope "Healing the Blind," a basic point he wants to communicate.

The question about the son of David (vv. 34-37) is another of those interesting insertions which moves the initiate away from traditional Messianic concerns just as surely as the previous controversies discouraged him or her from literalist interpretation of Scripture and from obsession with political issues — all of which, if not seen in the right perspective, distract from the spiritual life which must be lived if one is to enter the new age of the kingdom. It is not enough to merely think about the kingdom; it is not enough to be a martinet who steps carefully among the laws; it is incorrect to see oneself as a political citizen of a coming political kingdom. Jesus of Nazareth taught that one must paradoxically live for the kingdom in the face of its approach. The theology of Jesus of Nazareth is existential in its dynamic emphasis upon the celebration of God in present experiences. Jesus, as existential messenger, always confronts people with the present possibility of kingdom, and he always provides the means of actualizing that kingdom in their own experiences, no matter what their caste, class, politics, state of health, degree of sanity, or anything else. The gospel as told by Mark, through its double exposure, makes it clear that this attitude continues in the risen Christ who himself is a further realization of the approaching kingdom. Mark closes the controversy section by underscoring the basic theme. One must be real before God. Establishing the contrast between the posturing scribes (12:38-40) and widow who gave everything (vv. 41-44) allows the evangelist to underscore his theme. As Jesus said in another place, "God is spirit, and those who worship him must worship in spirit and in truth" (John 4:24).

Chapter 13, the section following the controversies, has been called the "Little Apocalypse." Together with the controversy section which precedes it, it provides the sayings portion of Mark's Jerusalem section. While we insist on no formal recursion here (since no easily identified doublets enclose the material), we can observe that Mark nonetheless organizes the Jerusalem experience much in the same way in which he composed the envelopes: he places a package of thematic sayings at a strategic point in the action. In this Jerusalem section, he places the sayings, significantly, before the passion of Jesus.

Mark introduces these apocalyptic sayings with a brief exchange between Jesus and his disciples concerning the temple: "Look, Teacher, what large stones and what large buildings!" (13:1). Then

Jesus asked him, "Do you see these great buildings? Not one stone will be left here upon another; all will be thrown down" (v. 2). Thus, Mark chooses the symbol of the temple as the entrance to his apocalypse, because what will happen to the temple will happen to the whole world. Never has the "yes/but" method of Mark been so sharply abrupt as in his treatment of the temple. First, Jesus, hailed by some as Messiah, enters Jerusalem and immediately cleanses the temple, which to the establishment stands as the guarantor of tradition. And here, in the brief space of two lines, the evangelist both praises and damns the temple. The implicit parallels with the fig tree are inescapable. Coming to Jerusalem has brought Jesus face to face with the opposition. The controversy theme, then, is appropriately capped with a prophecy of the destruction of the temple.

When Jesus prophesies the end of the world (13:7-37), he prophesies, in part, the end of nature ruled by the powers which he has confronted so far in this gospel story. This ending will terminate the power of the stormy forces which whip the sea into frenzy and drive humanity into demoniacal madness. Mark has already depicted these same evil powers as afflicting every part of the human body; his gospel has shown Jesus healing the leprosy-infected skin, the paralysis of limbs, the deafness of ears, the blindness of eyes, the afflictions of speech. Just as Jesus healed these infirmities, the apocalypse which he initiates will begin the healing of the world. Apocalypse will be the turbulence which levels the world to prepare it for the establishment of God's kingdom. Mark's apocalypse, therefore, looks back upon his preceding story of Jesus as healer as well as forward to the prophesies of future destruction.

Jesus leaves no doubt that the end of the world will come because of God's supernatural intervention, but he also portrays the process of apocalypse as manifest, at least partially, within the dimensions of space and time inhabited by humankind. In response to Jesus' temple prophecy, some of the disciples ask when these things will occur. And Jesus says that "nation will rise against nation, and kingdom against kingdom; there will be earthquakes in various places; there will be famines. This is but the beginning of the birthpangs" (13:8). Using the same metaphor Paul uses (Rom 8:22), Jesus portrays our present state of being, ontologically speaking, as suffering in the labor of childbirth. The kingdom will be born, he says, but only after much turbulence afflicts history.

Mark's portrayal of the reality in Capernaum and on the road to Jerusalem was obviously presenting the same world view as that the evangelist portrayed in chapter thirteen. Jesus, as God's messenger, initiates a cosmic crisis; he approaches the demon-afflicted reality of the time, and as messenger he causes a violent reaction. The forces to be defeated recognize him. These are the very forces which must perish before the kingdom can enter. But just as they have been obstinate in this gospel, causing Jesus to make multiple attempts at healing, so these powers will put up a fight as God moves to eliminate them completely. Ironically, these forces, also unwittingly participate in the kingdom's arrival by turning the face of nemesis toward God's son and messenger. In driving Jesus toward his death, they help construct the cross through which people may achieve eternal life. The metaphors behind this cataclysmic end are mixed: birth pangs, messengers, and fights. The common denominator beneath all the images, nonetheless, is the suffering necessary before deliverance.

Jesus prophesies specifically concerning the suffering of the disciples: they will be "beaten in synagogues," and "stand before governors and kings" for the sake of Jesus "as a testimony to them. And the good news must first be proclaimed to all nations. When they bring you to trial and hand you over, do not worry beforehand about what you are to say; but say whatever is given you at that time, for it is not you who speak, but the Holy Spirit" (13:9-11).

This is only the second time Mark has mentioned the Holy Spirit. The first was when Jesus was criticized during the Beelzebul controversy and criticism of his spirit was considered to be criticism of the Holy Spirit (3:21-30). In these passages Mark is revealing something of himself as the author of the gospel. We have seen how he has chosen the relatively detached point of view and he has used the device of double exposure, i.e., portraying the life and character of the risen Christ within the persona of Jesus of Nazareth. In these Holy Spirit passages, however, he drops this double exposure method and briefly moves forward, in author-to-reader comments, to become redactor and commentator, speaking of the Holy Spirit in the high emotion of apocalypse. In fact, he may have believed as much in the Holy Spirit as the author of John's gospel. Both he and that evangelist necessarily look back upon the life of Jesus through the lens of the Holy Spirit, because of the Spirit's connection with resurrection and its interpretation by the disciples and the other witnesses. Mark does not choose to tell the gospel story with constant reference to the Spirit but depends upon his dramatic and literary techniques to present the full portrait of Christ to the audience, who would certainly recognize the comfort and counsel of the Holy Spirit in the actions and words of Jesus of Nazareth.

In this Little Apocalypse, Mark is above all concerned to stress to his audience the historical struggles which are yet to come, the period of fire and testing. Mark still stands on the mount of transfiguration and still prophesies the kingdom "now, but not yet." His apocalypse may be primarily addressed to those who like Simon Peter wanted to build some dwellings to house their revelations. Placing Jesus' prophetic words in this context, Mark makes it clear that this is not the time, within this perishing dimension, to build a dwelling place for the Christ. The apocalypse must come first, in order to clear the way for God's arrival. Without the preparation, God will not dwell with humankind.

Much suffering which will take place during those days of "suffering, such has not been from the beginning of the creation which God created until now" (13:19), but Mark speaks of the elect for whom God shortened the days of tribulation and whom he will save (13:20). After the tribulation will come the final transfiguration of nature itself:

> But in those days, after that suffering,
> the sun will be darkened,
> and the moon will not give its light,
> and the stars will be falling from heaven,
> and the powers in the heavens will be shaken.
> Then they will see "the Son of Man coming in clouds" with
> great power and glory. Then he will send out the angels,
> and gather his elect from the four winds, from the ends of
> the earth to the ends of heaven (13:24-27).

Mark dramatizes the great power and glory of Christ by his complex intertwining of the person of Jesus with the person of Christ. They are one, and not two. They are theologically identical but need a gospel story to make them understood. And as we have stated before, it is Mark's combination of historical Jesus and risen Christ which creates his religious text. He senses a tremendous power in Jesus' person which will initiate the *peirasmos*. His historical existence so coincides with the beginning of the end; it is as if the world is not able to tolerate him, but cries out to him the way its demons did, and then dissolves away, leaving only the Christ. This is actually the experience of the disciples at the transfiguration: Moses and Elijah disappear, and only Christ remains. Now, at the end, the world itself will fade away, once and for all leaving before humans the true ground of his being: Jesus Christ.

Most apocalyptic writers do not know when to stop, but seem to go on and on with their depictions of the end of the world.[159] But Mark's chapter is brief and powerful; and he concludes it skillfully by bringing the reader back down to earth with the organic metaphor, once again, of the fig tree. This time, the lesson from the fig tree is "as soon as its branch becomes tender and puts forth its leaves, you know that summer is near. So also, when you see these things taking place, you know that he is near, at the very gates" (13:28-29).

After the fig parable, there is the statement that "this generation will not pass away before all these things have taken place. Heaven and earth will pass away, but my words will not pass away" (vv. 30-31). Just before the transfiguration, Jesus made another prophecy concerning the kingdom, predicting that many would not "taste death" before the kingdom arrived (9:1). Evidently Mark believed that all the wars and rumors of wars and other elements of the turbulence would occur within the span of a few decades. Mark sees himself standing in that dark time-frame portrayed in his gospel story, looking wearily at the continued heavy passage of time and the suffering it continues to bring. He wants to encourage the persecuted and to assure them that Jesus will soon come to them.

Although Mark is convinced of the imminence of the arrival of the kingdom, he is not dogmatic nor does he fear ambiguities. He portrays Jesus as reluctant to give a sign and thus stresses the impossibility of knowing the time of apocalypse. The precise time of the end of the world is not really of final importance; what is critical for Mark—and he seems to take this from Jesus himself—is the way the believer responds to the crisis of end time:

> But about that day or hour no one knows, neither the angels in heaven, nor the Son, but only the Father. Beware, keep alert, for you do not know when the time will come. It is like a man going on a journey, when he leaves home and puts his slaves in charge, each with his work, and commands the doorkeeper to be on the watch. Therefore, keep

> awake—for you do not know when the master of the house will come, in the evening, or at midnight, or at cockcrow, or at dawn—or else he may find you asleep when he comes suddenly. And what I say to you I say to all: Keep awake (13:32-37).

The metaphor of God the Father as head of the household is one of the major symbols under which Jesus of Nazareth organized his teaching. That familiar symbol would have established in Jesus' listeners a sense of the immediacy of the kingdom. Mark, the teacher, has learned from Jesus, the teacher. This attempt at immediacy of experience is one of the salient and defining characteristics of Mark's religious text. This immediacy is what is intended later, possibly, with the abrupt ending of the gospel, for above all Mark wants his congregation to live with an alert expectancy of the end and at the same time to be the kind of people who can receive the seeds of the growing kingdom.

Providing the transition from the apocalypse is a brief passage about the chief priests and scribes, "looking for a way to arrest Jesus by stealth and kill him" (14:1). Actually, it is more than transition, since it serves to advance the plot toward the death of Jesus. Appropriately, Mark chooses the pericope that follows, the anointing at Bethany, to introduce the Passion because for him it portrays the real triumphal entry of Jesus into Jerusalem. Those who scattered "leafy branches" before Jesus and dreamed of a Davidic king did not understand Jesus or his necessary fate. The woman who anoints Jesus does understand. After she anoints Jesus, the disciples are outraged by the waste of expensive ointment, pointing out that it could have been sold and given to the poor. But Jesus says to them:

> Let her alone, why do you trouble her? She has performed a good service for me. For you always have the poor with you, and you can show kindness to them whenever you wish; but you will not always have me. She has done what she could; she has anointed my body beforehand for its burial. Truly, I tell you, wherever the good news is proclaimed in the whole world, what she has done will be told in remembrance of her (14:6-9).

Jesus predicts his death here much in the same way he did in "Healing Many," when he spoke of the bridegroom who will be taken away. The difference now is in the marked transition to first person. In effect, Jesus here identifies himself as the bridegroom. The focus, which has been gradually shifting throughout the gospel, became clearer with the multiple healings in "Healing the Blind"; and now Mark swiftly sharpens the focus, for he is preparing for the Passover and the betrayal. For emphasis, he employs a recursive construction from 14:1 to 14:11:

> A   Chief priests and scribes plot the death of Jesus.
>     B   The anointing at Bethany.
> A´  Judas betrays Jesus to the chief priests.

Mark's dramatic advancement of the plot with the betrayal of Jesus gives an added sense of inevitability to the action. We shall note, in the epilogue to this book, how tragedy casts a net of fate, and how the end of most tragedies is implicit in their very beginning. Here, we can observe how smoothly events prepare the way for fate and how Jesus is in tune with this flow. He knows precisely where the road now leads, even down to some of the specific details:

> On the first day of Unleavened Bread, when the Passover lamb is sacrificed, his disciples said to him, "Where do you want us to go and make the preparations for you to eat the Passover?" So he sent two of his disciples, saying to them, "Go into the city, and a man carrying a jar of water will meet you; follow him, and wherever he enters, say to the owner of the house, 'The Teacher asks, Where is my guest room, where I may eat the Passover with my disciples?' He will show you a large room upstairs,[160] furnished and ready. Make preparations for us there." So the disciples set out and went to the city, and found everything as he had told them; and they prepared the Passover meal (14:12-16).

When Mark composed the feedings section, he was composing an introduction to the Passover story. That introduction linked the mission of Jesus in Galilee to his activity in Jerusalem. In other words, what the feedings envelope does is to demonstrate to the initiate the unity and integrity of Jesus' life. This is, of course, the final effect of all the envelopes as they unify Jesus' life around basic themes. When Jesus fed the five thousand and the four thousand, he integrated manna and Eucharist; he combined Moses and Elijah midrash with his interpretative actions at the Last Supper. He also moved closer to the first person Jesus who would sacrificially give of himself. Jesus' actions now become explicitly sacrificial. The first portion of the Last Supper pericope, however, is concerned with betrayal, which Mark will now skillfully interweave as a subplot. That subsidiary plot also includes Peter's denials of Jesus. Mark has prepared us for Judas's betrayal when he introduced the twelve disciples, revealing that Judas would betray Jesus (3:19). Likewise, we have been prepared for Peter's denial, because Mark has used him so frequently as a teaching tool. In regard to Judas, when Jesus chooses the twelve, Mark mentions Judas last and immediately yokes the announcement of his betrayal with the harsh Beelzebul pericope (3:20-27). Now, at the beginning of the Passover meal, Jesus prophecies his imminent betrayal by Judas: "Truly I tell you, one of you will betray me, one who is eating with me" (14:18). While prophesying this betrayal, Jesus refers to himself again as the "Son of Man" (14:21), a title closely allied to the Suffering Servant motif which has finally become the dominant theme in Mark's portrait of Jesus.

Even while existing under the oppressive weight of this betrayal and death, Jesus thinks of his relationship to the kingdom:

> While they were eating, he took a loaf of bread, and after blessing it he broke it, gave it to them, and said, "Take; this is my body." Then he took a cup, and after giving thanks he gave it to them, and all of them drank from it. He said to them, "This is my blood of the covenant, which is poured out for many. Truly I tell you, I will never again drink of the fruit of the vine until that day when I drink it new in the kingdom of God" (14:22-25).

Mark now presents a concentric construction of betrayal-sacrifice-betrayal, again with the key sayings placed at the center. For just as the supper was preceded by a reference to betrayal so is it followed by Jesus' references to the desertion by his disciples and to Peter's betrayal.

> When they had sung the hymn, they went out to the Mount of Olives. And Jesus said to them, "You will all become

deserters; for it is written, 'I will strike the shepherd, and the sheep will be scattered.' But after I am raised up, I will go before you to Galilee." Peter said to him, "Even though all become deserters, I will not." Jesus said to him, "Truly I tell you, this day, this very night, before the cock crows twice, you will deny me three times." But he said vehemently, "Even though I must die with you, I will not deny you." And all of them said the same (14:26-31).

Mark's construction can be represented in the following form:

A   Prophecy of Betrayal.
   B   Last Supper.
A´   Prohecies of Desertion and Denial (14:17-31).

The pericope which follows contains the Gethsemane story. After their arrival in the garden, Jesus asks the disciples to sit and wait for him while he prays. He tells them, "I am deeply grieved, even to death; remain here, and keep awake." Then he prays, "Abba, Father, for you all things are possible; remove this cup from me; yet not what I want, but what you want." When he returns, he finds the disciples sleeping. He criticizes them sharply, focusing upon Simon Peter: "Simon, are you asleep? Could you not keep awake one hour? Keep awake and pray that you may not come into the time of trial; the spirit indeed is willing, but the flesh is weak." And he went away and prayed, saying the same words (14:34-39). Just as the disciples have fallen short in both understanding and behavior throughout the gospel so far, they now drift off into sleep. When Jesus returns a third time, he upbraids them: "Are you still sleeping and taking your rest? Enough! The hour has come; the Son of Man is betrayed into the hands of sinners. Get up, let us be going. See, my betrayer is at hand" (14:40-42).

The Gethsemane scene thus forms an interesting "chain":

A   Jesus tells the disciples to remain and watch.
   B   Jesus prays.
A   Jesus returns to find the disciples asleep.
   B   Jesus prays.
A   Jesus returns a third time to find the disciples asleep (14:32-42).

More interesting than the form of the scene is its apparent relationship to apocalypse. The Greek word for watch—*gregorete*—is the word used by Jesus in his long discourse on apocalypse (13:35-37). There is a possible redactive criticism of Peter, James, and John, as if they did not remain alert after the resurrection of Jesus. One could certainly be excused, it seems to me, for concluding at this point that Mark's severely critical focus upon these three is motivated by some hostility toward them—provoked, perhaps, by painful memories of their tardy support of the gentile mission. This, of course, is speculation; the didactic function performed by these three disciples outweighs other considerations, in my opinion.[161]

What impresses most of all, however, is Mark's skill in taking these old traditions and creating a psychological drama of them. Polished or not, the stories of Jesus as Mark tells them remain dynamic. In this episode, he creates the atmosphere of a novel, a later genre which would have great freedom to move into the thoughts of its characters.

Mark now fills in the portrait of Jesus in some depth, portraying him as "distressed and agitated" and quoting him as saying, "I am deeply grieved, even to death" (14:33-34; cf. Heb 5:7). We have been prepared by the three prophecies, explicitly recalled in verse 41: "the Son of Man is betrayed into the hands of sinners." Yet, the story of Jesus is not stilted by any rigid structure. In this Gethsemane scene, Mark is careful to show that Jesus is not a suicidal martinet determined to shape his life in accordance with biblical prophecies. He is fully a human being who acts in freedom. Here that freedom is alive in his dread of death; and he wants very much to choose some other path, or to drink from some other cup. And so he asks God to remove this cup of suffering and death. God does not. By not running away, Jesus demonstrates that he chooses freely to fulfill his role. Thus, the salvation offered to humankind is an offer made in the context of freedom. Even though the tragedy of death brings a heavy sense of fate, by running away, Jesus would have created another all too human tragedy. In other words, Jesus could have disobeyed what he knew was God's will. He did not; he chose to make the sacrifice which he foresaw, with increasing awareness, at least since the time when he compared himself with the bridegroom.

Mark's portrayal of Jesus' freedom as a human being highlights an important soteriological aspect. By this, Mark suggests that we, too, are free to choose. Christianity is not a cut and dried process or a lifeless series of rituals. Jesus himself had to be open to the winds of fate; and even with the knowledge given by prophecy, he paused to doubt and to ask to be acquitted of this duty. The members of a persecuted church who listened attentively to Mark's gospel would have been moved by Mark's portrayal; for they themselves had likely experienced, and were perhaps still experiencing, the same emotions. The Messiah prophesied by John the Baptist has proven to be someone intimately related to their own psychological experiences. Thus, Mark moves further and further into first-person portrayal of the Christ—a Christ who was like you, he says to the believer, and a Christ who is still with you.

The betrayal and arrest of Jesus, as well as Peter's denials, follow immediately after the Gethsemane ordeal. These events represent the sad culmination of all the ironic misunderstandings of Jesus which Mark has so far dramatized. Not to know, not to understand—these were the negatives interlaced within all the envelopes. It is an irony among ironies that the officials who arrest Jesus do not know him sufficiently even to pick him out of a crowd, so that Judas has to kiss Jesus in order to identify him to them. It is ironic as well that Peter on the occasion of one of the denials says, "I do not know this man you are talking about" (14:71). In Sophocles' drama, *Oedipus the King*, it is the ignorance of Oedipus, the protagonist, which is a mainspring of tragic action. In Mark's telling of the gospel story, it is ignorance which contributes to Jesus' crucifixion. Neither his friends nor his enemies understand the nature of the kingdom Jesus announces. Both groups assume that Jesus, in some way, seeks political or at least earthly power. As a result, his friends cannot fully live up to the demands of discipleship and desert him at the end of his life; his enemies simply decide to kill him.

In this series of betrayal, trial, and denial scenes, Mark employs another of his concentric constructions. He builds this structure by placing the Sanhedrin trial of Jesus within the borders of the story of Peter's denials.

    A    Peter in the courtyard by the fire.
        B    The testimony of Jesus before the Sanhedrin.
    A´   Peter's denials (his own ironic testimony) (14:53–72).

Peter denies knowledge of Jesus, and his denials stand in absolute contradiction to his earlier confession (8:29–30). Mark is portraying Peter as an earnest but stumbling follower. He does have the courage to leave Capernaum with Jesus and to go to Jerusalem with him, but during the critical moment his misunderstandings of Jesus overwhelm him. To be sure, he is no villain as is Judas. Peter is a man of good heart, as we can tell from the heart-wrenching conclusion to the denial scene:

> At that moment the cock crowed for the second time. Then Peter remembered that Jesus had said to him, "Before the cock crows twice, you will deny me three times." And he broke down and wept (14:72).

While Peter is denying him, Jesus stands before the Sanhedrin. He finally reveals his identity, or at least tells more than he has ever before. The dramatic significance of this is that Simon Peter now stands outside the place of confession in order to deny Jesus. Meanwhile, Jesus is questioned by the the high priest:

> Are you the Messiah, the Son of the Blessed One? Jesus said, "I am; and 'you will see the Son of Man seated at the right hand of the Power,' and 'coming with the clouds of heaven.'" Then the high priest tore his clothes, and said, "Why do we still need witnesses? You have heard his blasphemy! What is your decision?" All of them condemned him as deserving death. Some began to spit on him, to blindfold him, and to strike him, saying to him, "Prophesy!" The guards also took him over and beat him (14:61-65).

This is the first of two mockeries, the second one occurring after the trial before Pilate (15:16-20). While Jesus is being struck and mocked, Peter, filled with remorse, is literally an outsider. Given this extreme deterioration of relationship, it seems that nothing now could ever reunite Jesus with his disciples. Most of them appear to have already run away; and it is as if the scattered controversies which have surrounded Jesus throughout Mark's story, now unite into one fierce judgment of him. This is especially so in the trial before Pilate. The theme of misunderstanding, of Jesus Incognito, is the basis of this final controversy. Pilate, as so many others have done, asks Jesus who he is:

> Pilate asked him, "Are you the King of the Jews?" He answered him, "You say so." Then the chief priests accused him of many things. Pilate asked him again, "Have you no answer? See how many charges they bring against you." But Jesus made no further reply, so that Pilate was amazed (15:2-5).

The Barabbas scene which follows presents the crowd-chorus at its most menacing. Mark's view of any crowd action is not ever really favorable. The crowds which press against the door in Capernaum are almost threatening in their eagerness; even in the open countryside, the crowds press against Jesus and the disciples and present logistical problems of feeding, comfort, etc.

This time, however, there is no controlling or escaping the crowd, which has taken on the character of a crowd of demons. It is the same legion who possess human beings and even nature; for in the voices of the crowd, we hear the roar of the sea. Not in Capernaum now, Jesus cannot choose the ground for this final battle. He is in enemy territory, and the final assault is terrible.

Pilate offers to release Jesus since "at the festival he used to release a prisoner for them, anyone for whom they asked" (15:6).

> But the chief priests stirred up the crowd to have him release Barabbas for them instead. Pilate spoke to them again, "Then what do you wish me to do with the man you call the King of the Jews?" They shouted back, "Crucify him." Pilate asked them, "Why, what evil has he done?" But they shouted all the more, "Crucify him!" So Pilate, wishing to satisfy the crowd, released Barabbas for them; and after flogging Jesus, he handed him over to be crucified (15:11-15).

Jesus, from Galilee to Jérusalem, has never really been a consistent crowd pleaser. Even though the healings pleased people, Jesus called people, to love God and do God's will. He also placed some severe demands upon them as individuals. Rather than being addressed to crowds, Jesus' call to *metanoia* ("turning about") is always ultimately addressed to the individual, who must soberly and prayerfully reflect upon his or her life. Time and again, Jesus moved away from crowds in order to pray and escape their turmoil. Now Mark demonstrates, in the vicious ugliness of this crowd, that Jesus

# JERUSALEM

indeed had reason to move away from the threats of mob psychology and turn, as he so often did, to the individual conscience.

Following the death sentence, a group of soldiers mocks Jesus. Mark establishes ironic parallels between this mockery of Jesus and the acclamation made at his triumphal entry into Jerusalem. By way of contrast, the mockery is actually a mock-triumphal exit from Jerusalem. Considering these passages side by side, we find few formal parallels, but the formal topical contrast is very strong.

> Many people spread their cloaks on the road, and others spread leafy branches that they had cut in the fields. Then those who went ahead and those who followed were shouting,
> > "Hosanna!
> > Blessed is the one who comes in the name of the Lord!
> > Blessed is the coming kingdom of our ancestor David!
> > Then he entered Jerusalem . . ." (11:8-10).

> Then the soldiers led him into the courtyard of the palace (that is, the governor's headquarters); and they called together the whole cohort. And they clothed him in a purple cloak; and after twisting some thorns into a crown, they put it on him. And they began saluting him, "Hail, King of the Jews!" They struck his head with a reed, spat upon him, and knelt down in homage to him. After mocking him, they stripped him of the purple cloak and put his own clothes on him. Then they led him out to crucify him (15:16-20).

In the triumphal entry, Jesus is hailed as king; so is he now during the exit. The first of hosannas is to the one coming in the "name of the Lord"; the other consists of "Hail, King of the Jews." The first passage portrays the entry into Jerusalem, the other an ignominious exit. These are the only pronounced correspondences, although one might add to them a few other less certain parallels. For instance, the garments also thrown down before the triumphal entry of the king become the garments placed mockingly upon Jesus. The basic parallel, however, is in the inverse echo of triumph with mockery set in the context of exit and entry.

We cannot fail to notice, too, that neither group, during entry or exit, really identifies the Christ. No one can discern him through any political lens. Only the initiate, stumbling onstage with the disciples, knows that to identify the Christ one must always be aware of the pattern of his existence as it unfolds before them. What is now happening to Jesus—mockery and crucifixion—are themselves the events which are answering the riddle and revealing the messianic secret. But one must have eyes to see this public unfolding of the truth. The power of the gospel story is that the telling of the problem gives the answer to the riddle, if one is willing to live that riddle. Jesus who healed and forgave was crucified and resurrected. The whole pattern calls for mimesis, even to the extent of submitting to persecution and mockery. This is what Mark seems to be telling his audience.

Mark uses the Jerusalem section to bring to completion the themes introduced in the envelopes. In so doing, he is able to complete his christological portrait. Even though the parallels between the triumphal entry and the "triumphal exit" do not immediately identify these as doublet twins, it is possible that Mark also constructed this Jerusalem section on the same recursive model that he used to build the envelopes.

The outline on page 169, because it lacks easily identifiable doublets, is not a candidate to be included among the four envelopes. (In order to establish some control over the material, I have not insisted upon any recursion not bounded by the doublets.) But if Mark did intend a recursion, with the sayings at the Lord's Supper as a center (G), we can draw some exciting conclusions from the comparisons between the parallel members of the structure. The entry and exit parallels, at A and A´, when read side by side provide a powerful statement about earthly triumph and spiritual victory. Jesus' triumphal entry was supported by a misconception about his identity, so that it was not really a triumph. The ignominious exit was also prompted by confusion concerning his identity, so that it was actually a triumph.

There are also other significant thematic parallels. A comparison between B and B´, reveals the connection between the death of the fig tree and the prophesied death of the temple (B) with the death sentence given to Jesus (B´). Such a recursion could reflect historical accuracy, since it is probable that Jesus' cleansing of the temple and his sayings about its fall led to his crucifixion. After the temple incidents, Jesus' authority is questioned (C), just as it is later questioned by Pontius Pilate (C'). Both B and C, then, provide incidents which mirror future, more deadly events. The same is true of D, the parable of the vineyard, for that story is acted out by D', in Jesus' trial before the Sanhedrin, who obviously can represent the evil men of the parable who accosted the son of the landowner. The brief reference to the plot to kill Jesus (E), when Judas conspires with the authorities, anticipates parallels at E', where Judas kisses Jesus, and betrays him to the authorities. The Anointing at Bethany (F) is a preparation for death, a mirror anticipating Gethsemane (F'), another preparation for death. The centerpiece of this recursion is the Last Supper, where the central sayings are the eucharistic words of Jesus.

The mockery of Jesus and his being led out for crucifixion provide the close of the construction by presenting the ironic contrasts between exit and entry. The procession out of Jerusalem stops at Golgotha, "the place of the skull" (15:22). There, while being crucified, Jesus is mocked again by passersby, by chief priests and scribes. Because of its importance to the gospel story and to our analysis, I quote the full description of the crucifixion:

> And they offered him wine mingled with myrrh; but he did not take it. And they crucified him, and divided his clothes among them, casting lots to decide what each should take. It was nine o'clock in the morning when they crucified him. The inscription of the charge against him read, "The King of the Jews." And with him they crucified two bandits, one on his right and one on his left. Those who passed by derided him, shaking their heads and saying, "Aha! You who would destroy the temple and build it in three days, save yourself, and come down from the cross!" In the same way the chief priests, along with the scribes, were also mocking him among themselves and saying, "He saved others; he cannot save himself. Let the Messiah, the King of Israel, come down from the cross now, so that we may see and believe." Those who were crucified with him also taunted him.
>
> When it was noon, darkness came over the whole land until three in the afternoon. At three o'clock Jesus cried out

with a loud voice, *Eloi, Eloi, lema sabachthani*? which means, "My God, my God, why have you forsaken me?" When some of the bystanders heard it, they said, "Listen, he is calling for Elijah." And someone ran, filled a sponge with sour wine, put it on a stick, and gave it to him to drink, saying, "Wait, let us see whether Elijah will come to take him down." Then Jesus gave a loud cry and breathed his last. And the curtain of the temple was torn in two, from top to bottom. Now when the centurion, who stood facing him, saw that in this way he breathed his last, he said, "Truly this man was God's Son!" (15:23-39).

Mark has once again combined midrash on Hebrew Scripture with elements of the new religion. In "The Feedings," for instance, he combined manna with Eucharist. In the crucifixion account, he incorporates numerous allusions to the psalms. Jesus' cry to *Eloi* is from the opening lines of Psalm 22. This psalm also was a source of other dramatic details:

> For dogs are all around me;
>> a company of evildoers encircles me.
>
> My hands and feet have shriveled;
> I can count all my bones.
> They stare and gloat over me;
> they divide my clothes among themselves,
>> and for my clothing they cast lots (vv. 16-18).

In Psalm 69, we find the possible source for the reference to the sour wine or vinegar reference (Mark 15:36).[162]

> I looked for pity, but there was none;
>> and for comforters, but I found none.
>
> They gave me poison for food,
>> and for my thirst they gave me vinegar to drink.
>
> (vv. 20-21)

In Ps 109:25, there is a reference to the "shaking" of heads: "I am an object of scorn to my accusers; when they see me, they shake their heads."

Understanding neither how Mark uses midrash to connect Jesus with the Hebrew past and its prophetic traditions, nor how the audience would expect these references, has led some scholars to conclude that Mark has created a fiction in his portrayal of the crucifixion.[163] All of the gospel writers have immersed their stories of Jesus in references to the Hebrew Scriptures. They did this for a very good reason. They wanted their readers to experience the link of Jesus both to the past and to the future prophesied by that past tradition. As was observed in the beginning, Mark's text is a religious text which was written to produce faith in the reader. The first-century Jewish Christians, whether Palestinian or of the Diaspora, were accustomed to midrash in a religious text; their acceptance of Jesus would depend upon their positive conviction that he stood in continuity with their tradition and probably that he was the fulfillment of their law. The God-fearers, the Gentiles who attended the synagogues, also would have known the Hebrew Scriptures and would have understood the portrayal of a present incident against the background of the past. Even the modern reader, with a knowledge of the Hebrew Scriptures, finds much of the significance of Christ's sacrifice in the context of its Hebraic background, as God continues to move closer to humankind. In the vocabulary of this book, Mark's use of psalms to tell this story is another instance of double exposure. In setting the crucifixion against its prophetic background in Israel, Mark affirms the transcendent identity of Jesus as it relates to the purpose and the very person of God.

The rending of the temple curtain recalls the splitting of the heavens at the baptism of Jesus (1:10). The arrival of Jesus as a messenger from God was, for Mark, not just the appearance of a historical person. Jesus' advent is an ontological breaching of a wall that has previously separated human from God. Not only is there a promise to the Gentile in the rending of the curtain, there is promise to all humankind that in the continuing life of the risen Christ there exists a direct avenue to God. Mark, like the author of Hebrews, is aware of Jesus as pioneer who has opened an entry into a new state of being.

> Therefore, my friends, since we have confidence to enter the sanctuary by the blood of Jesus, by the new and living way that he opened for us through the curtain (that is, through the flesh), and since we have a great priest over the house of God, let us approach with a true heart in full

> assurance of faith, with our hearts sprinkled clean from an evil conscience and our bodies washed with pure water (Heb 10:19-22).

It is extremely significant that the centurion, and not Simon Peter, has made the timely and accurate identification of the Son of God. There is no longer any question of a triumphant Messiah, and it is a Gentile who correctly identifies the Suffering Servant.

Mark certainly succeeds in portraying, through the use of understatement, the pain of the crucifixion. The political murder of an innocent man—this is what is portrayed here. Furthermore, this is the gentle person who spoke the parables. This crucified man is the same one who said to love your neighbor as yourself and to do to others as you would have them do to you. For any audience, this contrast of gentleness and murder is almost unbearable to witness. Yet this is the point which Mark has been preparing. Without the cross, after all, Jesus cannot be understood by either Jewish or Gentile Christian.

At Gethsemane, when Jesus continued to try to improve the understanding of the disciples and warned them to be alert, he implied that there were some surprises in store for them. In other words, John the Baptist's portrait would be finally filled in by two surprises. One was the crucifixion; the other was the resurrection (both of which were symbolized in the ritual of baptism).

The denouement, or falling action, of Mark's gospel does at first what the ending of a story usually does; loose ends are tied as we wait for someone onstage, perhaps the chorus, to comment on the action of the drama. So it is when Joseph of Arimethea appears; he is described as "a respected member of the council, who was also himself waiting expectantly for the kingdom of God" (15:43). Pilate allows Joseph to bury Jesus:

> Then Joseph bought a linen cloth, and taking down the body, wrapped it in the linen cloth, and laid it in a tomb that had been hewn out of the rock. He then rolled a stone against the door of the tomb. Mary Magdalene and Mary the mother of Joses saw where the body was laid.
> (15:46-47)

These women have just been mentioned (vv. 40-41), following the death of Jesus and just before the appearance of Joseph, in what at first appears to be a rather casual addition to the end of the drama. But they are the ones who will receive the first impact of the surprise.

> When the Sabbath was over, Mary Magdalene, and Mary the mother of James, and Salome bought spices, so that they might go and anoint him. And very early on the first day of the week, when the sun had risen, they went to the tomb. They had been saying to one another, "Who will roll away the stone for us from the entrance to the tomb?" When they looked up, they saw the stone, which was very large, had already been rolled back. As they entered the tomb, they saw a young man, dressed in a white robe, sitting on the right side; and they were alarmed. But he said to them, "Do not be alarmed; you are looking for Jesus of Nazareth, who was crucified. He has been raised; he is not here. Look, there is the place they laid him. But go, tell his disciples and Peter that he is going ahead of you to Galilee; there you will see him, just as he told you." So they went out and fled from the tomb, for terror and amazement had seized them; and they said nothing to anyone, for they were afraid (16:1-8).

Significantly, the young man tells the women that Jesus goes before them to Galilee. He is, perhaps, telling the initiate the same thing. If you want to see Jesus again, if you want to see him as the risen Christ, then go back to Galilee, to the beginning of the story, "there you will see him." He is saying that in rereading the story of Jesus of Nazareth, in the double-exposure technique of Mark, we will understand the character of the risen Christ, for he is there in everything Jesus said and did in Capernaum, and through the outward extension of his ministry into Galilee, along the road to Jerusalem, and in Jerusalem. The gospel thus becomes an eternal circle to be read and experienced, again and again, as an experience made available to us by the evangelist Mark. And before him, of course, there were those apostles who first shaped this circle with the religious purpose of sharing their experience of Jesus Christ.

The prologue and epilogue of the gospel, as we discussed early in the book, are themselves the enclosures of the story, reflecting one another as John prophesies at the beginning and as the young man in the tomb prophesies at the end of the story. Most scholars believe the story ends here — among other reasons, because the remainder of the text is so obviously written in a different style.[164] For many, this ending is too abrupt; they want to see the appearances of the risen Christ and to share the joy of the disciples. After all, have we not suffered all the way with the disciples as they struggled to understand? Why should we not be given the satisfaction of the ending of the story?

The answer may be that the darkened stage on which Mark leaves the women, and those of the audience who have participated, is the darkened stage of the present time — both Mark's present time and ours as well. After all, the women who go to the tomb experience what others in the gospel narrative experience when they attempt to know Jesus. They reach for him, and suddenly he appears to change or he is not there. Peter discovered this about Jesus on several occasions. We have referred to the evangelist's use of such occasions as a didactic attempt to educate the reader. But was not each such attempt during Jesus' life similar to this attempt at the tomb? Jesus, of course, was really present in the flesh among them, and not only apparently so, as Gnostics would later claim. There was always something transcendent about this man, however, and the reader will sense this in returning to Galilee and reliving these experiences. Mark is, after all, a biography. A biography of the risen Christ.

# Epilogue

Since I have referred to this gospel as a tragic drama and to Jesus as a tragic hero, it seems fitting to conclude the book with some consideration of tragedy, along with insights to be gained from viewing Jesus in such a context. Just as the preceding chapter summarized much of what was said about the themes of the envelope, here I will propose some conclusions about Jesus of Nazareth, both as a theological and a historical person. As we said in the introduction, we cannot intelligently analyze the gospel if we do not understand the nature of its genre. We must be careful, therefore, not to be reductive. To say that Mark's gospel is basically or only a tragedy, for instance, would warp the shape of the religious text and risk the misinterpretation of Christ's person and message.

It is possible — even necessary — for literary criticism to be aware of the mixture of elements within a genre. A tragedy can be written as poetry; epic can use elements of poetry, drama, and even the novel; the short story can use elements of the novel; a novel may be analyzed as a series of short stories, etc. Genres therefore are not unchanging, impermeable forms. On the other hand, neither can we ignore the influence of genre. One cannot read Hamlet as a novel and ignore the poetry or the dominant influences of drama and tragedy. *Moby Dick* contains elements of drama in those places where Melville was influenced by Shakespeare, but we must understand the dominating genre of novel to read the book intelligently.

Mark's gospel is a religious text which uses special symbolism, double-exposure, and a recursive structure to communicate the experience of faith. Furthermore, his religious text is characterized, in part, by the interpretation of Jesus' life through the lens of classical tragedy. This is not surprising, since the first century gives many examples of a "tragic" view of life. For example, the Greek philosophies of Stoicism and Cynicism as well as the Judaic wisdom traditions are imbued with a heavy awareness of the tragic fate of humanity.[165] It is not, therefore, too much to suggest that Mark could have seen Jesus against the background of classical tragedy. Insights gained from an analysis of tragedy in this gospel can significantly contribute to our understanding of the whole work.

Aristotle's definition of tragedy remains a useful definition, but certainly not the only one. He saw the tragic plot as consisting of the fall of a good person from a high place, a fall that occurs in such a way as to provide a catharsis, or purging, of the emotions of pity and fear. It is further characterized by the phenomenon of peripety, or reversal.[166] Events which begin to flow in a certain way, suddenly reverse themselves, frequently turning against the antagonist.

Even a brief rehearsal of Aristotle's definition will reveal how Jesus' life could be interpreted as a tragic life. This does not mean, of course, that Mark had read Aristotle; but it does imply that he knew some of the plays which Aristotle analyzed, or at least some of the Greek tragedies. In regard to the specifics of the definition, Jesus was certainly a good man who was placed in the highest of places. His crucifixion was certainly a fall, and his death was real, even though followed by resurrection. Pity and fear can be felt still, two thousand years later, not only in the Jesus plot as lived by the historical Jesus; but these emotions have continued to be experienced in the lives lived *imitatio Christi*. Modern Christians, in attempting in whatever small way to pattern their lives upon the life of Jesus, are involved in a tragedy; any real commitment is a step onstage to follow a tragic figure.

The later tragedies of Shakespeare add elements to plays that would surprise Mark, but the first-century Christian would understand how that English writer was using and interpreting classical traditions. Lear, for instance, like Oedipus, is a classical tragic hero. In his conflict with his daughters over the rule of his kingdom, Lear suffers greatly. The tragic reversals of this drama throw the king down from a high place. After being attacked by his monstrous daughters, he experiences a ripeness, however—the fullness of experience and wisdom which is the only redemptive feature of classical tragedy. This feature of ripeness can be seen as well in the blind Oedipus, tapping his cane before him, as he meditates upon the insights brought to him by his tragic experiences. One might well ask, Who needs it? Is wisdom any compensation for such suffering? The ancient audience, and many Elizabethans, would probably respond that the tragedian is merely presenting what is true.

Of course, who would not prefer a life free from suffering? Wisdom is the only reward possible.

Shakespeare really was interpreting a classical form of the genre when he composed his plays. For Shakespeare, too, the tragic hero lived in a state of being which involved the struggle of the forces of good and evil. Earlier, in Sophocles' *Oedipus*, nature itself has been wounded by Oedipus's crime. The populace of Thebes understands that justice must be done, some expiation effected, if nature will return to a less corrupted existence. Animals are dying; people are suffering—all because of the crime of Oedipus, which is hidden even from himself. That drama develops a strong identity theme as the king in searching for the truth is actually searching for his own past, his own true identity. The dramatic ironies, resulting from this basic fracture in nature and human consciousness, become so intense they set the teeth on edge. In *Macbeth*, Shakespeare captured such an atmosphere when the horses become carnivorous just before Duncan's murder, as if nature itself has been perverted by human evil. In *Hamlet*, too, this perversion of nature appears: "They say, the night ere Julius was killed, the sheeted dead did squeak and gibber in the streets."[167]

The tragic hero lives in a world wounded by evil; and frequently that hero must sacrifice himself, as Oedipus and Hamlet did, in order to restore both justice and nature's alternate state of harmony. "The time is out of joint," Hamlet says. "Cursed be the spite that I was born to set it right."[168]

At the end of the tragedy, order is frequently restored; but only at great cost. Invariably the best and the most interesting people are dead, and the stage is populated by those squares who want an orderly life in a settled society. Creon, the ultimate stuffed shirt, outlasts Oedipus. At the end of Romeo and Juliet, the audience is left with only the old Capulets and Montagues. Characteristic of the genre of tragedy is a sense of the waste of the good.

In Mark's instance, however, the idea of the tragic hero is complicated by the admixture of Palestinian Jewish notions. This is what is meant earlier when the statement was made that one must be careful not to ignore the integrity conferred by genre. Mark's presentation of Jesus can only finally be understood by analyzing both the Judaic and Helleniistic traditions. The typology of the prophet in the Hebrew Scriptures, as well as many elements of the exodus epic, must be included in any final analysis of Jesus. In Mark's genre, both traditions have affected the interpretation of Jesus' life. Although the Jewish background was the main influence upon this book, the Hellenistic notions of tragedy also provide significant interpretive analysis.[169] Against the background of tragic figures in the Hebrew Scriptures, it would have been natural for Jesus to interpret his own life as tragic; and it would not be surprising if the disciples and other of his contemporaries did as well.

After inheriting the mantle of John the Baptist, Jesus immediately was brought into conflict with authority. He stepped into the Elijah typology of apocalyptic end time, and thus he was pushed toward the turbulent center of his own time. His contemporaries, evidently at Qumran and elsewhere, during these years felt that people were existing in a time of waiting. It is not difficult to compare the perverted, hurt world sometimes portrayed in Greek and Shakespearean tragedy with the injured, dying world of first-century Palestine. A dominant hope seems to have been for supernatural deliverance from a corrupted world. The prophet Isaiah had spoken of a new time, a time when God would deliver even nature itself and when the "trees would clap their hands" (55:12). Jesus of Nazareth, then, came to help set these things right. Both Hellenistic and Judaic cultures would recognize such a rescuer. Like the later Hamlet, he had to suffer not only "spite" for his efforts, but also the crushing weight of nemesis, of all those forces which he provoked to move against him.

Like other tragic protagonists, Jesus' struggle has involved a search for identity. In this case, however, Mark dramatizes not so much Jesus' struggle to understand himself, but the struggle of his disciples and opponents to understand him. It was their misunderstandings which ultimately destroyed him.

There are strong implications, even in many of the traditions inherited by Mark, that Jesus did have to struggle with the nature of his identity and of his mission. This struggle was evident in the temptation by Satan in the wilderness, the retreat to the wilderness when he decided to extend his ministry, and at many other times in some place apart, when he needed to pray and meditate about his mission. Gethsemane, of course, was the climax of these temporary withdrawals. Jesus prayed in the garden that he not be required to drink the cup of martyrdom. Just as Mark has not hesitated to show the supernatural power inherent in Jesus, neither does he hesitate to present Jesus as a human being.

Thus, Jesus is not portrayed as a supernatural persona. Such a figure, like other superheroes, would experience no real defeat. This view, during the first century and later, characterizes the attitude of the Gnostics. The gnostic Christ, unlike the tragic figure, does not really suffer or die;[170] The gnostic Christ stands aside and laughs, watching his apparitional image die on the cross. Christianity, from the outset therefore, needed the leaven of tragedy—a sort of Hellenistic "leaven"—in order to preserve its integrity. Without that leaven, Christianity would be characterized by the brittle giddiness of gnostic cult. Mark therefore includes the characteristics of the tragic hero in his portrayal.

Under the image of the *pharmakos*, the scapegoat who should be killed by the community, Jesus represented the suffering of innocence. Unlike Oedipus, Jesus did not bring the net of fate down about him by some hot-headed hasty action. Jesus was born into the tragic end time where two ages—two states of being—were in imminent collision. His initial role was that of messenger, one continuing the work of John the Baptist. His role quickly changed, and in the face of nemesis, he was constantly challenged to maintain his integrity. He did.

Mark's gospel is different from classical tragedy in that there is a stronger hope for the eternal life of the human soul. Such a life would always, in a sense, provide a happy ending. But that eternal life is not entered without tragic suffering. Thus, tragedy is not just a possibility in the Christian context; many have even considered it an essential part of the Christian experience. Christians must live, homesick for heaven, in a tragic dying world. The best Christian tragedy, then, does not sentimentalize death and loss, simply because it looks in hope to an afterlife in heaven. In Hawthorne's *The Scarlet Letter*, we may assume that Dimmesdale and Hester may go to heaven, but what the plot of the story has dramatized is the insight the preacher and his lover gained through suffering. Hester Prynne, the sinner, became literally a minister to the needs of the community, placing herself at the disposal of suffering townspeople. They would not speak to her if they passed her on the streets, but she was the first they called when there was sickness in the community. Dimmesdale's suffering finally results in ripeness as well. The preacher gains the "tongue of flame" and since his tragic secret is not known, his congregation stands in awe of his power and wonder at his wisdom.

Christians actually suffer, and though they may not grieve as others do, they actually die. In the Hebrew Scriptures, Job's losses were recovered and his disease healed, but how he suffered! Jesus who died a full death is, of course, the prototype of the Christian tragic figure. His experience remains unique in many ways. In his life, the divine was intermingled with the human, and he appeared as God's messenger. His story tells of a contact between God and humanity; Christianity is a tragedy in the sense that the story involves the suffering and brutal murder of God's son. These events were real and were not made unreal by the offer of salvation (made in the context of tragedy). Jesus' story, combining suffering and transcendence, gives Mark his gospel, with its dimensions of tragedy and faith.

Jesus crosses the Jordan as the messenger from God. Who are the people which this messenger seeks out? Who, in other words, is God attempting to contact in this time of crisis? Jesus goes to the outcasts of society, the crippled, the insane, the diseased, the homeless, the broken. His commitment is, of course, to all humankind, but his specific approach to the suffering is what defines his tragedy and triumph. The beautiful paradox created by Mark's presentation is that the Son of God, identified with the divinity of his Father, committed himself to the lowliest of humanity. The tragic action of this plot, enacted historically by Jesus of Nazareth, takes shape from Jesus' unwavering commitment to these people. He comes to them at the time of turbulence: this age is giving way to a new one. The transition is not going to be easy, and everyone is not going to make it. John the Baptist assures all within earshot of that! People live on the edge of a whirlpool of impending crisis. This was the message of both John and Jesus. Between the two ages was thought to lie a period of trial or testing by fire. This would be the notorious time of *peirasmos*, or testing. John speaks of it often in terms of grain on the threshing floor and of the chaff being thrown into fire. Jesus spoke of it, as a time when people should have houses built upon rock and not sand. He calls for a readiness and alertness in the face of the approaching catastrophe. Jesus' mission is a tragic one, then, in that he has to function within a nature warped by all the dangers of this approaching transition. Not only in Mark's drama, but perhaps in the "self-consciousness" of Jesus of Nazareth, tragedy must precede kingdom.

# EPILOGUE

Satan, the prince of this world, is, appropriately, the first antagonist to face Jesus in Mark's gospel. One could conclude that Mark maintains that Satan does control the fate of Jesus and does orchestrate the discord that finally kills him. But Christian faith assigns this ultimate control of classical *moira*, or fate, to God; thus only with the permission of God can Satan maintain any sway over the life and times of Jesus. In a way, this is Satan's hour—his own period of triumph—into which Jesus is sent. In a grand chess game involving the fate of the cosmos, Satan apparently wins, as Jesus moves, following the fate of the tragic hero, toward Jerusalem and toward the cross.

By the time Jesus and the disciples reach Jerusalem, events take on an inevitable flow. Jesus prophesies concerning the arrangements for the ride into the city and the details concerning how to find the place at which they will stay in Jerusalem. There is a sense here that is found in all tragedy, the sense of necessity. The end of a tragedy is implicit in its beginning, as the protagonist becomes enmeshed in a net of fate. In this case, God wins the game, as it were, because all along Satan has been duped into causing just exactly the order and conclusion of events necessary for the salvation of humankind. The cross is the ironic "victory" of Satan which leads to the resurrection of the Son of God with the living and ongoing offer of salvation to humankind. To be sure, this is a simplistic statement of what happens; neither Mark nor any other evangelist says such things explicitly. But these patterns do shine through the stories about God's son and his experiences upon this earth.

If tragedy is transcended by the new faith, that transcendence owes its victory to Jesus' commitment to the real earth and its real suffering people. Jesus Christ, seeing the net falling about him, never deserts his mission and the suffering ones to whom he came. He transcends tragedy by accepting it. Far from being some ghostly, gnostic abstraction on a tour of the universe, Jesus of Nazareth finds his identity in serving those to whom God sent him. The historical Jesus came speaking of a great banquet, and he told stories of those living along the highways and hedges and how they would come to that great banquet. He transcended the world by immersing himself in it. He embraced his tragedy, once he discovered that it could not be avoided. Thus, he encouraged the first Christians, as well as those living some two thousand years later, to have faith that God is somehow behind the events of their lives. He encouraged people to believe something staggering: that God is interested in their personal histories, in all their struggles and hopes. It is not in abstraction, primarily, that we find the Christ, but in the world. In him, we remember not only the future as distance, but also the future as a dimension somehow enfolded with present events.

"Love calls us to things of this world."[171] In loving the men, women, and children of God's creation, God moved downward to identify with them in all their weakness, sin, and fallibility. Just as any lover must accept the imperfections and flaws of the beloved, so God approached humankind in spite of its flaws. God did not forgive casually, as with the wave of a hand. God, through Jesus, entered into the experiences of humankind so as to take its pains and burdens on himself. God not only forgave with the abstract forgiveness of theology; God forgave by entering into the trials of our existence and by demonstrating victory over those trials and limitations. God forgave humankind from the inside-out, not from the outside-in.

The good news of Jesus announces the arrival of God within our experience. By committing himself courageously to our existence, Jesus becomes the only tragic hero to transcend tragedy. Tragedy, it turns out, can be transcended through God's ultimate victory over the false identities imposed by the world upon suffering humanity. Looking into mirrors on earth we see only a reflection of who we really are. This, too, is the good news. This all-too-solid image of my earthly life, this image given to me by my parents and by my culture—this image will die. When we stand with the women at the close of Mark's gospel and see the empty tomb, we know that our tragedy—our own fateful identity struggle will be transcended. Down to the earth and into and through the earth, Jesus was given. He makes possible the achievement of final identity :

> See, the home of God is among mortals.
> He will dwell with them as their God;
> they will be his peoples,
> and God himself will be with them;
> he will wipe every tear from their eyes.
> Death will be no more;
> mourning and crying and pain will be no more,
> for the first things have passed away (Rev 21:3-4).

We, like Jesus, journey incognito through this world. We hope, however, for the confirmation and continuation of our identity as children of God:

To everyone who conquers I will give some of the hidden manna, and I will give a white stone, and on the white stone is written a new name that no one knows except the one who receives it (Rev 2:17).

# Appendix
## Mark's Concentric Constructions and the Synoptic Problem

A near consensus exists among New Testament scholars that Matthew and Luke used Mark's gospel. While not nearly as certain as they once were about this synoptic relationship, most find it improbable that Mark, if his gospel were secondary, would have omitted the Sermon on the Mount, for instance, along with most of the parables.[172] A comparative study of the three gospels' usage of concentric constructions might prove to be an effective tool for suggesting an answer to this perennial problem of New Testament criticism.

Both Mark's prologue (including the baptism, brief temptation, teaching summary, synagogue; 1:1-28) and his epilogue have parallel structures embodying some of the major themes of the gospel. If Mark's gospel is primary, his prologue is largely dismantled and then absorbed by both Matthew and Luke into their own stories about Jesus' birth or youth. Matthew's wise men, the flight into Egypt, and the extended temptation story form the bulk of his own prologue, with John's baptism of Jesus lacking much of the emphasis given by Mark. Luke emphasizes the baptism of Jesus even less. Both turn their attention to an expanded version of John's activity, and both give largely parallel (Q) examples of John's own teachings. The expansion of the temptation scene by both is a strong departure from Mark. Much of the power of Mark's introduction was provided by its stark brevity, highlighting above all Jesus' connection with Hebrew scriptures in the person of John the Baptist. Mark uses simple dramatic scenes to portray this theme, while Matthew and Luke use more explicit references to the Hebrew Scripture and focus attention upon stories concerning Jesus' birth or youth.

The envelope, "Healing Many," (1:29 - 3:12) consists of the following pericopes: healing many, a tour, the leper, the paralytic, the calling of Levi, the fasting sayings, the plucking of grain, the man with the withered hand, and the second half of the healing-many doublet. Luke, if he used Mark's construction, remains closest to him, for he not only preserves most of Mark's concentric construction, he also comes very near creating one of his own by introducing another closely related pair—the calling and choosing of disciples. Compare the following diagram of Luke's construction (4:38 - 6:19) to my diagram of Mark's "Healing Many" on page 51.

(Healing many-tour)
    Calling disciples
        Healing leper
            Healing paralytic
                Calling Levi—sayings
                Fasting—sayings
            Plucking grain
        Healing man (withered hand)
    Choosing twelve
(Healing many)

This is not a polished construction, but it is extremely close and is intriguing because it provides a new envelope-frame for much of Mark's material. If Mark used Luke's gospel, he might have found his basic organizational ideas in Luke's pattern. If Luke used Mark, however, the material represents a "shank" of Mark's writing excised to preserve its concentric construction and then inserted within another arrangement.

Matthew, after his pericope concerning the calling of four fishermen, uses the healing-many scene (4:23-25), but then introduces his Sermon on the Mount (5:1 - 7:29). The sermon is immediately followed by the cleansing of the leper (8:1-4), after which he includes another healing-many scene (8:14-17). The paralytic scene begins the ninth chapter. Matthew then reverts to Mark's order by placing the calling of Matthew (Levi) next (9:9-13). Whereas Luke used Mark's material to structure a significant part of his own gospel, Matthew is not, at this point, very interested in Mark's organization. (Those wishing to find support for the view that Mark used the other two synoptic gospels may find some very interesting comparisons here, since Mark would have sacrificed the Sermon on the Mount in order to follow the dramatic series of actions presented by Luke.)

In Mark, the envelope of the twelve included the following scenes: choosing twelve, the Beelzebul incident, the mother and brothers, the parables section (seed and light), the calming of the storm, the Gerasene demoniac, the pericope of Jairus's daughter and healing the woman, the rejection at Nazareth, and the sending of the twelve. Matthew preserves some of Mark's order by placing the mother-brothers scene (3:31-35) immediately before the parable of the sower. There is, too, another interesting parallel. Mark placed the Beelzebul incident just before the mother-brothers scene; Matthew precedes the family scene, not with Beelzebul, but with Jesus' sayings about another demonic subject, the return of the unclean spirit (Matt 12:43-45). This at least suggests that most of the oral traditions relied heavily upon *theme* to organize its material. Matthew also keeps the storm-demoniac continuity (4:35 - 5:20), where once again a thematic "organizer" can be inferred as healing of the mind is associated with the healing of nature, creating the double exposure of earthly Jesus and risen Christ.

Luke has already, as we have seen, made his own use of the calling and choosing of the twelve. Once again a thematic pattern remains constant even though the specific pericope is different. For example, Mark precedes the parable of the sower with a reference to Jesus' mother; Luke chooses the same position for his apparent digression concerning the women who followed Jesus (8:1-3). Luke also keeps the storm and demoniac passages as a symbolic pair (8:22-39). By proceeding immediately from the demoniac into the combined stories of Jairus and the woman's faith (8:40-54), Luke, for a space, follows Mark. Luke's most well-known change from Mark's order involves the moving of the rejection of Jesus at Nazareth forward to Luke 4:16-30, where it is revised to be used as a part of the prologue to Luke's gospel! If, on the other hand, Mark used Luke, he revised Luke's scene and placed the rejection just before the sending of the twelve, perhaps providing motive for Jesus' expansion of his ministry both in numbers of disciples needed against increased resistance and also a possible motive for his moving out away from Nazareth—just as he had previously moved out beyond the region of Capernaum.

Mark's envelope bordered by the feedings of five thousand and four thousand is constituted by the following scenes and groups of sayings: The old (death of John the Baptist), feeding five thousand, walking on water, healing the sick, tradition of elders (sayings), the gentile woman, the deaf and dumb man, the demand for a sign, and the old (the caution about the leaven of the Pharisees and of Herod). Like Mark, Matthew precedes the first feeding scene with the death of John (14:1-12), suggesting that he also finds it significant that Jesus' ministry surpasses John's. Jesus, for example, is not shown baptizing, but as doing much more: healing the bodies and minds of the people, and providing new manna for Israel. Walking on water immediately follows the first feeding in Matthew as well (14:22-33), as we see Jesus already revealing the power of the risen Christ, who rules over all powers. As Matthew continues to follow Mark with healing the sick, the traditions of the elders, and the Canaanite woman (Matt 14:22 - 15:28), we realize that it is Matthew, instead of Luke, who is closely conforming to Mark. Matthew does interpose his own healing-many pericope before the feeding of the four thousand (15:29-31), but aside from this "intrusion," Matthew virtually adopts Mark's concentric construction here, just as Luke had adopted much of the healing-many construction. (It is significant, say those who believe Mark conflated the other two synoptic gospels, that when Mark follows Luke's order, his Greek is closer in style to Luke's, and when he follows Matthew's order, his Greek style is closer to Matthew's.)[173]

Mark's envelope, "Healing the Blind," is ordered as follows: first blind man, Peter's confession and caution, first prophecy, central teachings, transfiguration, the possessed boy, second prophecy, who is greatest?, sayings (little children), rich man, third prophecy, request of James and John, and the second blind man.

Matthew's arrangement is somewhat similar. What one immediately notices is the absence of the first blind man (Mark's unique pericope). In other words, the demand for a sign and the caution about the leaven of the Pharisees (and now Saducees, 16:1-12) is followed immediately, not by the blind man at Bethsaida, but instead by Peter's declaration (16:13-20). Then Matthew again follows Mark's presentation by giving the first prophecy by Jesus of his death and maintaining that order through the second prophecy (17:22ff. Matthew now will include the "Markan" temptations-to-sin material (18:6-9) and the divorce teachings (19:1-12), but these teachings now begin to be interspersed among Matthew's parables (18:10 - 20:16). He still loosely maintains Mark's sequence, however, with teachings about divorce, little children, rich man, third prophecy, and the request of James and John (19:1 - 20:28). This is even though the parables interrupt the progression. Matthew also concludes the approach to Jerusalem with a healing of the blind. If Mark is secondary, this scene could have given Mark his idea for creating his doublet around a thematic envelope. Matthew, if secondary, after the blindness of the *two* disciples, has Jesus heal *two* blind men (20:29-34)! He would thus have his own way of preserving Mark's duality. This is a good example of how these constructions could be compared in order to understand the relationship between texts.

Which is the most probable? Did Mark get an idea from Matthew's symbolic healing and then construct his powerful envelope? Or did Matthew dismantle Mark's blindness doublet and recount only the healing at the end of the section? There is a strong argument, at least in this instance, that Mark has strengthened Matthew's version by relating blindness specifically to Peter's confession as well. It seems to me as improbable that Matthew would weaken Mark, as it seems to some that Mark would ignore the Sermon on the Mount. By creating the doublet, Mark has paralleled his other sections on healing, choosing, and feeding which are also organized within doublets. One must not forget, however, that even though Matthew continues to present *sayings* of Jesus within concentric constructions, he does not seem as concerned with arranging the *doings* (Lund's distinction, see chapter 3 above) in such a manner. In Luke as well, there may have been a historical tendency away from "chiasmus" even though such constructions remained and were obviously still appreciated.

In Luke's gospel, the feeding of the five thousand immediately precedes Peter's confession. Significantly, again, a thematic pattern among the synoptics emerges: instead of yoking the death of John (involving Herod) with the feeding, as Mark does, Luke writes instead of Herod's anxiety just before this feeding. Thus, even though the pericopes change, the theme remains constant. Once again, there is evidence of thematic ordering of oral materials in the synoptic tradition. This may seem too obvious to emphasize, but I call attention to it, since it is my hypothesis that the envelopes, as presented by Mark, take their basic order, not from a rigid chiastic model, but from less formal concentric constructions organized by theme. An ancient writer, of course, would not have used modern critical terms to describe this phenomena, but probably would have worked from typological and ideological similarities to achieve the unity of the gospels. The modern conception of theme, however, is extremely useful in revealing the patterns which have been established.

Luke's main divergence from Mark is, of course, due to his inclusion of the parables into his "journey to Jerusalem" section. Following the transfiguration (Luke 9:28-36). Luke tells of the unsuccessful attempts to heal the boy, once more prophesies his death, and presents some of the same teachings Mark did (9:37-50). Then, however, there follows much of Luke's unique material, including the parable of the good Samaritan (10:25-37). Not until much later (chapter 19) does Luke describe the triumphal entry of Jesus into Jerusalem.

This general overview can only suggest guiding ideas for further research into the literary structure of the gospels. My own opinion is that the relationship between the three synoptic texts is extremely complicated because they represent strands of interrelated oral traditions. In addition, there are undoubtedly missing written texts which represent versions of each of these gospels. Concentric constructions appear, however, to have been operative in oral and written traditions, and thus they provide a common denominator to help study all the synoptics. They might also provide useful clues, at least, concerning the interdependence of texts. Only a careful, close analysis can attempt to clarify this aspect of the synoptic problem.

This general comparison suggests that Mark could well have used the idea of concentric constructions as a structural guide and criteria for his summary of the other gospels. His addition, for instance, of the blind-man pericope to introduce one of his envelopes makes more sense, at first glance, than the later discarding of that story by Matthew and Luke. Mark's unique blind-man story is, of course, "redundant" in that it is half of a doublet he created; neither Matthew nor Luke, however, are bothered by doublets. Matthew, for instance, retains both feeding scenes, just as does Mark. Scholars could, I believe, find many instances where Mark wrote to improve the presentation of the gospel story by heightening dramatic tension, placing scenes in climactic order, and radically eliminating Jesus' teachings not directly applicable to Mark's story. In every envelope, for instance, the sayings are usually placed at or near the center, and invariably express the theme of each envelope.

Arguments concerning the priority of the synoptic gospels, however, are notoriously circular and scholars would have to walk carefully through a field thickly carpeted with land mines. They must necessarily demonstrate, for instance, the strong probability that Mark had good reasons for each change he made, and they would have to counter effectively the currently prevailing view that Matthew and Luke infused Mark's plot with the parables and other sayings of Jesus and in such a manner changed Mark's organizational patterns. I believe, nonetheless, that such a study should be made. These concentric constructions as they appear in Mark's gospel are, after all, not only interesting for the formal and theological insights they provide into his gospel, they are also tools to be used in further examination of the synoptic tradition.

# Notes

See bibliography for complete citations.
For abbreviations see *Journal of Biblical Literature*, 107(1988):588-596.

1. The reader interested in NT criticism should read the works by Bultmann and Dibelius listed in the bibliography. These are both seminal works of form criticism. For a general introduction, see McKnight.
2. The two most influential works of redaction criticism are those of Bornkamm and Conzelmann. I also recommend Perrin's little book.
3. See Kümmel.
4. A full discussion of the transfiguration is given in chapter 6.
5. Johnson, 11.
6. One of the best introductions to the relationship of faith and criticism is Ladd. This book is especially valuable for the believer who is troubled by modern critical approaches to the Bible.
7. See Talbert.
8. Schillebeeckx (*Jesus*, 327) writes of the disciples "Once more going after Jesus" and discusses the relationship of interpretation and repentance.
9. Schillebeeckx, *Jesus*.
10. Several critics have noticed how the baptism scenes and the burial and resurrection scenes could be the framework enclosing the entire gospel and portraying it as a large concentric construction. Mack (332ff) has suggested the following pattern for the gospel of Mark:

    A    John the Baptist (who points back to old-story expectations).
        B    Jesus' Baptism (mythic transition).
            C    Temptation (encounter with demonic).
                D    Call of disciples (positive response).
                    E    Teaching in synagogue (cleansing).
                        F    Mission in Galilee (power).
                            G    Transfiguration (mythic transition).
                        F´    Way to Jerusalem (passion).
                    E´    Way to Jerusalem (cleansing).
                D´    Response of disciples (negative response).
            C´    Temptation and trial (encounter with authorities).
        B´    Crucifixion (mythic transition).
    A´    Angel at tomb (points to renewed expectations).

11. Aristotle, "Aristotle's Poetics," trans. W. H. Fyfe, in *Aristotle, The Poetics, "Longinus," On the Sublime, and Demetrius, On Style*, Loeb Classical Library (Cambridge, Mass.: Harvard Univ. Press, 1932), 4-118.

12. Kingsbury, 27.

13. Kingsbury, 28-29.

14. Williams, 28.

15. Rather than refer both to reader and listener, I shall refer hereafter only to reader. Because the Gospels retain much of the oral tradition and because they were surely read aloud, all references to reader will always imply listener as well.

16. Travis, 153-164.

17. "Ars Poetica," in *The New Oxford Book of American Verse* (New York: Oxford Univ. Press, 1976), 624-625.

18. See especially Meagher.

19. Our notions of plot, character, and theme—of literary analysis—may seem at first to provide an artificial approach to Scripture. But the study of the Gospels as drama is surely long overdue. Historical material, after all, may still be true when cast in the form of drama. In fact, the emphasis given sayings and actions by dramatic form may point to a historical reality the author wanted to stress. It is necessary, therefore, to consider a writing in the context provided both by genre and by milieu.

20. Stock, 103. Stock goes on to say that "both Mark and Jesus himself may have seen Greek dramas performed." Herod Antipas had chosen nearby Sepphoris "as the site of his new capital and royal residence and there he built a beautiful Hellenistic city with a theater seating between 4,000 and 5,000 people." Sepphoris, Stock reminds us, "is midway between the Mediterranean Sea and Lake Gennesaret and the main highway leading south went through Nazareth six kilometers away, an hour's walk. The reconstruction of Sepphoris began about 2 BC and lasted until AD 8 or 10." The intriguing possibility arises that Jesus attended this theater! Stock says that when "Sepphoris and its theater is projected into the landscape, Jesus' youth takes on a very different aspect." And he believes that this new city with its theater "definitely left traces in the Gospels."

21. Stock, 202-203.

22. Kingsbury, vii.

23. *Harper's Bible Dictionary*, (1985), 635.

24. Ibid., 366.

25. Bailey, et al, 42-43. Bailey finds these forms of Midrash in Porter, 55-92.

26. Bailey 156-157.

27. In ancient Roman mythology, Janus was pictured as having two bearded faces, one facing forward, the other backward. He was a god who ruled beginnings and was often seen as the custodian of the universe and the guardian of doors and gates. The name of the first month of the year derives from his name.

28. The first half of this quotation is actually from Mal 3:1. The remainder is taken from Isa 40:3.

29. As the number of references which I make to him will attest, I am most indebted to Stock, whom I have already quoted. See also Van Iersal.

30. Stock, 46.

31. Petersen has shown how John's prophecies help unify this gospel. See especially pages 50ff.

32. Stock, 50.

33. Ps 2:7; Isa 42:1.

34. See Stock, 418. Since this book depends upon the doublets to introduce and define Mark's envelopes, the prologue is not presented as a concentric construction. The reader should notice, however, that such a construction is possibly intended by Mark:

    A    John preaches to many and baptizes Jesus (1–11).
        B    Jesus confronts Satan (12–13).
            C    Jesus begins ministry (sayings at center, 14–15).
            C´   Jesus calls four (16–20).
        B´   Jesus confronts demon in possessed man (21–28).
    A´   Jesus heals and preaches to many (29–34).

35. Stock, 160.

36. Kelber, 15–16. Quoted in Stock, 162–163.

37. Even though there will be storms and turmoils in the gospel, Mark achieves a degree of understatement in brief but powerful scenes in order to dramatize this evil. If Mark knew the so-called Q tradition, he seems to have preferred not to use those heavily dramatic scenes which tend to show Jesus' early triumph over the world (as for instance in the temptation scenes as dramatized by Matthew and Luke). For Mark, Jesus' triumph will come only with the cross.

38. *Eremos*, according to BAGD, 309, as an adjective describes a place "abandoned, empty," or "desolate." As a noun, it can refer to "desert, grassland," or "wilderness," lonely places "which stand in contrast to cultivated and inhabited country."

39. Nineham (p. 70) writes, "It is impossible to be sure whether St. Mark here understood the gospel to mean simply 'the good news'... or whether, as is perhaps more probable in view of his usage elsewhere, he understood it in its full Christian sense and pictured Jesus as using the

later Christian terminology . . . Certainly repent and believe in the gospel is exactly how the later Christian preachers summarized what men must do to be saved."

40. Although each can be interpreted as having concentric form, these boundaries of prologue and epilogue are established somewhat by default, in that they represent material on either side of the body of the four envelopes and the Jerusalem narrative. It is primarily the shared symbols which establish their existence as "frames." The author was careful not to insist upon the presence of recursions unless they were framed within doublets. The formal boundaries established by the doublets, then, are critical to the identification of the envelopes.

41. Stock, 229.
42. Dewey, 110.
43. Bailey, 178.
44. Welch, 9-12.
45. Both terms will be largely replaced by the term "recursion" which is Clark's word and which best describes Mark's constructions.
46. H. G. Liddell and R. Scott, *A Greek-English Lexicon*. Revised edition (1940) with 1968 supplement. (Oxford: Clarendon Press, 1940; 1968), p. 1991.
47. Talbert. This is one of the finest examples of the application of literary critical methods in the study of the New Testament.
48. Welch, 255-256.
49. Welch, 261.
50. The three examples are from Lund, 37-43.
51. Lund, 51ff.
52. Bailey, 182.
53. Lund, 263ff.
54. Lund, 266.
55. Welch, 248.
56. Lund, xvi-xviii.
57. Welch, note, 214.
58. See Lund's example, 34. The NRSV hides the original Greek order, represented by B´. In the Greek, therefore, the order of the chiasmus is present.
59. Lund, 303.
60. Welch, 9-10.
61. Welch, 12.
62. Ibid.
63. Several other critics have found the construction here, although each may find some minor difference. Dewey mentions Giuseppe G. Gamba (1966) as the "first scholar to recognize a symmetrical pattern in

Mark 2:1 - 3:6." She says further that "... in 1973 Mourlon Baernert and I presented independently of each other somewhat different proposed concentric patterns for Mark 2:1 - 3:6" (Dewey, 137). These works are Gamba, Giuseppe G. "Considerazioni in margine alla poetica di Mc. 2, 1-12," *Salesianum* 238 (1966):324-349 and Mourlon Baernaert in "Jesus controverse: Structure et theologie de Marc 2:1 - 3:6," *NRT* 95 (1973):129-149 and also his "Structure litterraire et lecture theologique de Marc 14, 17-523," *L'evangile selon Marc: Tradition et redaction*. Edited by M. Sabbe. BETL 34. Gembloux: J. Duculot, 1974. pp. 241-267. In addition to Lund's version given above, David L. Clark, in the seventies, worked hard in this area. He sees the concentric construction here extending from the John the Baptist introduction to the healing summary which concludes at verses 3-12. Concentric constructions have been identified in this and/or other sections of Mark not only by Lund, Welch, Clark, and Dewey, but also by Bas Van Iersal and Augustine Stock. I shall be referring to their contributions throughout the book.

To interject a personal note, I was initially surprised to discover this consensus, for of all the doublets which we shall analyze, this healing-many doublet was the least obvious to me. There are several references to it, nonetheless, while the function of the other doublets goes unnoticed. The parallels seem more obvious between choosing and sending disciples, the two feedings, and the two blind men; these pairs are extremely close, some of them involving verbatim repetitions. Their significance has usually been ignored both as frames enclosing text and also in their possible relationships to the concentric rhythms which they enclose.

64. Dewey, 110.
65. Ibid.
66. Dewey, 110-119.
67. Dewey, 112-113.
68. Her discussion (pp. 110-119) is built on the premise that C is central, both in the chiasm and in its statement of the large themes.
69. Lund, 40-41.
70. Dewey, 115-118.
71. Dewey, 119.
72. Welch, 13-14.
73. Dewey, 132-134.
74. Welch, 13-14.
75. Clark, 71.
76. If a scholar has no firm definition on which to stand, it is practically impossible to define most New Testament texts as concentric constructions. The area is incredibly slippery, and many overlapping and

even interlocking constructions can be found. In this discussion, I depend heavily upon the doublets as solid places to stand. In every construction interpreted to be a recursion, the position of the material within the doublets has guided my analysis. Even then the surface is slippery! But painful experience with "shifting chiasmus" has made me determined to be careful in defining these structures by ascertaining their limits, their centers, and their interrelationships.

77. For the purposes of this analysis, a doublet may be defined as two passages which closely resemble each other in form and content. In this book, doublet usually refers to that pair of passages which enclose, and thus create the frame of, an envelope. Many scholars object, rightly, to the casual identification of doublets. In other words, if an author is merely carelessly repeating something, then a doublet can have no real significance. In this book, I establish the existence of a doublet by answering the question: Does the material within the doublets exhibit structural integrity? If that integrity is demonstrable, then the doublet was almost certainly an intentional construction.

78. Nineham (p. 82), however, refers to the first passage (1:32-34) as describing the conclusion of a "specimen day." Taylor (p. 180) says it is not a summary passage because it is "a story about Jesus connected with a particular time and place which records things recalled at the close of a memorable day."

79. BAGD, 410, states that the word, in some classical writers and in the Septuagint, means "nearly always 'pursue' in a hostile sense." Nineham (p. 85) says that this Greek word "is used in nine other places in Mark and always in a derogatory sense; it refers either to actual persecution or to seeking Jesus in a wrong and unacceptable way (cf. especially 3:32 and 16:6).

80. See Philip Shuler, *A Genre for the Gospels*. (Philadelphia: Fortress, 1982).

81. Thompson, 47.

82. Thompson, 27.

83. Thompson, 174.

84. The Greek word translated as "sternly charged" is a form of *embrimaomai*, which in Aeschylus could be translated "snort." It can also be translated as "scold, censure, or warn sternly." It is, it seems to me, a strong word considering the context in Mark. See BAGD, 254.

85. Nineham, 86-87.

86. There may be something else in this leper story, as well. Mark surprises us by saying that Jesus sent the leper to a priest. Jesus is seen at his most conservative here. This is, after all, not the Gospel of Matthew, where this pericope finds a more comfortable home at 8:1-4, right after

the Sermon on the Mount. Matthew is never shy about emphasizing Jesus' Jewish "conservatism." This is, of course, just what the historical Jesus would probably have done—send the man to the priest, as was commanded by Moses. But in Mark's gospel, there may emerge a dramatic explanation for this as we examine the following scenes, which demonstrate a progression toward radical newness in Jesus' behavior: his reference to new wine, for instance, and new patches on old garments; his challenges, in the last scenes of the envelope, to the Sabbath laws. The leper episode would be the first conservative episode in a progression toward the radical views of Jesus of Nazareth.

87. Stock, 241.
88. Stock, 241, quoting Kingsbury, 167.
89. In this first detailed analysis of a recursion, it seemed best to move back and forth from the linear plot to the recursive order. In this way, the reader is spared the necessity of reading back through the story again, and it is possible to discuss scene by scene both Mark's linear and recursive comparisons. In regard to the other three envelopes, the recursive analysis, for the most part, will not begin until the center of the construction is reached. In that way, the reader can observe, in the episodes after the sayings, how Mark is comparing the second arm of the recursion with the first.
90. Nineham, 106.
91. See the discussion beginning on p. 119 in Dewey.
92. Nineham, 103.
93. Ibid.
94. This has been noted by many, e.g., Kingsbury, passim.
95. Stock, 125.
96. Here again is apparently a pre-Marcan link between crowds and eating, as if this introduction once served as the beginning of a feeding pericope.
97. "He has gone out of his mind" involves a translation from the Greek verb *exesti* (third person singular of *existemi*), which in classical literature could be translated variously as "change, displace," "become separated" or "astound" in our literature refers only to "spiritual and mental balance." It means to "lose one's mind, be out of one's senses." BAGD, 276.
98. Joachim Jeremias (230 and note) writes, "For he has been manifested whose veiled kingliness shines through every word and every parable—the Savior." And he adds that in the parables are found the "veiled christological self-attestation of the historical Jesus."
99. Williams, passim.
100. Williams, 43.

101. Williams, 45.
102. Williams, 45-46.
103. Ibid. Italics mine.
104. Williams, 47-48.
105. Williams, 190-191. Metonymy is a figure of speech which substitutes the name of a thing or idea for the name of another related object. For example, in the substitution of "scepter" or "crown" for "sovereignty" or of "bottle" for alcoholic drink.
106. Williams, 181.
107. *Harper's Bible Dictionary* (p. 215) identifies the Decapolis as "a federation of ten cities of Hellenistic culture in an area east of Samaria and Galilee. The Roman scholar Pliny the Elder ... lists them as Damascus, Philadelphia, Raphana, Scythopolis, Gadara, Hippos, Dion, Pella, Gerasa, and Canatha."
108. See especially Stock, 165ff. Other references to "the other side" in Mark occur at 4:35; 5:1; 5:21; 6:45; and 8:13.
109. So Helms, by revealing midrash, tends to debunk the gospel story.
110. While structural clues reveal that this antithesis was important for Mark, more significant is the continuing development of Mark's christology. Using the symbolism of the Eucharist, Mark makes meaningful additions to the developing portrait of Christ, as he continues to fill in the blank spaces left by the prophecies of John.
111. Stegner, 77-81.
112. Stock, 217.
113. Williams, 125.
114. Stock, 223ff.
115. Kingsbury, 99-102.
116. Stock, 162-163.
117. Kelber, 16.
118. Stock, 76.
119. Stock, 102.
120. Williams, 114.
121. Williams, 118-120.
122. Williams, 99-101.
123. Williams, 99.
124. Stock, 121.
125. This is, of course, Mark's notoriously confusing description of an itinerary from the region of Tyre toward Galilee: "Then he returned from the region of Tyre, and went by way of Sidon towards the Sea of Galilee, in the region of the Decapolis" (7:31). In this English translation, as well as in the Greek, the description ends with the Decapolis and turns

immediately to the healing of the deaf man who seems to be, logically, in the last described location. It is the placing of this deaf man's scene next to the healing of the Syro-phoenician woman's scene (7:24-30) which increases the probability that these were both gentile healings. Another crossing of the sea does not occur until the second feeding, at which time Jesus and the disciples go to the region of Dalmanutha (8:10). Some authorities say Magdala instead, which is on the western side of the sea. That would, of course, further support the idea that previous scenes were to the east, in gentile territory. It is after making this crossing, furthermore, that Jesus encounters the Pharisees (8:11ff), as one would expect to happen upon the return to the Jewish "side" of the sea.

126. Quoted in Nineham, 207-208.

127. In Greek mythology, Prometheus was the Titan who stole fire from Olympus in spite of warnings from Zeus. As punishment for thus helping humankind, Zeus caused him to be chained to a rock while an eagle constantly tore at his liver. Prometheus was finally released by Hercules.

128. One should not, of course, read Mark as a Pauline document, but the similarities are there.

129. Stock, 286, also p. 28.

130. Stock, 32.

131. Taylor (p. 380) writes that the Greek verb (appearing as well in Matt 16:23; Acts 28:22; Phlm 22; 1 Tim 6:17) means "'to be minded'... either of reflection or purpose ... the verb keeps in view the direction which thought (of a practical kind) takes." BAGD, 866, notes that, followed by the accusative, as it is here, the verb can imply setting one's mind upon something, being intent upon it, or even taking someone's side or espousing their cause.

132. Nineham, 227-228.

133. Cranfield, 277.

134. "This section consists of excerpts from a collection of sayings and is inserted at this point for topical reasons." Taylor, 122.

135. Quentin Quesnell, quoted in Stock, 34.

136. Nineham, 232.

137. For a useful summary of criticism regarding the transfiguration as a rearranged appearance episode, see Gundry, 471ff.

138. According to Thrall, Peter makes his primary mistake in seeing Jesus as only the equal of Elijah and Moses.

139. In regard to divine commission, voice, and light (luminosity), see especially Enoch 14:17-21; Ezek 1:26-28; Dan 7:9-10 and 8:17; Isa 6:1-2 (compare also the three accounts of Paul's conversion in Acts 9:1-19; 22:3-21; 26:9-18). These parallels are discussed in Munck, 31ff. He cites

them as the background for Luke's descriptions of Paul's conversion experience. Just as Luke undoubtedly used the Hebrew Scriptures to affirm Paul's divine commission, Mark probably has these same Scriptures in mind to affirm Jesus' identity and purpose.

140. Schnackenburg, discussed and quoted in Stock, 247-248.

141. I have difficulty finding critics who share this idea. Nineham, 245-246, does admit the possibility that Mark has Moses in mind, but he sees the comparison as being very general with very few close verbal parallels.

142. See Childs's provocative discussion of NT writers as canonizers, especially his discussion of Mark on pp. 82-95. Some may think that the process could not have begun as early as the first century, but have already seen some internal features of Mark's gospel which suggest that he is deviating from another interpretation of tradition. From the beginnings of the church, and perhaps especially then, it was necessary to choose among competing traditions, whether oral or written.

143. One is reminded here of Talbert's (pp. 5ff) excellent analysis of Luke's tripartite portrayal in Acts of Paul's conversion experience. His discussion of "architectonic design" is especially interesting. Talbert discusses how many ancient writers, including Homer and Virgil, repeat key verses or scenes not only for emphasis but also to achieve esthetic balance. He also shows how the New Testament writers were influenced by this mode of composition. In his discussion of the Old Testament, Alter (92-95) has also called attention to what he calls "the technique of repetition."

144. See Aries. Crossan (28-29) gives examples of the child in apprenticeship in the first century.

145. Nineham makes the same speculation, 253-254.

146. There is a possibility, too, that "little ones" here refers to the devout Christians who were persecuted. If so, a new dimension of meaning appears, in that the vehement evocations of hell fire in this section could be parabolically directed toward the recent persecutors of Christians in Rome.

147. Clark's diagram appears in Welch, 234.

A   Healing blind man at Bethsaida.
   B   Peter's confession.
      C   First prophecy.
         D   Transfiguration.
            E   Healing boy.
               F   Second prophecy; central instructions.
                  (Includes who is greatest?).
            E´  Blessing children.
         D´  Leaving all to enter kingdom (includes rich man).
      C´  Third prophecy.
   B´  Request of James and John.
A´  Healing blind Bartimaeus.

148. There is an interesting stylistic parallel here between this saying and the parable of the sower. Both the manifold growth of seed in the sower parable and now the manifold reward for discipleship are dependent upon the same idea of abundant rewards for good discipleship. Mark's symbols gain weight, as it were, by accumulating additional meaning every time they appear and reappear. On a second reading through this gospel, we can find much more in the parable of the sower and can do so without reading into the text. Again, this is the effect of Mark's hermeneutic circle, of his charging the component parts of his gospel with the message of the whole, and of enriching the whole of the gospel with the energy emanating from the parts. It is the Suffering Servant which now enriches, in retrospect, the parable of the sower. There is a price to pay for discipleship; and even when Jesus promises rewards, he adds the lessons taken from the child: "But many who are first will be last, and the last will be first." (10:31).

149. Clark, quoted in Welch, 234.

150. Luke's use of theophany is discussed in Lohfink, passim.

151. This is the first reference to ransom in Mark, and he does not elaborate upon that metaphor. But there is some connection between the root meaning, which refers to redemption from slavery, and the meaning the Suffering Servant theme has acquired up to this point in the gospel. BAGD, 205-206, defines Mark's word *lutron* as "price of release" or "ransom." It also comments that *lutron*, mostly when used in the plural, can denote "the ransom money for the manumission of slaves."

152. Crossan (43-71) presents an interesting discussion of first-century social stratification.

153. In fact, he has been as Isaiah prophesied: "A bruised reed he will not break, and a dimly burning wick he will not quench" (Isa 42:3).

154. Cullman, 12-25, provides an excellent analysis of early church ritual.

155. Concerning the symbolism of the fig tree, Nineham (p. 209) writes that the "manner and place of its insertion strongly suggest that the story was intended to make a didactic point, the fate of the fig tree symbolizing the fate that awaited Jerusalem and the Jewish people and religion." He says this interpretation is strengthened "by the parable in Luke 13:6-9, where the fig tree clearly represents the house of Israel, and also by such Old Testament passages as Jer 8:13, Joel 2:7, Ezek 17:24, Mic 7:1-6, and Hos 9:10, 16-17."

156. Nineham (p. 305) sees the "Have faith in God" sentence (v. 22) as "probably a Marcan addition . . . to effect the transition from the story to the teaching which follows."

157. Thomas Merton explores similarities between these two religions in regard to the experiences of grace and detachment.

158. The political dimension of the Saducees' religious points of view is summarized in Stambaugh and Balch, 97-99.

159. As Schillebeeckx put it (*Christ*, 460), "Apocalyptic writers constantly go round in circles and cannot manage to end."

160. Jesus' approach toward crisis is reflected in the narrowing of setting. Gone are the spacious sea and the hills of Galilee, as the tragic action funnels down from freedom of movement across large tracts of land and expanses of sea to a fateful encounter in a room.

161. I would encourage the reader to look at Weeden's work for a discussion of Mark's possible redactions in his presentation of the disciples.

162. Mark's Greek word is *oxous*, which the NRSV translates as "sour wine," but which the RSV translates as "vinegar." The Greek word could be translated either way in Mark's context. BAGD translates the word to mean "sour wine, wine vinegar"; noting that it relieved thirst more effectively than water; and, because it was cheaper than regular wine, was a favorite beverage of the lower ranks of society and of those in moderate circumstances." It adds that it was especially favored by soldiers (p. 574).

163. See especially Helms.

164. According to Nineham, 439, "The undisputed facts are that everything which follows 16:8 in any surviving MS. can confidently be declared non-Marcan on grounds of attestation, style, and content; thus the gospel in the earliest form in which we can trace it ended at 16:8. Moreover the evidence of both St. Matthew and St. Luke shows that it ended there in the versions of it known to them."

165. Dudly provides a good introduction to the Cynic philosophers. The philosophy most often compared to some parts of Christ's message is the Stoic philosophy of Epictetus. His works are collected in the Loeb Classical Library, *Epictetus: The Discourses as Reported by Arrian, the Manual, and Fragments*, trans. W. A. Oldfather, 2 vols. (Cambridge: Harvard Univ. Press, 1925/1928).

166. *Aristotle's Poetics*, see pages 27, 39, and 41 for Aristotle's definitions of peripety.

167. William Shakespeare, *Hamlet* I. i. 114-116. *London Shakespeare*, vol. 5, 379.

168. Ibid. I. v., 188-189. p. 418.

169. Aristotle's definition, by the way, says much about the tragedies portrayed in Hebrew Scriptures as well: consider Samson as tragic hero (as Milton did in *Samson Agonistes*), consider Job's suffering, the life of David, etc.

170. St. Irenaeus of Lyon gives this example of the gnostic Christ in his *Against Heresies* 1.24.4. Taken from Bentley Layton, ed., *The Gnostic Scriptures* (Garden City, NY: Doubleday, 1987), 423.

171. A line from one of Richard Wilbur's poems, see pp. 5-6.

172. For a discussion of this aspect of the synoptic problem, see William Farmer, *The Synoptic Problem* (London & NY: Macmillan), 1964, and Arthur Bellazoni, ed., *The Two Source Hypothesis* (Macon: Mercer University Press, 1985). A good recent bibliography is Longstaff and Thomas, *The Synoptic Problem: A Bibliography*, 1716-1988 (Macon: Mercer Univ. Press), 1988.

173. For a detailed discussion, see Harold Riley, *The Making of Mark: An Exploration* (Macon, GA: Mercer University Press, 1989).

# Works Cited

Achtemeier, Paul J., ed. *Harper's Bible Dictionary*. San Francisco: Harper & Row, 1985.

Aland, Kurt, et al., eds. *The Greek New Testament*. Third edition (Corrected).United Bible Societies, 1983.

Aries, Phillipe. *Centuries of Childhood*. New York: Random House, 1965.

Alter, Robert. *The Art of Biblical Narrative*. New York: Basic Books, 1981.

Aristotle. *The Poetics in Aristotle's Rhetoric and Poetics*. Translated by Ingram Bywater. New York: Random House, 1954.

Bailey, James et al. *Literary Forms in the New Testament*. Louisville: Knox, 1992.

Bauer, Walter. *A Greek-English Lexicon of the New Testament and Other Early Christian Literature*. 2nd. Ed. rev. and augmented by F. W. Gingrich and Frederick Danker. Chicago: University Press, 1979.

Bornkamm, Günther, et al. *Tradition and Interpretation in Matthew*. London: SCM Press, 1963.

Bultmann, Rudolph. *History of the Synoptic Tradition*. Oxford: Basil Blackwell, 1963.

Childs, Brevard. *The New Testament as Canon: An Introduction*. Philadelphia: Fortress Press, 1984.

Clark, David J. "Criteria for Identifying Chiasm." *Linguistica Biblica* 35 (75):63-72.

Conzelmann, Hans. *The Theology of St. Luke*. New York: Harper & Row, 1961.

Cranfield, E. B. *The Gospel According to St. Mark*. Cambridge: University Press, 1963.

Crossan, John Dominic. *The Historical Jesus*. San Francisco: Harper, 1991.

Cullmann, Oscar. *Early Christian Worship*. London: SCM Press, 1953.

Dewey, Joanna. *Marcan Public Debate*. Chico, California: Scholars Press, 1980.

Dibelius, Martin. *From Tradition to Gospel*. Greenwood: South Carolina: Attic Press, 1983.

Dudley, Donald R. *A History of Cynicism from Diogenes to the Sixth Century A.D.* London: Methuen, 1937.

Fuller, Reginald. *The Formation of the Resurrection Narratives*. New York: Macmillan, 1971.
Gundry, Robert H. *Mark: A Commentary on His Apology for the Cross*. Grand Rapids: Eerdmans, 1993.
Helms, Randall. *Gospel Fictions*. Buffalo: Prometheus Books, 1988.
Jeremias, Joachim. *The Parables of Jesus*. Rev. edition. New York: Scribners, 1963.
Johnson, Luke T. *The Writings of the New Testament: An Interpretation*. Philadelphia: Fortress Press, 1986.
Kelber, Werner. *The Kingdom in Mark: A New Place and a New Time*. Philadelphia: Fortress Press, 1974.
Kingsbury, Jack D. *Conflict in Mark*. Minneapolis: Fortress Press, 1989.
Kümmel, Werner. *Introduction to the New Testament*. Revised English Version. Nashville: Abingdon Press, 1975.
Ladd, George Eldon. *The New Testament and Criticism*. Grand Rapids: William R. Eerdmans, 1967).
Liddell, H. G. and Scott, R., eds. *A Greek-English Lexicon*. 1940 edition, rev. with 1968 supplement. Oxford: Clarendon Press, 1940/1968.
Lohfink, Gerhard. *The Conversion of St. Paul*. Chicago: Franciscan Herald Press, 1967.
Lund, Nils. *Chiasmus in the New Testament*. Sweden: Gleerup, 1966.
MacLeish, Archibald. "Ars Poetica." in *The New Oxford Book of American Verse*, pp. 624–625. New York: Oxford University Press, 1976.
Marrou, H. I. *A History of Education in Antiquity*. New York: Sheed & Ward, 1956.
McKnight, Edgar V. *What is Form Criticism?* Philadelphia: Fortress Press, 1989.
Munck, Johannes. *Paul and the Salvation of Mankind*. Richmond: John Knox Press, 1959.
Meagher, John C. *Clumsy Construction in Mark*. New York and Toronto: Edwin Mellen Press, 1979.
Merton, Thomas. *Mystics & Zen Masters*. New York: Dell Publishing Co., 1961.
Nineham, D. E. *Saint Mark*. The Pelican New Testament Commentaries. New York: Viking Penguin, 1969.
Perrin, Norman. *What is Redaction Criticism?* Philadelphia: Fortress Press, 1970.
Petersen, Norman R. *Literary Criticism for New Testament Critics*. Philadelphia: Fortress Press, 1978.
Porter, Gary G. "Defining Midrash." In *The Study of Ancient Judaism*. Vol. 1. Edited by Jacob Neusner. New York: KTAV, 1981, pp. 55–92.

Quesnell, Quentin. *The Mind of Mark.* Analecta Biblica 38. Rome: Pontifical Biblical Institute, 1969.
Radday, Y. T. "Chiasmus in Hebrew Biblical Narrative." In *Chiasmus in Antiquity*, edited by John Welch, 50–117. Hildescheim: Gersteberg, 1981.
Schillebeeckx, Edward. *Christ: The Experience of Jesus as Lord.* New York: The Crossroad Publishing Co., 1983.
_____, *Jesus: An Experiment in Christology.* New York: The Crossroad Publishing Co., 1979. [New York: Random House, Vintage Books edition, 1981.]
Schnackenburg, R. *The Gospel According to St. Mark.* 2 vols. New York: Herder and Herder, 1971.
Shakespeare, William. *William Shakespeare: The Complete Works.* Edited by A. Harbage. Baltimore: Penguin Books, 1969.
Stambaugh, John E. and David L. Balch. *The New Testament in its Social Environment.* Philadelphia: Westminster, 1986.
Stegner, William R. *Narrative Theology in Early Jewish Christianity.* Louisville: Westminster/John Knox Press, 1989.
Stock, Augustine. *The Method and Message of Mark.* Wilmington: Michael Glazier, 1989.
Talbert, Charles H. *Literary Patterns, Theological Themes, and the Genre of Luke-Acts.* Missoula, Montana: Scholars Press, 1974.
Taylor, Vincent. *The Gospel According to Mark.* 2nd. ed. London: St. Martin's Press, 1966.
Thompson, Mary S. *The Role of Disbelief in Mark.* New York: Paulist Press, 1989.
Thrall, Margaret. "Elijah and Moses in Mark's Account of the Transfiguration." *NTS* 16 (1970):305–316.
Travis, Stephen H. *New Testament Interpretation: Essays on Principles and Methods.* Edited by I. H. Marshall. Grand Rapids: Eerdmans, 1977.
Van Iersal, Bas. *Reading Mark.* Collegeville, MN: The Liturgical Press, 1988.
Weeden, Theodore J. *Mark: Traditions in Conflict.* Philadelphia: Fortress Press, 1971.
Welch, John. *Chiasmus in Antiquity.* Hildescheim: Gersteberg, 1981.
Wilbur, Richard. "Love Calls Us to the Things of This World." *Things of This World: Poems by Richard Wilbur.* (New York: Harcourt, Brace, 1956), pp. 5–6.
Williams, James. *Gospel against Parable: Mark's Language of Mystery.* Bible and Literature 12. Sheffield, Engl.: Almond Press, 1985.
Wrede, William. *The Messianic Secret.* Greenwood, SC: The Attic Press, 1971.

## Other Titles Available from BIBAL Press

| Balla | *The Four Centuries Between the Testaments* | $ 7.95 |
| Braulik | *The Theology of Deuteronomy* | 18.95 |
| Christensen | *Prophecy and War in Ancient Israel* | 14.95 |
| Christensen | *Experiencing the Exodus from Egypt* | 7.95 |
| Clements | *Wisdom for a Changing World* | 7.95 |
| Elliott | *Seven-Color Greek Verb Chart* | 3.50 |
| Gunkel | *The Stories of Genesis* | 15.95 |
| Haïk-Vantoura | *The Music of the Bible Revealed* | 29.95 |
| Lohfink | *Option for the Poor* | 7.95 |
| Lohfink | *The Inerrancy of Scripture and Other Essays* | 13.95 |
| Mynatt | *The Sub Loco Notes in the Torah of BHS* | 18.95 |
| Reid | *Enoch and Daniel* | 12.95 |
| Schneck | *Isaiah in the Gospel of Mark, I-VIII* | 19.95 |
| Scott | *A Simplified Guide to BHS* | 7.95 |
| Scott | *Guia para el Uso de la BHS* | 6.95 |
| Sinclair | *Jesus Christ According to Paul* | 12.95 |
| Sinclair | *Revelation: A Book for the Rest of Us* | 12.95 |
| Sinclair | *The Road and the Truth: The Editing of John's Gospel* | 12.95 |
| St. Clair | *Prayers for People Like Me* | 6.95 |
| St. Clair | *Co-Discovery: The Theory and Practice of Experiential Theology* | 12.95 |

Prices subject to change

Postage & Handling: (for USA addresses) $2.00 for first copy + 50¢ for each additional copy

California residents add 7.25% sales tax
Texas residents add 7.75% sales tax

Write for a free catalog:
BIBAL Press
P.O. Box 821653
N. Richland Hills, TX 76182

GENERAL THEOLOGICAL SEMINARY
NEW YORK